T0372737

DEMOCRACY IN TIMES OF PANDEMIC

Different Futures Imagined

The COVID-19 pandemic has presented an important case study, on a global scale, of how democracy works – and fails to work – today. From leadership to citizenship, from due process to checks and balances, from globalization to misinformation, from solidarity within and across borders to the role of expertise, key democratic concepts both old and new are being put to the test. The future of democracy around the world is at issue as today's governments manage their responses to the pandemic.

Bringing together some of today's most creative thinkers, these essays offer a variety of inquiries into democracy during the global pandemic with a view to imagining post-crisis political conditions. Representing different regions and disciplines, including law, politics, philosophy, religion, and sociology, eighteen voices offer different outlooks – optimistic and pessimistic – on the future.

MIGUEL POIARES MADURO was the founding Director of the School of Transnational Governance of the European University Institute in Florence where he is currently a Professor. He has been Advocate General at the European Court of Justice and a Government Minister in Portugal.

PAUL W. KAHN is Robert W. Winner Professor of Law and the Humanities, and Director of the Orville H. Schell, Jr. Center for International Human Rights at Yale Law School. He is the author of a dozen books in law, political theory, and moral philosophy. His most recent book was *The Origins of Order* (2019).

DEMOCRACY IN TIMES OF PANDEMIC

Different Futures Imagined

Edited by

MIGUEL POIARES MADURO
European University Institute, Florence

PAUL W. KAHN
Yale Law School, Connecticut

CAMBRIDGE
UNIVERSITY PRESS

University Printing House, Cambridge CB2 8BS, United Kingdom

One Liberty Plaza, 20th Floor, New York, NY 10006, USA

477 Williamstown Road, Port Melbourne, VIC 3207, Australia

314–321, 3rd Floor, Plot 3, Splendor Forum, Jasola District Centre, New Delhi – 110025, India

79 Anson Road, #06–04/06, Singapore 079906

Cambridge University Press is part of the University of Cambridge.

It furthers the University's mission by disseminating knowledge in the pursuit of education, learning, and research at the highest international levels of excellence.

www.cambridge.org
Information on this title: www.cambridge.org/9781108845366
DOI: 10.1017/9781108955690

© Cambridge University Press 2020

This publication is in copyright. Subject to statutory exception and to the provisions of relevant collective licensing agreements, no reproduction of any part may take place without the written permission of Cambridge University Press.

First published 2020

A catalogue record for this publication is available from the British Library.

ISBN 978-1-108-84536-6 Hardback

Cambridge University Press has no responsibility for the persistence or accuracy of URLs for external or third-party internet websites referred to in this publication and does not guarantee that any content on such websites is, or will remain, accurate or appropriate.

CONTENTS

CONTRIBUTORS

OLIVIER BEAUD is Professor of Public Law at University Paris 2 Panthéon-Assas and has chaired the Michel-Villey Institute for Legal Culture and the Philosophy of Law since December 2006.

DEVAL DESAI is Lecturer in International Economic Law at the University of Edinburgh, and research fellow at the Albert Hirschman Centre on Democracy, Graduate Institute, Geneva. He studies the administrative state across the global North and South, in legal, political, and social theoretic perspectives.

ROBERTO GARGARELLA is a professor of Constitutional Theory and Political Philosophy at the Universidad de Buenos Aires and at the Universidad Torcuato Di Tella.

MOSHE HALBERTAL is Gruss Professor of Law at NYU School of Law. Halbertal received his PhD from Hebrew University in 1989, and from 1988 to 1992 he was a fellow at the Society of Fellows at Harvard University.

STANLEY HAUERWAS is an American theologian, ethicist, and public intellectual. Hauerwas was a longtime professor at Duke University, serving as the Gilbert T. Rowe Professor of Theological Ethics at Duke Divinity School with a joint appointment at the Duke University School of Law.

MICHAEL IGNATIEFF is Rector and President of Central European University in Vienna and Budapest. He holds a doctorate in history from Harvard University and has held academic posts at Harvard Kennedy School, King's College, Cambridge, the University of Toronto and the University of British Columbia.

DANIEL INNERARITY is Ikerbasque Research Professor for Political Philosophy at the University of Basque Country and visiting professor in the European University Institute of Florence.

PAUL W. KAHN is Robert W. Winner Professor of Law and the Humanities, and Director of the Orville H. Schell, Jr. Center for International Human Rights at Yale Law School. He is the author of a dozen books in law, political theory, and moral philosophy. His most recent book was *The Origins of Order* (2019).

CHRISTINE LUTRINGER is executive director and senior researcher at the Albert Hirschman Centre on Democracy. Trained in political science and international history, she studied in Strasbourg (Institut d'études politiques), Rome (Sapienza University and LUISS) and Geneva at the Graduate Institute where she received her PhD. in international history and politics in 2009.

MIGUEL POIARES MADURO is a professor at Universidade Católica Portuguesa Global School of Law. He was the founding Director of the School of Transnational Governance of the European University Institute in Florence where he currently is a professor. He has been Advocate General at the European Court of Justice and a Government Minister in Portugal.

SAMUEL MOYN is Henry R. Luce Professor of Jurisprudence at Yale Law School and Professor of History at Yale University. His areas of interest in legal scholarship include international law, human rights, the law of war, and legal thought, in both historical and current perspective.

SUSAN NEIMAN is director of the Einstein Forum. Neiman studied philosophy at Harvard and the Free University of Berlin. She was professor of philosophy at Yale University and Tel Aviv University before coming to the Einstein Forum in 2000.

KALYPSO NICOLAIDIS is Professorial Chair at the School of Transnational Governance at EUI, Florence, and formerly professor of international relations at Oxford and Harvard Universities. Her latest book is *Exodus, Reckoning, Sacrifice: Three Meanings of Brexit*.

DAVID POZEN is Vice Dean for Intellectual Life and Charles Keller Beekman Professor of Law at Columbia Law School. He teaches and writes about constitutional law, information law, and nonprofit law, among other topics.

SHALINI RANDERIA is Rector of the Institute for Human Sciences (IWM), Vienna; and Professor of Social Anthropology and Sociology at the Graduate Institute, Geneva, where she also directs the Albert

Hirschman Centre on Democracy. Her research focuses on the state, law, and policy under neo-liberal globalization; civil society; multiple modernities; and post-colonial knowledge production.

KIM LANE SCHEPPELE is the Laurance S. Rockefeller Professor of Sociology and International Affairs in the Woodrow Wilson School and the University Center for Human Values at Princeton University. Scheppele's work focuses on the intersection of constitutional and international law, particularly in constitutional systems under stress.

NEIL WALKER has held the Regius Chair of Public Law and the Law of Nature and Nations at the University of Edinburgh since 2008. Previously he taught public law at Edinburgh for ten years (1986–96), was Professor of Legal and Constitutional Theory at the University of Aberdeen (1996–2000), and then Professor of European Law at the European University Institute in Florence (2000–8), where he was also the first Dean of Studies (2002–5).

J. H. H. WEILER is Joseph Strauss Professor of Law at NYU Law School. Weiler studied law (LLB and LLM) in the United Kingdom (Sussex and Cambridge) and at the European University Institute in Florence, Italy (PhD), where he later served as professor of law, head of the Department of Law, and most recently as President.

Introduction: A New Beginning

MIGUEL POIARES MADURO AND PAUL W. KAHN

The best apocalyptic movies (from *Mad Max* to *The Stalker*) are less about the apocalypse than what follows it. They focus on the systemic changes triggered by the apocalypse. About the apocalypse itself, little can be said. Speech begins again with survival. Likewise, in the middle of the current pandemic, we operate under the law of necessity. For this reason, nations with very different political systems have converged on the same practices of lockdown, social distancing, testing, and tracing. Nations that refuse to accept the law of necessity demonstrate not political strength, but weakness. They suffer the consequences, for the virus recognizes no excuses. Consider the ravages of the pandemic in Brazil and the United States.

Only when the end of the pandemic begins to come within view does a proper politics of reasonable analysis begin again. For those nations that held to the course during the worse of the epidemic, new political problems are just beginning to emerge. Contrary to the view expressed by Samuel Moyn in this volume, we do not believe that the pandemic will register as only a brief detour from which we now return to normal politics. Rather, it has been a world-historical event which has devastated economies, national institutions, global arrangements, and public health. Events of this magnitude can lead to dramatic reconsiderations of relationships among citizens and between them and the state. Citizens everywhere are beginning to reimagine their relationship with each other and to government. How and whether they act on those new imaginings depends very much on how political leadership responds. Leadership, too, must rethink what it owes to the members of the community.

These projects of national reimagination have been displayed most forcefully in the explosive growth of the Black Lives Matter movement in the United States. Before the killing of George Floyd by the Minneapolis police on May 25, 2020, few would have thought the middle of a pandemic likely to be a moment of dramatic, sustained, public protest. Even fewer would have thought that protests begun in the American

Midwest would rapidly spread around the world. This is a confirmation, even amid challenges to globalization, that politics too has turned global. Whatever the form that may take, from the cross-national fertilization of political movements and ideas to the development of transnational political spaces and organizations, politics has moved beyond the borders of states.

Just as nations are reconsidering the fundamentals of the social contract, so too is this a moment for reimagining the relationships among states and the performance of transnational institutions. Remarkably, political organs of the United Nations have had no visible role in the pandemic, while the World Health Organization's (WHO's) performance has spawned major controversy. The reimagining of globalization will have to consider whether the problems of transnational organizations have been internal and bureaucratic or a consequence of the gap between national and transnational politics.

For those who study law and politics, the pandemic has presented a sort of natural experiment on a global scale. It can seem as if everything has been simultaneously put at issue, from constitutional order to health care delivery, from due process to quarantine, from wealth redistribution to international trade. Different nations and transnational organizations have responded in different ways, providing tests in real time of competing theories, structures, and practices. Academics will be analyzing the variety of responses for a generation or longer. The world, however, does not operate on the academic calendar.

Responsible leadership has already begun to face the problem of drawing lessons from the experience of the pandemic. Released from the law of necessity, leaders everywhere will have to decide what to do in response to the devastation wrought. They will face tasks not just of economic recovery, but also of political recovery. Institutions that were "good enough" before the pandemic may not survive. In the short term, there will be a range of tactical issues of how to return people to work and reopen shuttered institutions, ranging from parliaments to universities. In the long term, serious attention will have to be given to addressing the failings of the old institutions and practices, in order to ameliorate the conditions under which we will deal with the next pandemic. Of this we can be certain – there will be a next.

The chapters in this volume have been written just at the moment when much of the world is tentatively beginning to reopen. By the time of publication, we are likely to know whether and which of those plans succeeded. We will also know whether we are likely to have a vaccine, putting an end to the pandemic. Like politics itself, writing about politics before the virus is defeated can be risky. Nevertheless, each of the authors has tried to consider the present from the perspective of an imagined future. Only so can we learn from the pandemic. This is no less true of law and politics than it is of public health.

This volume offers a variety of inquiries into democracy in times of pandemic with a view to discussing democracy beyond the pandemic. We have brought together some of today's most creative thinkers. They represent different disciplines and different regions. They include scholars of law, politics, religion, and sociology. Fifteen authors imagine fifteen different futures. The authors have widely different dispositions, ranging from optimistic to pessimistic. Some are sympathetic to the performance of leadership; others critical. The debate is lively and ongoing. In this Introduction, we do not try to summarize their different views. Instead, we offer a preliminary account of the terrain within which they all operate.

Multiple Emergencies

We begin with a sketch of the many emergencies created by the coronavirus. These began with public health, but have spread across the multiple dimensions of our public lives. Government is operating in an emergency mode in virtually every dimension: Hospitals, schools, courts, legislative bodies, regulatory affairs, and economic transfers. In an interconnected world, these emergencies begin at the local level of delivery of services, but extend to the transnational as borders close while information flows.

Communities have faced natural disasters before. Even pandemics are not new. Plague shaped European history; smallpox initiated the European conquest of the New World. Disaster creates the conditions for political change. Nevertheless, facts alone, even terrible facts, do not themselves determine "what comes next." A crisis brings new problems, but it also offers new opportunities. Sometimes, we make good use of those opportunities; sometimes, we do not. It may help to begin by trying to understand the scope of the crises of governance.

The COVID-19 pandemic initially presented a public health emergency. Over the past several months, an expert consensus has emerged on treatment – perhaps because there are so few treatment options available. Six months in, there are still no pharmaceutical interventions that can do more than ameliorate the symptoms for some of those who suffer the most. Doctors have, however, learned a lot about the proper administration of oxygen and the use of ventilators. They have also learned a lot about the way in which the disease spreads – none of it good. Silent transmission from asymptomatic carriers has made the disease notoriously difficult to contain. This is all common knowledge now, but so is the observation that populations subject to long-term lockdowns become increasingly restless – and increasingly desperate. The number of unemployed has reached figures not seen since the Great Depression of the 1930s.

Management of the public health emergency has raised issues of democratic governance. As social and economic desperation increases, politics comes to weigh more heavily on the decision-makers. We might imagine a sort of balance between expert advice and political pressure. That balance changes over time. An initial lockdown becomes more and more difficult to maintain as social and economic desperation increases. A population can become desperate under lockdown, but equally desperate as the infection numbers soar. The metaphor of a balance should not hide from view the simple reality that there may be no stable point of compromise between the disease and the economy, between experts and politics. This makes the interface between expertise and democratic authority dynamic, rather than static. We are learning, as well, that it does not move only in one direction, but may cycle through different phases.

A pandemic threatening death and destruction is a public health crisis similar to a national security crisis. In this crisis, however, we cannot turn to the military for help. The new generals are the public health experts, but are they subject to the political accountability upon which democracy depends? Civilian control of the military is a fundamental principle of democratic governance. We have hundreds of years of experience – and learning – in dealing with this problem. Public health experts may have even more power than traditional generals, but we have very little experience in the exercise of democratic control over them. They have made costly mistakes in some places, sometimes out of excusable ignorance, sometimes out of inexcusable bureaucratic failures. Our mechanisms of accountability have been weak, and are only just beginning to confront the problem.

In some nations, the pandemic has brought renewed trust in experts and support for their exercise of authority. In other places, public health experts have had to operate in an atmosphere of distrust: A legacy of populist movements that has long-targeted government by elites.

Resistance to wearing masks in some states grows out of this deep-rooted skepticism, which the often-changing recommendations of experts did little to decrease. It is enough to recall how the WHO's advice has changed on a multitude of issues from testing, to transmission, to masks. Because science develops through trial and error, new data will lead to new results. This might be good science, but it can be bad policy when the experts repeatedly change their advice on best practices.

When the advice has required sacrifices by a restive population, mistakes can fuel a political counterreaction. A destructive, downward cycle can set in, as we see with the large number of resignations of American public health officials who have found it impossible to operate in a hostile environment. This competition between trust and distrust will weigh heavily on the accountability mechanisms that have yet to be invented. We will no doubt need robust systems for evaluating how well the experts did, before we can settle on what their proper role should be in democratic politics in the future.

Experts contribute to democratic governance not just through offering rules, but also by contributing to the development of public opinion. A public health emergency, today, is always a public opinion emergency as well. Democratic governance requires the support of public opinion. We have witnessed a remarkable process of global education as citizens everywhere have learned about virology and public health. "Testing and tracking" have become part of our ordinary vocabulary. On the other hand, we also know that public opinion formation today can be driven by misinformation. There has been no lack of misinformation flowing through social media, sometimes encouraged by mistaken information flowing from official sources.

Democratic governance is both a product of and a contributor to public opinion formation. For this reason, the reformed politics coming out of the pandemic will sweep beyond the formal institutions of the state to include regulation of the sources of public opinion. The major tech companies – Facebook, Google, and Twitter – are all reconsidering their own policies and responsibilities for the democratic formation of public opinion. In the end, it may be harder to settle on a regime to control the viral character of misinformation than on a regime to control the coronavirus itself. The former will no doubt survive well beyond the demise of the latter.

The pandemic has also created social and economic emergencies of national and global dimensions. Responses to the economic crisis will pit claims of nationalism and protectionism against policies of globalism and free trade. They will put at issue fiscal and monetary policy, triggering huge domestic contests over how to manage the public debt within politically acceptable levels of unemployment. In Europe, for example, the current crisis may redefine the ethos of the European Union (EU). Fiscal discipline, the core policy of the Euro area, has been suspended and the EU has introduced new forms of risk-sharing, increased its budget capacity, and may, de facto, acquire tax powers. The political stakes in these decisions will be as high as they can possibly be, for a breakdown of economic security can lead to a breakdown of the state itself. We are all very aware of the political transformations that followed from the Great Depression. These were not minor adjustments of tax and welfare policies, but revolutions in the ends and means of governance. Reflecting these concerns, some of the chapters imagine a post-pandemic reconstruction of the social contract.

Finally, if the pandemic pushes us to a reconsideration of the nature of the political, it necessarily confronts us as an ethical emergency. The ethics of health care delivery has been very much on our minds, as nations have had to confront overwhelmed hospital facilities, shortages of medical personnel, and a lack of personal protective equipment (PPE) for those on the frontlines of response. Populations have been taught new lessons in interdependence as they have come to see that the truly "essential workers" are often those who were least appreciated before the pandemic. Democratic nations will have to confront difficult questions of redistribution and reward. To whom do we have a duty of care? How do these responsibilities fall on public and private actors? What are our obligations toward the worst-off at home and abroad?

The ethical crisis of the pandemic cannot be limited to social and economic responsibility. In our society which is increasingly digital and dependent on artificial intelligence (AI), responses to the pandemic have raised a series of concerns about privacy. How and to what extent should privacy concerns give way to the protection of health and life? Some of these questions parallel the concerns about misinformation. Others are unique. Our capabilities to deal with tracking, for example, may offer us the ability to go further than we dare go.

We confront here a variant of the traditional national security issue of "dual use" technologies: That which we do for public health reasons today may be used tomorrow not to keep us safe, but to keep us down. This is the cyber equivalent of the constitutional problem of government seizing extraordinary powers to manage the emergency, and then retaining those powers after the emergency ends. Where democracies may be reluctant to deploy power commensurate with the crisis, authoritarian regimes may see the crisis as an opportunity for consolidation. Political and legal tools developed to control the spread of the virus may become tools simply to control us. This threat of dual use is raised in a number of the chapters in this volume.

These diverse forms of crisis raise multiple issues that sometimes coincide, but sometimes point in different directions. Preliminarily, they center around three themes: Power, knowledge, and citizenship. Democracy understands citizenship as a relationship between power and knowledge. Thus, relationships among these terms are necessarily at the core of the inquiries into leadership, expertise, institutions, and responsibility that follow. Power is found both wanting and abused by leaders and institutions. Expert knowledge must contend with public opinion – a relationship that can be conflicted or harmonious. Citizenship appears as both a claim for care and a responsibility to act.

Power, knowledge, and citizenship take center stage in democratic practice as well as in democratic theory. They structure responses to the crises of the pandemic, but they will also, no doubt, be reconstructed by the experience of the pandemic. We are confident in this prediction because it is already clear that, for many people in many places, democracy itself has become the subject of the pandemic. Issues of power, knowledge, and citizenship bear on leaders and citizens as we all decide, individually and collectively, how to move forward. Some responses may be transformative; others may only amplify or limit ongoing transformations. While we have no crystal ball, we do think that we are far enough along to begin a discussion of what we might learn for our future from our recent past.

Who Was Taking Care?

Why were we not prepared? By now, almost everybody has heard of Bill Gates's famous speech from 2015, warning that the biggest threat to humankind was not military conflict but a pandemic. Many political leaders (including the previous two American presidents) also identified prevention of a pandemic as a strategic priority. Nevertheless, there was very little strategic preparation. Indeed, there was not even much tactical preparation once the virus was on the radar screen. In December, when the virus was already known to be spreading in China, governments on other continents did little to prepare. They did not even check their stockpiles of PPE, leaving many thousands of health care workers at risk of their lives.

Because this failure of preparation was nearly universal, an explanation cannot point to the personal failings of individual political leaders. Nor can we point to differences among political ideologies as an explanation. Spain had a Socialist government; Germany and Italy big or *sui generis* coalitions; the UK a Conservative government; Brazil and some states in eastern Europe populist governments; China and Russia variations of authoritarian regimes. None were prepared strategically; all fell into a desperate tactical effort only after the virus started killing their own citizens. Democratic states failed to take care of their most precious asset: Their people. Some argue that China, despite its authoritarianism, did a better job strategically and tactically, but that is increasingly put into question and the truth is that the nature of the regime prevents us from really knowing.

Most states – arguably all states – were not prepared for the pandemic, despite a decade of warnings. This widespread strategic failure indicates that, just like ordinary citizens, governments too have problems integrating future risk into public policy planning. The behavioral scientist will tell us that politicians are as susceptible to optimism bias as anyone else. But the political theorist will insist that politicians are responsible for planning in ways that overcome that bias. The constitutional lawyers will advise us on institutional structures that operate against the bias. All this expertise, but still governments failed. They failed on the most basic matter of life and death. They failed not just in preparations to fast-track production of vaccine; they failed in the production of paper masks that cost pennies.

The failure of anticipation and preparation was broad and deep. There were failures to pay attention as well as failures to respond. The failure of preparation extends to prevention, treatment, vaccines, and protection. More broadly, it includes a failure to prepare citizens for the possibility of a pandemic; that is, it includes a failure in the pedagogic responsibilities of the democratic state. How many states spent as much effort teaching their citizens of the risk of pandemic as teaching them to fear traditional enemies? Moreover, few populations had been prepared for the basic steps of a public health response: Quarantine. The result was panic and hoarding in some places, and a lack of preparation for a long lockdown virtually everywhere. The few states that were better prepared were those who previously experienced the SARS illness which emerged in 2003. That they did better is a visible sign that social learning is possible. But this will not happen if governments fail to take responsibility. Democratic populations will not hold their governments accountable when it counts most – before the crisis – if they have not been taught that the crisis is coming.

Can We Deal with Risk?

Democratic regimes will have to do a much better job of incorporating science into their planning and policy choices. This will be difficult because of a structural misalignment of benefits and costs. We prepare for the risks of tomorrow's pandemic by investing today. Political leaders must ask today's citizens to pay for protections they may never need. Bill Gates's prediction might not have come true for decades.

Of course, governments make similar investments in the future all the time. National security investments, for example, assess risks over several decades. Consider a decision made in the Middle Ages to build a cathedral: Construction could take a hundred years. Communities were effectively investing today to prevent risks to future generations. Stockpiling PPE might be today's equivalent of building a cathedral – a point supported by Stanley Hauerwas's claim that health has taken the place of faith in modern politics.

To notice that governments do make investments for future generations is hardly to say that they do so easily. As in so many other things, expectations are institutionalized. A society comes to have a normal range of investments. Bill Gates's speech was a reminder of the need to reconsider what falls within the range of "normal." The absence of response offers a lesson in how difficult it is to move the norm. Those with entrenched interests in existing investments will not easily support a shift of resources to respond to some other threat. Who in a democracy is watching out for the greater good of the future community? Bill Gates? But then he can afford to be future-regarding, and no one elected him.

What would have happened if governments had diverted resources in December 2019 into tactical preparations? Many people at that point still thought that the pandemic would "stay in China." What if government leaders had enforced an economic and social lockdown well before its inevitability was obvious to all? Scientists recommended these preventive measures, but were they politically feasible?

Citizens may literally need to see for themselves before they can support such harsh measures. Even today, many ordinary citizens disregard social-distancing rules in communities that have not yet *seen* the ravages of the virus. US President Donald Trump was not alone in his assessment that it was politically impossible to close down the country before anyone had even died of the virus in the US. Of course, closing down the country is one thing; stockpiling PPE is another. Still another is long-term preparation. Our failings, however, were across the board.

How to assess leadership's response to the uncertainty of the pandemic is a theme of several chapters, including those of Michael Ignatieff, Olivier Beaud, Daniel Innerarity, and Neil Walker. All emphasize the danger of hindsight – an omniscience bias. Just like political actors, we have to be careful to counter our own biases in assessment. Still, we must judge, if only to do better in the future.

The pandemic renders sadly visible the problem of insufficient internalization of future risks in today's policy choices. As we think about the shape of the problem and the proper response, we would do well to put the problem in the context of our longer discussion of climate change. For many years, scientists have been telling us that we are not doing nearly enough to prevent disastrous climate change. We have had many Bill Gates. Nevertheless, the structure of political incentives has undermined effective political action. The asymmetry between the long-term nature of the benefits and the immediate costs of preventive action short-circuits effective policies. Only when the effects start to appear to the community does political action become possible. As the pandemic has taught us, that is likely to be too late.

Bill Gates's warning was for naught. We need to introduce into the political system mechanisms that force the internalization of long-term risks. Only in doing so will we overcome our biases. These mechanisms may take the form of independent health and environmental agencies. They may also take the form of "signaling instruments" in the public space, such as environmental or health ratings or alerts. Whatever mechanisms we settle upon will have to have a strong transnational component, for the risks we face today are global. How to advance along these lines while maintaining democratic accountability within the organization of the nation state may be the defining question of constitutional construction for the next generation. These problems of institutional construction are taken up in the chapters by Roberto Gargarella, Olivier Beaud, and Kim Lane Scheppele and David Pozen.

Who Forms Public Opinion?

Democracy depends on the formation of the collective will. Today, that means the formation of public opinion. Because of the close relationship between public opinion and government legitimacy, a democracy is necessarily concerned with regulation of the public space within which public opinion forms. Authoritarian regimes tend to try to shut down this space. Democratic regimes are skeptical of regulation, but no longer do they have the luxury of relying upon a "free market of ideas." Such a market is as subject to monopolization and distortion as an economic market; neither is self-correcting. In addition, the digital space has transformed the public sphere: Easier access to information has undermined traditional authoritative sources of knowledge; information bubbles have multiplied and fed polarized politics; misinformation has expanded and become more insidious and dangerous. The pandemic as an information emergency has amplified these trends, making more pressing the problem of regulation.

The pandemic has also made clear that the public space of opinion formation is no longer a national space; it knows no borders. Just as goods, services, and viruses move globally, so does information. Some of that information directly bears on scientific research in response to the virus. The impact of transnational information flows to government policy is, however, much broader than scientific exchange. That information has fed a tendency toward "governing by comparison."

During the pandemic, the number of people infected by the virus and the number of related deaths in each country, and even each locale, were constantly set in comparison to each other. The general public and governments alike became attentive readers of graphs and charts, their own and those of others. These comparisons were often effective. No government could ignore successful responses by others. Despite the pressure, these comparisons were often based on unreliable and incomparable data. Different countries used different criteria to test, and therefore to measure the number of infected. They also used different criteria to account for pandemic deaths. Reliability of data also varied greatly; countries at very different points in the pandemic were compared.

Despite the problems with this information system, it shaped public debates and, as a consequence, political responses. Misdirection can be caused by misinformation even when it is not intentional. The collection, reliability, and comparability of data was weak, controversial, and disputed. There were no clear criteria put forward for such data. Open access did not become the standard, as public authorities limited access to their own data resources. Transparency and cooperation remained aspirational. In a world where access to data has never been easier, data has never been so contested.

Countries were trying to learn from each other, but in the absence of reliable data, how insightful were those lessons? These problems were exacerbated by calculated disinformation. Fake news is not a new phenomenon, but social networks and the internet have increased its scope, speed of dissemination, amplification, and means of credibility, thereby making it much more dangerous. The pandemic offers a case study on the risks of disinformation.[1] It has also presented an opportunity for new forms of regulation. Social networks were much more proactive in identifying and blocking false content regarding the pandemic and the virus. Many governments also adopted special laws penalizing the dissemination of such information.

Some public and private actors are now transferring the practice of fighting disinformation during the pandemic into a broader program of responding to disinformation in general. The further one moves toward political debate and away from issues of science and health, the more controversial this becomes. There is no democracy without truth, but in democracy truth must be grounded in pluralism. The problem of fake news is that it uses democratic pluralism to undermine pluralism by creating information bubbles and rejecting traditional forms of debate with opponents. The pandemic has made trolling and fake news matters of life and death for individuals and for their political practices.

What is the Role of Science in Democratic Decision-Making?

Government responses to the virus rely upon forms of scientific expertise that are not easily understood by citizens. This raises extremely difficult issues of popular accountability, for how can citizens act responsibly in areas that they do not understand? Professional fields discipline themselves; they do not subject their work to popular review. Politics does not have this luxury, yet it too must rely on forms of expert knowledge. Political rationality can be at risk from forms of democratic accountability, including the most basic form – elections. This is a theme touched upon in the chapters by J. H. H. Weiler and Paul W. Kahn, both of whom worry about populism and democratic rationality.

[1] A *NewsGuard* report has tracked Twitter accounts that are "super-spreaders" of COVID-19 misinformation in several European countries, showing that, combined, these accounts reach about 616,600 followers, who can spread fake news further on their own social media accounts. M. Richter, C. Labbé, V. Padovese, and K. McDonald, "Tracking Twitter's European COVID-19 Misinformation 'Super-spreaders,'" NewsGuard (May 2020), www.newsguardtech.com/twitter-superspreaders-europe/.

In the pandemic, individuals fear for themselves and their families. Even when they are being very careful, they cannot know if they will become infected. Ordinary activities can be life-threatening for vulnerable individuals. Government decision-making works with populations (groups), not individuals. Government cannot assure any individual of their safety; at best, it can try to assure the community that it will keep the infection rate low. Knowing that a certain percentage of the population will require care allows governments to plan, but that certainty about the aggregate does little to assuage the fear of the individual. In a pandemic, accordingly, even a well-performing government operates in a situation of considerable citizen fear.

The virus puts this paradox of governmental certainty coupled with individual uncertainty at the center of politics. We see this uncomfortable conjunction acted out everywhere. Universities, for example, might decide to reopen as long as they can keep the infection rate under 3 percent. They make sure that there will be facilities to treat the sick and quarantine the exposed. But their planning for the collective does not reassure individuals, who must ask themselves whether a 3 percent chance of illness is acceptable. Individuals are notoriously bad at evaluating the meaning of such a risk to themselves. The problem is everywhere, from restaurants to meatpacking plants.

A decision-maker rationally evaluating costs and benefits may not garner much political support in the face of fear of individual illness. Politicians are faced with contradictory demands: People want to be safe but they also want to keep their jobs; they want the pandemic not to spread but they also want the economy to open. Politicians must respond but they can have no assurance that a "rational" response will be accepted as such.

These asymmetrical attitudes toward risk raise the question of the conditions under which governments and citizens will defer to expertise. Governments place themselves at greater risk of popular rejection if they act against the consensus view of the experts. Trump and Brazil's President Jair Bolsonaro have quickly lost popular support for this reason. But this hardly means that the population will respond positively to expert instructions. There are risks to political leadership in aligning with or against the scientists, particularly when their advice might involve immediate economic and social costs. Unfortunately – or fortunately – all politics is risky when citizens live in fear.

The pandemic has brought an incredible entry of science into the public sphere. From social networks to mainstream media, everybody shares and discusses epidemiological, viral, and mathematical/scientific articles. But here, as elsewhere, familiarity can breed contempt. When politicians try to frame social-distancing policies as recommendations based on scientific expertise, we frequently see widespread rejection. Recommendations do not work because there is a mismatch between that which determines public support (evidence "you can see") and the scientific literacy necessary to understand public risks (evidence "to be reasoned with"). For this reason, there is an inevitable tendency to move from policy recommendations to legal requirements. Wear a face mask starts as good advice but ends as a rule that will be enforced by legal sanctions. Under these circumstances, science is at risk of becoming a scapegoat for whatever goes wrong.[2]

All this requires rethinking the relationship of the public spheres of science and politics. They do not automatically coincide. The crisis has the potential to bring them together or drive them apart. This relationship, too, may be more dynamic than static. It will be driven in part by results but also by opportunistic politicians seeking a scapegoat. Elections may become battlegrounds in which the underlying issue is the modern concept of reason itself. The pandemic will provide a great test of the attractiveness of the anti-elitist element of populist politics. As Moyn's chapter points out, we should not assume that we know which side will win in these elections.

Can Democratic Politics Deliver?

The problematic place of science in the democratic formation of policy points to a larger and ongoing crisis of democratic effectiveness. There are both output and input dimensions to this crisis.

The output dimension is obvious and pressing. Democracy is no longer equated with strong levels of economic growth and social justice. As Walker puts it, "confidence in the capacity, and trust in the willingness of the political system and its leaders to respond to major social and

---

[2] This may explain why, contrary to the assumption of many, initial data does not seem to suggest that the pandemic has brought about a renewed trust in science. A survey from the European Council on Foreign Relations (ECFR) conducted after the pandemic began shows instead that a majority of citizens in most EU Member States do not trust experts and the authorities. "Among those who expressed an opinion on the issue, only 35 per cent of respondents believe experts' work can be beneficial to them, while 38 per cent believe politicians have instrumentalised experts and concealed information from the public, and 27 per cent profess little faith in experts in general." I. Krastev and M. Leonard, "*Europe's Pandemic Politics: How the Virus Has Changed the Public's Worldview*," European Council on Foreign Relations (June 2020), pp. 6–10, www.ecfr.eu/page/-/europes_pandemic_poli tics_how_the_virus_has_changed_the_publics_worldview.pdf.

economic problems and promote effective social change decline across all constituencies." In many democratic countries, growing inequality levels, lower social mobility, and economic insecurity have accompanied increased economic stagnation. These trends have been exacerbated by the pandemic. Masses of workers have lost their positions; families have exhausted their savings. Yet, the stock market has mostly recovered, after an initial fall. In recent years, while Western democracies have stagnated, nondemocratic regimes, led by China, have been successful in taking people out of poverty and developing a middle class. Those same economically successful regimes contained the pandemic at an apparently much lower cost to their populations. The ineffectiveness of democracies was already straining the social contract before the pandemic. If only the stock market comes out of the crisis without suffering major loss, we are likely to face a deep crisis over the terms of governance.

The input dimension refers to the viability of the democratic process as a self-correcting political system. Around the world, democratic politics displays deadlock among parties. Elections do not bring change, but only more of the same. Deadlock favors the status quo and the elites who thrive in it. Alternatives within the political system no longer seem possible, as the possibilities for change narrow. People feel disempowered, as if no longer represented.

Under these conditions, politics increasingly takes place outside of formal, political institutions. Those institutions were constitutionally designed to make the system lean toward deliberation, reason, and moderation. A politics free of institutional constraint moves forward in a rather different epistemological space – one in which emotion trumps reason. This is often the space of social media, which produces populist and demagogic leaders who then make their way back into the political system. In this way, we can end up with political leaders who conduct the nation's business on Twitter. At that point, constitutional construction has fallen apart.

In its initial phases, the pandemic reinforced trust in existing political authorities. Faced with an exogenous shock, people rallied behind the flag. With few exceptions political leaders saw their popularity rise, including (or particularly) in countries in which the pandemic was severe.[3] In many

---

[3] Recent polls suggest that almost all world leaders except for Brazil's Bolsonaro have seen their popularity rates increase between 10 and 18 percent from February to April 2020. M. Armstrong, "The Coronavirus Crisis and Leader Approval Ratings," Statista (April 21, 2020), www.statista.com/chart/21437/coronavirus-and-leader-approval-rat ings/. For European leaders, see the analysis of M. Holroyd and L. Chadwick, "Coronavirus: Why Did European Leaders' Approval Ratings Rise during Lockdown?"

countries, though not in all, a political consensus emerged, leading to a pause in the ever-increasing polarization of national politics. Consensus opened a space for a renewed belief in reason, suggesting that reason in politics always depends upon trust by citizens in political authority. But, as the crisis moves from a health emergency to a social and economic crisis, this trust is unlikely to continue. As the severity of the crisis leads to greater social and political gaps, there will be plenty of reasons not to trust leadership, however much they claim to be standing on reason. Beaud's chapter presents one illustration of how traditional institutional practices – criminal law – can be dangerously repurposed when trust in ordinary democratic institutions disappears.

Can Citizens Hold Themselves Accountable?

We would learn only half of the lessons of the pandemic if we limit our inquiries to those of leadership performance and effectiveness. The pandemic raises issues not only of what government owes citizens, but of what citizens owe to each other. As Kahn suggests, we have all been drafted into a kind of stay-at-home army. Each of us has the potential to damage our family members, friends, fellow workers, and other members of the community. We have moral and political obligations to take care, which cannot be put off on leadership or the political system.

It may be too soon to know the impact the pandemic will have on our practices of citizenship, but a number of the authors in this volume express concern. Weiler puts his finger where it hurts by reminding us that populist leaders succeed only because they are popular. Citizens must hold themselves accountable for the success of authoritarian, xenophobic, and discriminatory ideas. Weiler, along with Susan Neiman, believes there is a certain political psychology at stake. Where she criticizes the ethos of interests, which led to neoliberalism, he criticizes an ethos of individual rights that has displaced republican political values. To these critiques, we should add the voice of Hauerwas, who assesses these changes in political psychology as a failure of a genuinely Christian ethos of care.

In response to concerns about the decline of political virtue, some authors see indications that the pandemic might lead to new practices of citizenship. Neiman sees new forms of solidarity emerging as people extend recognition and care under difficult circumstances. Kalypso Nicolaidis too sees the possibility of a creative reimagining of democracy as a consequence of the horizontal, informal, and decentralized forms of organizing that emerged as the pandemic intertwined with social protest movements. The pandemic did not suspend politics, as some had feared. Instead, it has, paradoxically, pushed politics into the streets – real and metaphoric.

The pandemic teaches us that politics is choice not destiny, as Innerarity also reminds us. The pandemic has offered a crash course in collective responsibility. For our social space to be free, we all have to be responsible. It is enough that one of us is not safe for all of us to be unsafe. To be social now is, in the first place, to really care for and protect the other. Still, the pandemic is also a lesson on how this collective responsibility is hard to develop. Free riding is rampant as individuals neglect the social-distancing rules. Cleavages have emerged along the lines of greater and lesser risk: The old against the young, and those with underlying conditions against the otherwise healthy. These cleavages can translate into social and economic cleavages. If, initially, the virus nurtured our collective bounds through multiple forms of solidarity and mutual responsibility, with time individual self-interest has gained ground. As Deval Desai, Shalini Randeria, and Christine Lutringer describe, there can be competition even among the needy.

The pandemic, then, forces yet another consideration of the relationship between rights and responsibilities, liberalism and republicanism, self-interest and altruism. Limited environmental and financial resources, along with stagnant economies, will require hard trade-offs and redistributive choices. Democracy will not be able to continue to develop only by expanding rights. This theme is developed as a matter of constitutional law in Olivier Beaud's contribution; it informs the political philosophy in Moshe Halbertal's chapter.

The Pandemic and Emergency Powers: How Have Democracies Coped?

Democracies need extraordinary tools to respond to the multiple crises of the pandemic. Some have formally invoked emergency powers under their constitutions. Emergency powers and democratic governance are always uncomfortable partners. Pessimists point to three different risks attached to the use of emergency powers. First, there is a possible perception that authoritarian regimes are more effective in addressing the crisis, which will undermine trust in democratic leadership. Second, there is a well-grounded fear that populists will use the extraordinary powers necessary to address certain aspects of this crisis further to erode the principles of liberal democracy. Third, there is a fear of a resurgence of nationalism as some politicians blame other nations and immigrants for the pandemic. We have seen all three in action in this crisis and, often, together. Several authors describe how political leaders have exploited the pandemic to entrench themselves further into power by curtailing any checks.

This trend too is best seen as an opportunistic effort to further political practices well underway. The reduced conception of democracy opened the door to populism. The pandemic just pushed many through that door. When citizens elect authoritarian populists, they should not expect them to change their manner of operation under the pressure of the pandemic. It is not an accident that the countries with the worst public health response are those with populist, authoritarian leaders. The democratic culture had already entered its own state of emergency in those nations, for democratic culture had been reduced to a practice of counting heads. Democracy has been confused with majority voting. The failure of political culture is the theme of many chapters, including those of Weiler, Kahn, and Halbertal.

The pandemic has also made patently clear that politics today is as much about controlling political narratives as it is about effectiveness. To the narratives of fear that may be the natural response to the crises of the pandemic, we can begin to see our way to a new narrative of optimism. That narrative is based on the renewed awareness for our relational nature. Competing with the democratic pathologies running through the pandemic is a more hopeful story of solidarity. The pandemic called upon our democratic and civic duties as well as on our rights. Alongside critique, we may also see increased support for political elites and for the editors of our democracy, from the media to experts in the field. Renewed support and trust in scientific expertise can open new paths for a more rational and epistemologically sound democratic engagement. Citizens have demanded transparency and public disclosure of information. These may be the tools by which ultimately to win the public opinion battle that is taking place nationally and internationally. From here, we can imagine a new beginning in which democracy is again connected with reason, pluralism, a civic ethos, and liberal constitutionalism.

PART I

Power

Introduction

The appearance of COVID-19 raised an immediate question for every political leader around the world: What could be done to prevent, cure, and mitigate the disease and its economic and social effects. This was a public health issue, raising issues of expert knowledge that we treat in Part II, but it was also a question of political power. Pandemic response was a test of leadership, but also a test of governmentality. Individual leaders had to make decisions, but they were empowered or constrained by the constitutional structures within which they operate. Alongside of these formal structures, there were also patterns of civil society and political competition that closed down some possibilities while opening others. The COVID-19 crisis put leadership under the intensely critical eye of an aroused population, for citizens were asked to take extraordinary measures, including substantial sacrifices, to deal with the virus. While leadership might initially benefit from the rallying behind the flag effect, it could also expect to be judged harshly for failure, while success might be difficult to measure.

An important feature of the arrival of the virus was that it began in China. Once the Chinese government realized the threat it confronted, it acted very aggressively. Absent democratic constraints, leadership was free to pursue something analogous to a military campaign to stop the spread of the virus. Democratic leadership does not ordinarily have the same power, but results count in responding to the virus. Many saw in the pandemic a test of two systems of power: One without constraint and one with substantial constraints. Did democratic systems provide government with power commensurate with the threat? Democracies have an additional worry: Would some political leaders use any award of emergency powers for public health purposes to consolidate their power even after the emergency has passed?

Even within democratic regimes, the virus happened to arrive at a moment when a vast experiment in populist politics was happening in countries spread across the globe. Here too, the pandemic created a natural experiment. Can populist leaders, elected to dismantle much of the existing state apparatus, exercise the sort of positive power needed to contain the disease? Beyond populist regimes, traditional structures of democratic, representative government were confronting issues of legitimacy even before the virus arrived. The need to respond to the virus layered an emergency – some would say a "state of exception" – on top of an ongoing crisis of democratic institutions. The pandemic created a set of conditions under which citizens could judge the adequacy of their political institutions, as well as the competency of their individual leaders.

The chapters in Part I take up these issues of the exercise of power. Each takes crisis response as a point of access for examining broader, structural issues of leadership today. Several try to think through the standards citizens should deploy to measure the exercise of power by their leaders. Others take a more institutional perspective, asking why some institutions performed and others failed in the crisis. Still others raise the question of how and to whom political leadership should be accountable.

Neil Walker presents a theory of interconnection between the ongoing crisis of democratic leadership and the sudden and "real world" COVID-19 crisis. He argues that the "hollowing" of contemporary democracy has opened a void between rulers and ruled, undermining the capacities of national political leaders to respond to citizen aspirations for well-being. Against this background, the COVID-19 pandemic has further revealed the weaknesses and blind spots of democratic governance. Yet it may also offer a turning point and an opportunity to change course.

David Pozen and Kim Lane Scheppele write about the risks of executive overreach and underreach during the COVID-19 pandemic. They define the former as the expansion of executive powers during emergencies at the expense of democratic values and institutions. Executive overreach is certainly the most feared political consequence of a state of emergency, and they provide examples of it. Yet, Pozen and Scheppele argue that executive underreach has resulted in even greater damage during the COVID-19 crisis. Executive underreach occurs when leaders refuse to take adequate measures to face or control an emergency even when they have the capacity to act and are informed of the threat and its risks. Against this backdrop, the authors argue that constitutions should be better equipped to confront and correct for executive underreach alongside executive overreach.

Governmental failure to act is also the topic addressed by Olivier Beaud in his case study of the troubling turn of French politics to the criminal law to hold officials accountable for their official decisions. Beaud shows that the COVID-19 state of emergency has spurred a surge of criminal complaints against French ministers – a phenomenon he names "penal populism." He argues that this flood of criminal complaints arises out of institutional misdesign, which simultaneously limited the possibility of political accountability and opened an avenue of criminal prosecution. Standard practice in parliamentary regimes is to hold ministers politically accountable for their mistakes. Beaud explains why that has not worked in France, leading civil society to look for other means of accountability. Yet, the replacement of political accountability with criminal liability promotes penal populism and is a sign of the worrying state of democracy in France.

The chapter by Roberto Gargarella focuses on the constitutional framework of the institutional choices made by Latin American countries in response to the COVID-19 crisis. Even as the pandemic has exacerbated previous economic and social inequalities in the region, government choices have tended to undermine institutional and constitutional structures. Many regional leaders have used the excuse of the pandemic to gain additional powers to rule beyond constitutional limits. Reflecting on Latin America's history of political authoritarianism and democratic backsliding, Gargarella suggests extreme caution in conceding any additional powers to executives to restrict constitutional rights.

Stanley Hauerwas's chapter is a philosophical and theological reflection connecting democracy, politics, and religion. He focuses on the political responsibility of Christians, and fears that American Christians have not properly held the US President to account. He worries that too many American Christians are acting as many German Christians did by conforming during the Nazi era. Confronting the problem of Christian accountability in response to President Trump's claims on the faithful, he pushes back forcefully against the politicization of the faith. Hauerwas argues that Christians should endorse and promote a democratic narrative based on an ethic of mutual care, rather than on a fear of death. Thus, the pandemic can be an opportunity to reclaim a Christian response grounded in acts of neighborly love.

1

The Crisis of Democratic Leadership in Times of Pandemic

NEIL WALKER

The word 'crisis' has two different shades of meaning, both central to the topic of this chapter. A crisis can refer to an unstable situation in political or social affairs that persists and intensifies over the relatively long term. Modeled on the original Greek meaning of *krisis*, denoting the turning point in a disease, a crisis can also refer to a traumatic episode or condition whose resolution remains unclear and replete with danger. The crisis of democratic leadership is a crisis of the first sort – a slow burn tending toward meltdown. The coronavirus pandemic is a crisis of the second sort – a traumatic event spiraling into an uncertain and perilous future. My argument is that the crisis of the first sort – the crisis in democratic leadership – is currently feeding into and feeding off the crisis of the second sort – the "real world" crisis posed by COVID-19. Indeed, compared to many other potential real world crises, COVID-19 is especially revealing of the problems of democratic governance. It shines a particularly searching light on deficiencies in the steering of contemporary democratic regimes. In so doing, the pandemic exacerbates the democratic leadership crisis. But, in the way of crisis events, it may also offer a turning point, and some salutary lessons on how to plot a better course.

***

Let us begin with the crisis in democratic leadership. That crisis, I contend, is merely one aspect of a broader crisis of democratic governance. It might seem obvious that one should be closely bound up with the other, but just how the difficulties of democracy today manifest themselves as particularly urgent problems of leadership repays close consideration.

When we talk about democratic systems of governance, our paradigm case is that of liberal representative democracy. Here the composition of legislatures and executives, and the title to govern claimed on behalf of these institutions and roles, derive from periodic contested elections. A key distinction holds between politician and citizen, ruler and ruled, elected elites and voting non-elites. Citizens enjoy equal political rights and associated freedoms (speech, assembly, privacy, etc.). Rulers are held to account not only through the ballot box but also under the rule of law, and by dint of the checks and balances inherent in the division of governmental powers.

The strict division between rulers and ruled offers a first general reason why the ills of representative democracy tend to manifest themselves as problems of leadership. Representative democracy implies a passive rather than an active form of citizen involvement. The rulers are seen as the standard bearers of the system, and to many of the ruled they are the true instrument and best measure of democracy's success or failure. The sheer dominance of the model of representative democracy offers a second general reason for the focus on the quality of its leadership. While the world knows many – too many – de facto alternative political systems, and a few *de jure* ones, whether totalitarian, authoritarian or epistocratic, most of us live in systems that fly under the banner of representative democracy. Most of us continue to prefer this to any nondemocratic system. We also tend to prefer the representative model to any more participatory variant of democracy – whether plebiscitary or deliberative – or at least hold it to be more plausible than any emphatically participatory model. As we will shortly see, however, that general preference does not mean there is not widespread dissatisfaction with particular democratic regimes, or even with certain general tendencies across regimes. This leaves us in something of a bind. As Claus Offe summarizes, "we may ... say that abstract liberal democracy is celebrating its near-global victory, while concrete and existing democracies are widely looked at with discontent and frustration over failures of both the legitimacy and effectiveness of democratic rule."[1] Unable or unwilling to ditch representative democracy, we are more likely to express our discontent and vent our frustration by criticizing the system's operators and the standard of their operation.

What are the more particular factors feeding this general discontent? Much of this is captured in the notion of the "hollowing"[2] of

---

[1] C. Offe, "Referendum versus Institutionalized Deliberation: What Democratic Theorists Can Learn from the 2016 Brexit Decision," *Daedalus*, 146(3) (2017), 14–27, 15.

[2] P. Mair, *Ruling the Void: The Hollowing of Western Democracy* (London: Verso, 2013).

contemporary democracy. On the one hand, the passivity that is a structural feature of representative democracy can morph into expressions of apathy and alienation. This is especially so in those political systems that are long established, and so have become adept at suppressing the very triggers of violence or disorder that have often provided democracy's formative impetus, while failing to address the tenacious underlying roots of unrest.[3] These attitudes of withdrawal are particularly prevalent within the most disadvantaged sectors of the population. Those suffering from economic or educational inequality, or from structural discrimination on the basis of gender, race, age, or other minority status, are less likely to feel a stake in the democratic system and more likely to opt out of participation as party members, or even as voters. On the other hand, and contributing to a self-reinforcing cycle, governing elites within and beyond the political parties become disconnected from these sectors. Policy priorities are increasingly set by groups whose privileged access to the levers of political influence is as entrenched as is the exclusion of other groups. In particular, employers, investors, and various other organized interests possess the economic resources, the strategic know-how, and the cultural confidence to shape the political agenda in ways that secure their privilege and respond to their own concerns at the expense of others.

The trend, however, is not just toward reinforcement of prevailing patterns of privilege – of the distribution of winners and losers. It is also toward the erosion of the general steering capacity of the political system. The "void"[4] that opens up between rulers and ruled not only leads to the disempowerment of certain types of constituency and their interests, but contributes to a general depletion of democratic political capital in its traditional home of the nation state. Confidence and trust in the capacity and willingness of the political system and its leaders to respond to major social and economic problems and promote effective social change decline across all constituencies. Once more, a self-fulfilling dynamic comes into play. As issues such as social exclusion, deepening inequality, environmental degradation, and international conflict – both old wars between states and the "new wars"[5] of nonstate actors – are increasingly seen as beyond the policy reach of any particular governing party or coalition, "the perceived political purchasing power of the ballot

---

[3] D. Runciman, *How Democracy Ends* (London: Profile, 2018), ch. 2.
[4] Mair, *Ruling the Void.*
[5] M. Kaldor, *New and Old Wars: Organized Violence in a Global Era*, 3rd ed. (Cambridge: Polity, 2012).

declines."[6] Citizens of all stripes are less likely to invest their efforts in making the system more fully fit for purpose, or to respond to the overtures of governing elites to make the kinds of collective commitments necessary to deliver social reform. Major political parties, with declining room for maneuver, provide a narrowing and increasingly similar menu of outcomes, and even of aspirations. In turn, this leads to an artificial competitive emphasis on those matters where distinctions remain palpable, such as the personalities of leaders.

Another key contributory factor to the narrowing of political vision is the impact of economic globalization. Its latest wave begun with the postwar development of the Bretton Woods institutions, globalization has been reinforced by the growing influence of neoliberal governing ideologies in leading Western polities from the 1970s onwards. Transnational imperatives of competitiveness, capital mobility, and tax competition, and the associated disciplines of debt consolidation and austerity have generally prevailed. This has dovetailed with a rescaling of economic decision-making from national to the supranational level. And in the gradual transfer of authority from the democratic state to supranational technocratic elites, we see, yet again, a self-reinforcing feedback. Yet for all their new ascendancy, the room for these new elites to maneuver also remains restricted. Even in the relatively broadly purposed and democratically accountable case of the EU, supranational capacity has tended to be limited to mitigating some of the harsher effects of the operation of transnational markets on workers, savers, or public service recipients.

Overall, the hollowing of democracy has led to a situation where the governing capacity of nation states becomes less adequate and less responsive to the aspirations and well-being of the citizenry as a whole. Terms such as "post-democracy"[7] and "competitive authoritarianism"[8] have been coined to capture some of the diverse consequences of this drift. These include both the technocratic turn to "output legitimacy" over "input legitimacy"[9] and the development of more selective and emotionally charged forms of electoral coalition-building. For in

---

[6] Offe, "Referendum versus Institutionalized Deliberation," p. 16.

[7] C. Crouch, *Post-Democracy* (Cambridge: Polity, 2014).

[8] S. Levitsky and L. Way, *Competitive Authoritarianism: Hybrid Regimes after the Cold War* (Cambridge University Press, 2010).

[9] F. Scharpf, *Governing in Europe: Effective and Democratic?* (Oxford University Press, 2010).

a context of limited political capital, citizens may come to be treated by political elites merely as the rationally self-interested consumers of a finite pool of public goods and private benefits. Or, partly in reaction to the arms-length, deracinating style and its distributive patterns, a particular category of citizens may instead be mobilized and rewarded as holders of a privileged social and political identity.

Leadership is emphasized in either case, both in the "cool" technocratic mode and, more emphatically, in the recently resurgent "hot" populist form. Contemporary populism, boosted by the recruitment to its cause of the leaders of global or regional powers such as Donald Trump, Vladimir Putin, Jair Bolsonaro, Narendra Modi, Recep Erdoğan, and Viktor Orbán, comes in many shades. But in its most vivid colors it works by explicitly rejecting an inclusive and ecumenical conception of the common good.[10] Instead it appeals to the ethical particularity of "left behind" nativist identities, setting these in confrontation with cosmopolitan elites, internal minorities, "foreign" forces, and others who have frustrated and would continue to deny the birthright of the "real" people. Populist movements and parties often foreground an expressive agenda of identity assertion. They rely less on the development of a detailed policy portfolio and, even once voted into power, dwell more on a symbolic politics of resentment, protest, and obstruction. They not only target marginal groups but also frame an amorphous "Establishment" or "deep state" as the scapegoat for the longstanding failure of "normal" politics to recognize them or their aspirations. "Strongman" leaders are an important part of this package. They offer both a galvanizing force to set in performative contrast with the conservatism or cramped ambition of the political mainstream, and a way of lending shape and coherence to an approach that lacks clear policy vision. Such leaders, moreover, tend to treat the classic constraints of liberal constitutionalism, including the separation of powers and minority rights, with casual disregard. They are at best rules to be strategically managed and at worst impediments to a project of electoral authoritarianism that seeks to sustain itself more by the acclamation of its base than the acceptance of the wider population.

The hollowing out of democracy, in a nutshell, places democratic leadership in a critical spotlight. Democratic governance is seen to become less close, less capacious, less responsive, less trusted, less recognizably representative of those it is intended to represent, yet

---

[10] J.-W. Muller, *What is Populism?* (Philadelphia, PA: University of Pennsylvania Press, 2016).

still the only form of governance that most citizens would wish to contemplate. In consequence, the burden falls on leaders to turn the tide – to offer a fuller and more appetizing version of the same dish. But the problems remain structural, concerning the limited traction that political decision-making, treating all citizens as formal equals, has over circuits of economic and social power that are unequally possessed and distributed, and that in any case stretch well beyond the decision-making purview of the nation state. And since, in addition, those who steer the system often exhibit the very "elitist" qualities that for many citizens indict the system as a whole, democratic leadership always treads a treacherous path. In the name of efficiency, there may be a retreat into a technocratic style that increases the affective disconnect with the democratic audience and undermines the capacity to mobilize future political capital. Or in the name of popular identification, there may be a retreat into a connective style that draws its political capital from a limited section of the population and undermines the classic democratic ambition to represent the people as a whole.

***

COVID-19 has had an extraordinary effect on the political landscape we have just sketched. Its challenge to democratic leadership and to the paradigm of representative democracy more generally may be framed by reference to a number of key features. First, the pandemic may be considered as a *premonitory* event. Second, it poses various acute problems of *collective action*, both within and beyond the polity. Third, it highlights the dense *interconnectedness* of the issues that form our political agenda. And fourth, it *suspends* many aspects of social and political life, both pausing our capacity to act and interrupting the flow of the world we act upon. Each of these features has double-edged implications for our capacity to steer our democracies. Each threatens to reinforce democratic impotence, but each also offers some hope of democratic renewal.

Premonition

More so than ever before, today we live in the shadow of the threat of global catastrophe. Since the bombing of Hiroshima and the near misses of the Cold War, the menace of nuclear calamity has been ever present. The dangers posed by climate change entered public consciousness later and more gradually. But today, despite the continuing economic and political strength of climate change denial, this is increasingly seen as a similarly profound risk to species survival.

Both types of existential risk reinforce the sense of relative impotence that figures so importantly in the hollowing of democracy. One part of the explanation is obvious. Eradication or even significant mitigation of these risks is simply beyond the capacity of any political system, and perhaps even of all the political systems of the world working together. That objective truth colors subjective attitudes. Impotence can lead, if not necessarily to denial, then at least to a wishful relegation of the threat to the margins of democratic attention. This is a tendency that is reinforced by the ways in which the pressures of the electoral cycle prioritize the short term over the long term, the everyday over the exceptional, the manifest over the concealed. In addition, nuclear calamity and climate change each carry a contrasting element of uncertainty. This further undermines the democratic capacity to respond, or even to focus on the need to respond.[11] In the case of nuclear calamity, we are dealing with an all-or-nothing phenomenon. It is a low-risk, high-cost event that we have somehow avoided in the past without fashioning any stable political mechanism that would guarantee its continued avoidance in the future. In the case of climate change, uncertainty is due to the vagaries of what is, by contrast, an emergent and incremental pattern of destruction. We remain unsure about the speed and pattern of long-term environmental degradation, and the tipping point of irreversibility. In either case, uncertainty about how to respond provides cover for our unwillingness to confront the gravity of what is at stake, while also compounding that unwillingness.

How does the coronavirus pandemic compare to these existential threats? It comes with a premonitory message – a cautionary tale – that is not available to either. Given the lethality of contemporary nuclear weaponry, a nuclear strike is unlikely to provide any learning opportunities for the next time. There will simply be no next time, or at least none in sufficiently similar circumstances to be usefully informed by past experience. Given the incrementalism of climate change, or of other looming long-term threats such as the development of super-intelligent forms of artificial intelligence (AI) beyond human control, there are here neither clearly pivotal events nor neatly bookmarked cautionary episodes from which we can learn. Instead, there is an unending sequence of reactions and feedback loops.

[11] Runciman, *How Democracy Ends*, p. 96.

With coronavirus it is different. As of the end of June 2020, the number of deaths by COVID-19 recorded by the WHO was half a million and counting. But whatever the final toll of the tragedy, this is not an existential event for a global population of nearly eight billion. We also know that it is not the first twenty-first century pandemic, and will assuredly not be the last. It is in fact the sixth Public Health Emergency of International Concern (PEIC) to be declared by the WHO since 2007. All of these have taken place against a global background of large-scale environmental engineering. An expanding human population disturbs local ecologies (such as the Amazon) and destroys wilderness in ways that allow animal-borne infections to jump more easily to humans, who then exploit the availability of mass air travel to accelerate disease transmission. If alongside the natural and accidental we factor in the possibilities of bio-terrorism that advances in bio-engineering allow, it is difficult to view the coronavirus as anything other than the precursor of even greater pandemic threats.

In some respects, the availability of coronavirus as a cautionary tale, and as a rehearsal for future struggles, reinforces democratic impotence. The significance of the event is palpable. It cannot either be pushed to the edges of our democratic consciousness as just one other factor in an incremental sequence, or mourned as a *fait accompli*. It is neither too early nor too late, but a challenge calling to be addressed in real time, and also an experience to be learned from for future reference. Yet the problems of joint action, as we shall shortly see, remain profound. In addition, the complexity of dealing with the knock-on effects of the pandemic in other areas of social and economic life are formidable. Democratic governments across the world have been left badly exposed by COVID-19; by their limited success in dealing with the clear and instant danger of the virus, and also by how much it has advertised deficiencies of democratic capacity and social policy beyond the domain of public health. Governments also undoubtedly fear exposure of their limited capacity to address future iterations, whose inevitability is now much more broadly appreciated among their populations than before. But with the greater certainty of exposure may also come a renewed sense of accountability, and, in turn, of collective responsibility and agency. If an unchallenged curtailing of ambition, and even defeatism – perhaps even fatalism, is part of the self-reinforcing pattern of modern democratic decline, then coronavirus could be an important circuit-breaker.

Collective Action

Coronavirus poses new collective action problems for governments, both internally and externally. Most of the focus in the urgent early stages of the pandemic has rightly been internal, dealing with the collective response of the national population. But the question of international coordination assumes increasing significance as the epicenter of the virus shifts across continents, and as the issues of how to deal with secondary global effects and how to plan for future outbreaks take center stage.

During the initial spread of the virus, governments introduced a package of social disciplines of unprecedented scope and type. Citizens and denizens of all states, democratic or authoritarian, were required to participate in a general "lockdown" of movements and activities. This typically took the form of a quasi-curfew. Most people were required to stay at home except for essential journeys, and with obligatory observation of social distancing when people did meet outside the home. Most forms of non-home-based work or public gathering for the purposes of shopping and leisure were banned, impacting considerably on the economic well-being and broader amenity of many. An exception was made for various front-line services in areas such as medical treatment, social care, transport, supply of food and utilities, and civil security. Under test and trace regimes (of highly variable form, intensity, and success), those who were infected or feared infection were required to isolate, and those who had been in contact with known cases also had to submit to testing and isolation.

What marks this regime is the sheer range of participation combined with the relatively low cost of compliance for many, if by no means all. Hardly anyone was untouched by the measures. Yet with the sharp exception of front-line workers in hospitals and other care facilities, whose experience remained comparable to the "self-sacrifice"[12] of citizen soldiers in modern warfare, participation in these measures did not involve an additional direct risk to life. For large numbers, nevertheless, particularly the low paid and those in casual employment, the short- and middle-term economic consequences were disproportionately severe.

Given the citizen passivity of representative democracy in its present hollowed state, this experiment in popular participation possesses a double-edged quality. On the one hand, it is an opportunity to mobilize a national effort that is broadly inclusive and at least formally egalitarian

---

[12] P. Kahn, "Torture and Democratic Violence," *Ratio Juris*, 22 (2009), 244–59.

in the contribution it demands. For any democratic government, whether or not elected on a populist mandate, it is a rare chance to build political capital on a broad base, and to offer a reminder of what democratic authority can achieve. On the other hand, sustaining the required level of popular mobilization requires the government both to display high levels of strategic competence and to gain and retain trust in its commitment to ensuring a genuinely collective effort across all sectors of the population. Otherwise, if individuals feel that governmental competence is undermining their efforts or jeopardizing their safety, or that elites continue to receive privileged treatment and to free ride on the contribution of non-elites, then their commitment to maintaining the relevant levels of social discipline will ebb and their skepticism about the capacity and connective qualities of government will return.

Some governments have met this challenge more effectively and more sustainably than others. Notably less successful have been those led by populists. Typically they have been more comfortable traducing the Establishment than employing the state's administrative capacity in pursuit of an inclusive public good, and more concerned to showcase their iconoclastic exceptionalism than advertise their sustained subscription to a common plan. Those governments that have experienced particular difficulties include the three with the highest numbers of recorded deaths, namely USA, Brazil, and the UK. Each would offer an instructive case study, but the experience of the UK, which has had the highest overall coronavirus death rate of any large economy, will suffice to make the point. Despite a quick and effective reorganization of hospital provision within the National Health Service and a generous scheme to cover 80 percent of the salaries of workers "furloughed" due to the constraints of social distancing, the UK government's reputation for competence suffered as a result of repeated indecision and delay. The UK was late compared with its European neighbors to introduce the lockdown. It was slow to increase testing, to ask people to wear face masks in public, and to implement contact-tracing. It also failed to provide adequate PPE to its health workers, and was lax in imposing a protective ring around the elderly population of its care homes. In addition, trust in the government's commitment to ensuring a solidarity of effort across elites and non-elites was undermined when Prime Minister Boris Johnson's chief advisor, Dominic Cummings, was perceived by many observers to have broken the government's own rules about travel during lockdown, but kept his job. At the beginning of the pandemic, there was quite broadly based goodwill toward a government that had just been elected with a significant majority. But by June 2020 a YouGov poll suggested that, of twenty-two countries surveyed, only Mexicans thought worse of their government's performance during the pandemic than Britons.

The implications of the pandemic for capacity-building cooperation between democracies has been similarly double-edged. On the one hand, if we focus on the immediate public health agenda, the benefits to all of international cooperation are obvious. Global public goods tend to be of three kinds; "single best effort," "weakest link," and "aggregate effort."[13] All three are implicated in the treatment of infectious diseases by WHO and others. Single best efforts can produce vaccines and new types of effective antiviral drugs. Weakest link approaches can target vulnerable areas where a virus might persist or begin to spread. Aggregate effort approaches are relevant to the development and sustenance of capacity in different locales to deal with an ongoing international outbreak, as in the case of the current pandemic. In all types, the content of the public good and the basic strategy to achieve it is widely recognized and uncontroversial. Even in the case of the aggregate effort public good of pandemic management, where there is greater reliance on different sites of authority keeping to a common script, the basic method of surveillance, interruption of infection chains, and ramping up prevention and treatment capacity is unchallenged. And in all cases, such is the scale of the harm to every state of uncontrolled infection that any difficulties of overcoming disincentives to cooperate should not be insurmountable.

In certain respects, the pandemic has indeed showcased the benefits of global public health cooperation, both formally and through informal channels of mutual medical aid. Yet problems of incentivization and trust remain. Different countries with comparable levels of wealth have different levels of long-term investment and reactive capacity in pandemic management, and show little commitment to equalize to a high standard. Moreover, even in the case of best shot goods, various states, influenced by the "big pharma" lobby, have held out against a WHO initiative to share research on COVID-19 treatments and produce any final medicines patent-free.[14] And as Trump's basic attack on the funding basis of WHO indicates, even the very principle of a forum of international

---

[13] S. Barrett, *Why Cooperate: The Incentive to Supply Global Public Goods* (Oxford University Press, 2007).

[14] See N. Dearden, "As Others Pull Together on a Coronavirus Vaccine, Why Is the UK Siding with Big Pharma?" *The Guardian* (June 3, 2020), www.theguardian.com/commen tisfree/2020/jun/02/coronavirus-vaccine-uk-big-pharma.

cooperation on these matters can be challenged. Furthermore, the fact that the challenge has been accompanied by the claim that WHO was unduly influenced by China at the beginning of the outbreak shows the precarious double-bind of international organizations in the face of powerful states that are skeptical of international cooperation. Too strong, and their willingness and ability to dictate matters to these states is feared and resented. Too weak, which is the likely outcome of persistent underfunding and rhetorical undercutting, and they may be criticized by these same states for their susceptibility to domination by rival strong states.

Interconnectedness

If it is difficult for democratic governments to rise to the challenge of "joined up" thinking and action, either with their citizens or with their fellow states over the public health aspects of the pandemic, it is all the harder to do so across the wider range of public policy matters implicated in the treatment of public health. Indeed, this is the most formidable question asked of democratic leadership in the pandemic, but for that very reason also the one where the answers may be most salutary.[15]

What threatens to overwhelm democratic systems in these circumstances is a combination of complexity, fragility, and structural amplification – the last referring to the latent tendency for changes within any interconnected system to reinforce existing preferences, biases, and inequalities. These various features are always present in the ecosystem of global public policy. But they are shown in stark relief when a single issue is "securitized" with such intensity and on such a scale.[16] For suddenly the trigger point and framing concerns for reform of the complex, fragile, and structurally amplificatory system as a whole are the existential threats that have arisen in that one particular sub-system.

Complexity and fragility in the present case are reinforced by the fact that public policy is so rarely viewed and steered from the perspective of public health. Yet the idea that interconnected areas as diverse as employment, investment, trade, housing, welfare, sport, transport, tourism, culture, education, security, and environmental management should all be understood through the prism of public health is refreshing. And the

---

[15] Runciman, *How Democracy Ends*, p. 112.

[16] N. Alexander-Sears, "The Securitization of COVID-19: Three Political Dilemmas," *Global Policy* (March 2020), www.globalpolicyjournal.com/blog/25/03/2020/securitiza tion-covid-19-three-political-dilemmas.

notion that public policy be adjusted to the immediate imperatives of public health rather than public health being treated as the dependent consideration, can liberate as well as intimidate. It is intimidating both politically and intellectually, as it goes against the grain of so many vested interests and established priorities, and as it requires a type of thinking that follows new lines of priority and causal sequencing. Yet that same novelty of thought can also be enabling. Previously counterfactual questions become real and engaged. What environmental and other benefits would accrue from a world without air travel? Can cycling become the default form of local public transport? What are the advantages and disadvantages of merging home place and work place? Does a universal predicament help make the case for universal basic income? Can education at a distance be fashioned into a general model rather than a second-best exception?

But there is also the problem of structural amplification. The interconnectedness of consequences may free up thinking about social reform, but it also compounds the stresses within the actually existing system. Those whose circumstances were precarious before lockdown – migrants, the insecurely employed, homeless persons, persons with compromised immune systems, victims of domestic abuse, and disadvantaged minorities of all types – will often find their situation exacerbated. It is they who are most likely to be rendered vulnerable by their disproportionate engagement in poorly rewarded front-line services, and to have their support services reduced, their concerns marginalized, and their long-term life chances left unattended.

In the national context, these wider structural concerns, and anxieties over the polity's response to these concerns, have tended to surface more clearly as the sticking plaster of the initial emergency response is removed. They do so against a rising conservative chorus for the augmented state subsidy of the economy and social welfare to be reduced in favor of a return to "business as usual." In the international context, by contrast, responsiveness to the problems of structural inequality runs in the opposite direction. However compromised their capacity, it is states rather than international institutions that remain the primary site of political solidarity and the first and minimal guarantor of citizen well-being. Yet political leadership that is able to recognize the indispensability of the international level in providing a long-term route out of structural inequality quickly become important. As of the end of June 2020, the EU had become intensely engaged in a political debate over the terms of delivery of an unprecedented package of centrally

guaranteed financial support. It undertook this initiative in recognition
of – and chastened by – its lack of solidarity with a fiscally challenged Italy
earlier in the pandemic. In the same moment, the International Monetary
Fund (IMF), faced with the prospect of the overall size of developing
economies shrinking for the first time in sixty years, was receiving requests
for financial assistance from more than a hundred countries that do not
possess the fiscal resources or the borrowing credentials to recover by
themselves.[17] Once again, by exposing the limits of the existing political
system so vividly, the coronavirus pandemic has also prompted renewed
consideration of the ways in which these limits might be challenged.

Suspension

Let us in conclusion note a final ambivalence. The coronavirus pandemic
left political leaders with little option but to hit the pause button on many
lives and countless activities. In some ways, this might be seen as the
crowning evidence of the gathering impotence of the democratic system.
Faced with a familiar challenge on an unprecedented scale – a known
unknown – the political system could only respond by advocating inertia.

Yet that would be a one-sided view. As an adult I have lived through
the fall of 1989, the chaos of 9/11, the crash of 2008. These were all events
with a claim to be more momentous than the coronavirus, not least
because they were the direct result of human agency rather than an
accident of the natural world. But none of these produced the same
intensity of "in time" reaction as the current pandemic. None produced
the range of instant predictions from political players and commentators
that the world would never be the same again; that history would forever
more be split into before and after, even if it was too early to discern the
shape of the after.

A flippant response would be that this is only to be expected when the
chattering classes are given license to chatter without distraction for
upwards of three months. A more serious follow-up would urge that
this chatter should not distract us from the propensity of the overall
system to reassert itself. But even if both these things are true, the many
intimations of change-to-come also speak to a deeper realization. We
have already noted how the prolonged pause allowed previously

[17] Christian Aid Report, "Tipping Point: How the COVID-19 Pandemic Threatens to Push
the World's Poorest to the Brink of Survival," (May 2020) www.christianaid.org.uk/sites/
default/files/2020–06/tipping-point-covid19-report-May2020.pdf.

counterfactual questions to be posed as live options. More than that, however, these questions were not just seminar inquiries. They also received practical answers that could stand as prefigurative models of change. For the pause was effective not only in providing unheard-of room for reflection on options for change, but in reminding us that things can *in fact* change at a speed and to an extent that would have been unimaginable before the intervention of a single random occurrence. In that sense, the pause has been not merely an interlude of the imagination but a reeducation in the art of the possible; in particular, it is to be hoped, our sense of what might be possible under conditions of renewed democratic leadership.

2

Executive Overreach and Underreach
in the Pandemic

KIM LANE SCHEPPELE AND DAVID POZEN

The pandemic that convulsed the globe in 2020 was long foretold but still surprising to many. Within a few months of its appearance, COVID-19 became one of the leading causes of death worldwide. Governments struggled at first to comprehend what was happening – and then reacted in very different ways. Most political leaders followed the advice of epidemiologists. Many declared states of emergency. A few pursued autocratic agendas. And some did almost nothing.[1]

During emergencies, constitutional scholars normally worry about executive aggrandizement at the expense of human rights and democratic values. Emergencies often require national executives to act quickly and forcefully to stave off threats. But emergencies also give national executives the opportunity to consolidate power, just when parliaments and courts are least keen to take responsibility. As we will show, the pandemic has provided a textbook example of this phenomenon, reinforcing what we know from the literature on emergencies that "executive overreach" is a serious problem.

We have also been witnessing in the pandemic a phenomenon that is much less familiar: "executive underreach."[2] This occurs when a leader

---

[1] For a global survey of legal responses by governments in the pandemic, see T. Ginsburg and M. Versteeg, "The Bound Executive: Emergency Powers During the Pandemic" (July 26, 2020), https://ssrn.com/abstract=3608974.

[2] For preliminary analyses, see J. Gould and D. Pozen, "How to Force the White House to Keep Us Safe in a Pandemic," *Slate* (April 6, 2020), https://slate.com/news-and-politics/2020/04/nancy-pelosi-white-house-covid-19-supplies.html; K. L. Scheppele, "Underreaction in a Time of Emergency: America as a Nearly Failed State," *Verfassungsblog* (April 9, 2020), https://verfassungsblog.de/underreaction-in-a-time-of-emergency-america-as-a-nearly-failed-state. We offer a more formal definition of executive underreach, and a defense of our definition, in a companion piece. D. Pozen and K. L. Scheppele, "Executive Underreach, in Pandemics and Otherwise," *AJIL*, 114 (forthcoming 2020).

has the legal and practical capacity to act in the face of a threat to the integrity or population of the country, yet fails to do so. Imagine a prime minister who knew that hostile foreign troops were planning to invade, and then went on holiday. Or imagine a president who knew that she could deploy engineers to stop a dam from breaking and killing thousands downstream, and then assigned the engineers to other tasks. In a well-functioning democracy, such behavior would normally cause the leader or her party to lose the next election, which is precisely why the phenomenon is unfamiliar. Executives in general want to act effectively to manage crises. Underreach may arise, however, when a leader fears that a more energetic response will alienate key constituencies, is resigned to losing office, or is simply unhinged. In some circumstances, underreach may allow leaders to *gain* power, by shifting blame to other actors or using the resulting chaos to their political advantage.

Not all oversights and omissions count as underreach. It is not executive underreach when a leader is unaware of a threat and fails to act out of ignorance, although it may approach underreach if the leader refuses to learn. And it is not executive underreach when a leader guesses wrongly about what will be effective, although waiting too long to take an educated guess may present a closer case. Executive underreach, in our sense, implies that a leader sees a significant threat coming, has access to information about what might mitigate or avert it, possesses the legal authority and practical means to set a potentially effective plan in motion, and refuses to pursue such a plan, putting the nation at risk.

Overreach and underreach have more in common than one might guess. Knowledge, resources, and the power to act decisively in a crisis are generally concentrated in the executive. Through either overreach or underreach, the executive may block other actors in the system from mustering a different response. Ill-motivated executives can exploit this blocking position to undermine political rivals and control the political narrative. Sometimes overreach will work better to dominate a situation; other times underreach will.

As we will argue, both overreach and underreach pose existential challenges to constitutional governance. With executive overreach, the danger lies chiefly in degrading checks and balances and violating civil liberties. That is why many constitutions protect against this sort of danger. But underreach, too, can destabilize political systems, corrode public trust in government, and jeopardize people's safety and security. Underreach can also lead to later overreach when problems are allowed to fester. Constitutions only rarely require executives to act, however, assuming that electoral and institutional incentives will supply sufficient motivation. It is therefore challenging to figure out how to move executives from underreach into responsible action.

To see both kinds of threats playing out during the pandemic, we will first consider Hungary, which exemplifies executive overreach. We will then examine the United States and Brazil to illustrate executive underreach. We will conclude by asking how constitutional governments can protect themselves from both dangers.

Executive Overreach

When the pandemic leapt from China to the rest of the world, national governments reacted in a largely uncoordinated manner. Many declared a state of emergency in the weeks that followed, notwithstanding preexisting health laws enabling authorities to cope with an outbreak of infectious disease.[3] By and large, however, emergency powers have been reserved for strategies recommended by epidemiologists, such as stay-at-home orders, curfews, limitations on large gatherings, social-distancing and mask-wearing requirements, and collection of cellphone data to track compliance. The recipe for dealing with the pandemic has involved more or less the same ingredients everywhere. Some of these policies have had drastic implications for economic and civil liberties, which we do not mean to minimize. Yet seen in historical perspective, what is most remarkable is how few governments failed, fell, or crashed their constitutions to fight the virus. "[I]n many countries, checks and balances have remained robustly in place."[4]

Against this backdrop, Hungarian Prime Minister Viktor Orbán's use of emergency powers has been unusual and extreme. Declaring a "state of danger" by executive decree on March 11, 2020, Orbán initially followed the Hungarian constitutional provisions for invoking a so-called special legal order, which has checks attached. While the prime minister can initiate a state of danger by decree, the Hungarian Parliament must explicitly extend the decree or it lapses after fifteen days. Instead of following this constitutional procedure, however, Orbán proposed a new law giving him unlimited decree powers for the duration of the COVID-19 crisis. Significantly, this law also bestowed upon Orbán the

[3] J. Grogan, "States of Emergency," *Verfassungsblog* (May 26, 2020), https://verfassungsblog.de/states-of-emergency.
[4] Ginsburg and Versteeg, "The Bound Executive," 5.

power to indefinitely renew his own decrees as long as the state of danger lasted. And who would determine its end date? Orbán himself.

To prevent a last-minute change of heart, the law barred Parliament from reconsidering the delegation of these powers by providing that it could not be repealed during a state of danger. Even when the state of danger was over, Parliament could only restore its powers by a two-thirds vote to repeal the law. Writing itself out of the pandemic response, Parliament passed this law on March 29, and it went into effect the next day.[5] The "Enabling Act," as it came to be called, expressly authorized Orbán to issue decrees that "suspend the application of certain Acts, derogate from the provisions of Acts and take other extraordinary measures." These decrees could be justified "in order to guarantee that life, health, person, property and rights of the citizens are protected, and to guarantee the stability of the national economy."

Even before the Enabling Act was passed, Orbán wasted no time issuing such decrees, extending all indefinitely. Many had little to do with the pandemic.[6] Military commanders were put in charge of every hospital and military teams were inserted into "strategic companies," allegedly to guide the pandemic response. The hospital commanders promptly forced out terminally and chronically ill patients to clear beds for pandemic victims.[7] The commanders also prevented data from escaping hospitals into the hands of journalists, assisted by a permanent change that the Enabling Act made to the criminal code, empowering the government-friendly public prosecutor to bring charges against anyone who states or disseminates "any untrue fact or any misrepresented true fact" regarding the pandemic. Once inside the strategic companies, military personnel exfiltrated data about employees, clients, and industrial processes for no apparent public health reason. At least one public

---

[5] *2020 évi XII. Törvény, a koronavírus elleni védekezésről* [Act XII of 2020 on the containment of coronavirus], English translation at https://perma.cc/9LMR-YS3L. For more on the mechanics and dangers of this law, see K. L. Scheppele, "Orbán's Emergency," *Verfassungsblog* (March 29, 2020), https://verfassungsblog.de/orbans-emergency.

[6] This paragraph draws on G. Halmai and K. L. Scheppele, "Don't Be Fooled by Autocrats," *Verfassungsblog* (April 22, 2020), https://verfassungsblog.de/dont-be-fooled-by-autocrats; G. Halmai and K. L. Scheppele, "Orbán is Still the Sole Judge of His Own Law," *Verfassungsblog* (April 30, 2020), https://verfassungsblog.de/orban-is-still-the-sole-judge-of-his-own-law.

[7] A nurse who cared for ten prematurely released patients reported that nine died shortly afterward. P. Dam, "Hungary Kicks Patients Out of Hospitals to Prepare for COVID-19," *Human Rights Watch* (May 6, 2020), www.hrw.org/news/2020/05/06/hungary-kicks-patients-out-hospitals-prepare-covid-19.

company traded on the Hungarian Stock Exchange had its board sacked and replaced by government cronies under a special decree, even though the manufacture of cardboard boxes did not seem pandemic-related. A number of Orbán's other decrees punished the political opposition by redirecting sources of tax revenue from cities where the opposition had won political control to county governments run by Orbán's party. These were not normal pandemic responses.

Orbán's Enabling Act was criticized by the European Parliament, which met to condemn his power grab. The international press attacked the measures in unison. The European Commission warned Orbán to renounce his new powers. By mid-June 2020, Orbán retreated and ended the state of danger. The Hungarian Parliament repealed the Enabling Act.

Yet in the same session in which it made this move, the Hungarian Parliament passed a complex law on "transitional provisions," which gave Orbán back under a different legal rubric nearly all of the powers he had ostensibly just relinquished.[8] This law created a new emergency framework, this time under the Health Act rather than under the constitutional provisions for special legal orders. It allowed Orbán to declare a "state of medical emergency," which he promptly did. He then decreed that the military would continue to run the hospitals and that the "Operational Staff" would continue to control Hungary's pandemic response along with the recently created "Economic Operational Staff," two extra-constitutional bodies with no accountability to Parliament. The decrees removing income from opposition-led local governments were converted into a statute. The military was granted expanded powers to use weapons against civilians inside Hungary "up to but not including death."[9] In short, the state of emergency continues, and most of the powers that Orbán grabbed in the initial phase of the pandemic are still his to use.

A healthy democracy would be unlikely to lose its constitutional soul so completely in a crisis. But Orbán had spent the decade before the pandemic eliminating potential sources of resistance and winning tainted elections. Having already captured all crucial state institutions, it was not hard for Orbán to remove the last remaining checks on his power when he assumed his critics would be distracted. While international pressure eventually led him to switch course, the new course is even worse than the

[8] G. Halmai, G. Mészáros, and K. L. Scheppele, "From Emergency to Disaster," *Verfassungsblog* (May 30, 2020), https://verfassungsblog.de/from-emergency-to-disaster.
[9] G. Halmai and K. L. Scheppele, "The Moment for Lies," *EURACTIV* (June 26, 2020), www.euractiv.com/section/justice-home-affairs/opinion/the-moment-for-lies.

old one. Orbán's response is perhaps the most extreme example of executive overreach in the pandemic.

Executive Underreach

In the two most populous countries in the Americas, we find a different constitutional danger emerging. The presidents of the United States and Brazil have denied that the pandemic is real and urged their supporters to act accordingly. Both Donald Trump and Jair Bolsonaro were widely seen as demagogic populists before COVID-19, as they flouted constitutional constraints, incited their supporters to intolerance and violence, and generally refused to perform up to the legal and ethical standards of their jobs.[10] One might have expected such leaders to welcome the pandemic with open arms for the opportunity it would give them to marginalize opponents, centralize power in the executive, and further trash the norms constraining them. Instead, Trump and Bolsonaro have flaunted their underreach.

Months into the pandemic, the powers that would have allowed the United States to mount an aggressive and concerted nationwide response were not invoked. On the contrary, the federal government was largely missing in action. For example, the President could have ordered the Centers for Disease Control and Prevention (CDC), the nation's health protection agency, to prioritize COVID-19 once it became a clear global threat in January 2020. Instead, Trump repeatedly minimized the threat, likening the virus to the common flu. Ignoring a National Security Council playbook on fighting infectious diseases, the CDC monopolized the creation and deployment of test kits (which didn't work), failed to track the spread of the disease (because there were no test kits), refused international offers of help that would have allowed the government to begin testing faster (America First!), and refused permission to states and private businesses that wanted to develop tests but needed federal approval to do so. By the time the Trump administration finally authorized other tests, the

---

[10] J. Chafetz and D. Pozen, "How Constitutional Norms Break Down," *UCLA Law Review*, 65 (2018), 1430–59; T. Daly, "Populism, Public Law, and Democratic Decay in Brazil: Understanding the Rise of Jair Bolsonaro" (January 2019), https://ssrn.com /abstract=3350098. For comparison of Trump's and Bolsonaro's responses to the pandemic, see S. Al-Arshani, "Brazilian President Bolsonaro's Response Mirrors the Trump Playbook from Praising Protesters to Touting Unproven Remedies – and the Death Toll Is Mounting," *Business Insider* (May 22, 2020), www.businessinsider.com/brazils-bolsonaro-mirrors-trump-playbook-for-coronavirus-response-2020-5.

WHO had already declared a global pandemic and most US states were already registering community transmission, in which the virus was spreading freely with no way to track its course.[11]

The US President is authorized under the Defense Production Act of 1950 (DPA) to order private companies to produce scarce supplies needed for national security. Test kits, ventilators, and PPE for health care workers could have been expedited. But Trump did not invoke the DPA until late March, and then only in a limited manner. By that point, the country was close to the anticipated peak of demand. Trump's reticence to deploy the DPA was especially surprising given the way the statute is typically used. As the *New York Times* reported, "[t]he Defense Department estimates that it has used the law's powers 300,000 times a year" in recent years.[12]

Under the Pandemic and All-Hazards Preparedness Act, the US government maintains a strategic national stockpile of pharmaceuticals and other medical supplies for use in a national health emergency. For weeks, however, the Trump administration refused to authorize distribution of relevant supplies to the states. Instead, Trump told governors that it was their responsibility to fend for themselves, even though the stockpiles existed precisely for this purpose. Trump's son-in-law Jared Kushner asserted that the national stockpile was not supposed to be used by the states except as a last resort; after governors protested, the program's website was changed to match Kushner's legally inaccurate statements.[13] When the reserve of medical supplies was finally dribbled out to the states in late March, states with Republican governors generally received the supplies they asked for, while Democratic governors came up short.[14] Trump seemed to be using a public health emergency to benefit his political allies and harm his political rivals.

[11] C. Peters, "A Detailed Timeline of All the Ways Trump Failed to Respond to the Coronavirus," *Vox* (June 8, 2020), www.vox.com/2020/6/8/21242003/trump-failed-coronavirus-response; D. Watkins et al., "How the Virus Won," *New York Times* (June 25, 2020), www.nytimes.com/interactive/2020/us/coronavirus-spread.html.

[12] Z. Kanno-Youngs and A. Swanson, "Wartime Production Law Has Been Used Routinely, but Not with Coronavirus," *New York Times* (March 31, 2020), www.nytimes.com/2020/03/31/us/politics/coronavirus-defense-production-act.html.

[13] A. Blake, "The Trump Administration Just Changed Its Description of the National Stockpile to Jibe with Jared Kushner's Controversial Claim," *Washington Post* (April 3, 2020), www.washingtonpost.com/politics/2020/04/03/jared-kushner-stands-trump-proceeds-offer-very-trumpian-claim-about-stockpiles.

[14] A. Rupar, "How Trump Turned Ventilators into a Form of Patronage," *Vox* (April 10, 2020), www.vox.com/2020/4/10/21215578/trump-ventilators-coronavirus-cory-gardner-colorado-jared-polis-patronage.

Meanwhile, after years of refusing to hold regular press conferences, Trump began to hold daily press briefings on the pandemic, in which he often made claims contradicting experts in the field. He also peddled unproven and downright dangerous cures. On the day when the CDC formally recommended that Americans should begin wearing masks (despite the fact that few were available at the time), Trump announced that he would not.

Eager to jumpstart the economy for the November election, Trump criticized governors who were reopening their states only gradually, following public health advice.[15] He demonized China for creating the "China Plague," threatened to withdraw from the WHO, and cheered on armed supporters who protested that their rights were being violated by stay-at-home orders. And long before his own health experts considered it safe to so do, Trump and his Vice-President started holding indoor rallies – with thousands of largely mask-free supporters – to gin up support for their reelection.[16] In the meantime, the virus continued to spread and, in late June, spiked again to the highest levels yet recorded.

The virus came to Brazil about a month after arriving in the United States, with the first confirmed case in late February. The results have been perhaps even more catastrophic there. Like President Trump, President Bolsonaro denied that the virus was a problem, touted unproven treatments, bashed the WHO, and refused to act. As in the United States, state governors in Brazil took the lead and imposed lockdowns when the public health threat became clear. As in the United States, the President berated the governors for doing so. Confronted by a reporter in late April as the death toll climbed past 5,000, Bolsonaro responded: "So what? . . . What do you want me to do?"[17]

In some respects, Bolsonaro has gone even further than Trump. He fired his first federal health minister, whose replacement quit after less than a month in the job. Bolsonaro then gave up on appointing public health experts to the position: The health minister at the time of writing is

[15] M. D. Shear and S. Mervosh, "Trump Encourages Protest Against Governors Who Have Imposed Virus Restrictions," *New York Times* (April 17, 2020), www.nytimes.com/2020/04/17/us/politics/trump-coronavirus-governors.html.

[16] D. Jackson, "Trump Will Return to Rallying," *USA Today* (June 10, 2020), www.usatoday.com/story/news/politics/2020/06/10/donald-trump-host-rallies-florida-okla-arizona-n-carolina/5325237002.

[17] T. Phillips, "'So What?': Bolsonaro Shrugs Off Brazil's Rising Coronavirus Death Toll," *Guardian* (April 29, 2020), www.theguardian.com/world/2020/apr/29/so-what-bolsonaro-shrugs-off-brazil-rising-coronavirus-death-toll.

an army general ignorant about pandemics.[18] On April 1, Bolsonaro issued Provisional Act 936 to try to prevent states from shutting down economic activities. While Bolsonaro fought those who would fight the virus, the courts intervened on multiple occasions and ordered several of his initiatives to be stopped.[19] The Brazilian Parliament also intervened to countermand several of Bolsonaro's measures and allocate more money to the poor as economic hardship increased. Even still, the number of confirmed COVID-19 cases has exceeded one million as we write, with more than 20,000 deaths, and Brazil is on track to become the worst-affected country in the world alongside the United States.

Both Trump and Bolsonaro, in short, refused to use the powers at their disposal to prevent catastrophic outcomes. Instead, they made things even worse by downplaying the virus and undermining the public health efforts of more responsible actors. Federalism kicked in to compensate for some of their failures, but with only limited success.

Executive underreach, as we have indicated, occurs when a national executive branch declines to address a significant public problem that it is legally and functionally equipped to address. Total passivity is not required. As the responses of Trump and Bolsonaro to COVID-19 demonstrate, the failure to confront a true threat is consistent with active efforts to change the subject, shift blame, and sow chaos. The examples of Trump and Bolsonaro also show how leaders may try to compensate for or distract from their underreach by overreaching on other axes, such as compelling states to reopen or deploying military force against protesters.[20]

Trump's and Bolsonaro's popularity ratings have plummeted in recent weeks,[21] which might suggest that extreme cases of underreach

---

[18] O. Encarnación, "Brazil Is Suffering. Bolsonaro Isn't." *Foreign Policy* (May 28, 2020), https://foreignpolicy.com/2020/05/28/brazil-is-suffering-bolsonaro-isnt.

[19] E. P. Neder Meyer and T. Buttamante, "Authoritarianism Without Emergency Powers: Brazil Under COVID-19," *Verfassungsblog* (April 8, 2020), https://verfassungsblog.de /authoritarianism-without-emergency-powers-brazil-under-covid-19.

[20] R. Farley, "Constitutional Experts: Trump Lacks Power to 'Open Up the States,'" *FactCheck* (April 14, 2020), www.factcheck.org/2020/04/constitutional-experts-trump-lacks-power-to-open-up-the-states; D. Superville et al., "Trump Threatens Military Force Against Protesters Nationwide," *AP News* (June 2, 2020), https://apnews.com /a2797b342b4fc509e43f404817a56aa9.

[21] A. Saraiva, "Poll: Bolsonaro Rejection Rates at All-Time High," *Brazilian Report* (May 2, 2020), https://brazilian.report/coronavirus-brazil-live-blog/2020/05/28/jair-bolsonaro-rejection-rates-in-brazil-at-all-time-high; E. Yokley, "Voter Sentiment on Trump's

EXECUTIVE OVERREACH & UNDERREACH IN THE PANDEMIC 47

will be self-correcting, over time, so long as elections remain free and fair. Prior to the pandemic, both presidents enjoyed significant success with political styles that relied heavily on distorting the truth and controlling the media narrative. A pandemic, however, cannot be "spun" out of existence. The reality of mass fatalities is too stark for most voters to deny. Yet even if COVID-19 does ultimately prove the political undoing of Trump and Bolsonaro – which is far from guaranteed – it will be too little, too late for the tens of thousands who have died. To reduce the risk of executive underreach, constitutional designers and reformers must do more than hope for outrageous facts to bring down bullies after the damage is done.

Preventing Overreach and Underreach

In *On Revolution*, Hannah Arendt argued that constitutions must perform two functions to be effective and durable. First, and perhaps most visibly, constitutions must limit power. Having led revolutions against overreaching monarchies, the constitution writers of the late eighteenth century were determined to find a way to tame unlimited executive power. As a result, to them,

> constitutional government was ... limited government in the sense in which the eighteenth century spoke of a "limited monarchy," namely, a monarchy limited in its power by virtue of laws ... However, the liberties which the laws of constitutional government guarantee are all of a negative character. ... [T]hey claim not a share in government but a safeguard against government.[22]

Executive overreach therefore is an old and familiar problem in constitutional design, arguably the canonical problem. Finding ways to force national leaders to govern with parliaments and to subject their decisions to judicial scrutiny while protecting the rights of citizens was at the heart of the constitutional project. Over time, the initial set of strategies came to be supplemented in new constitutions by a proliferation of institutions that provide additional constraints on executive power – ombudspersons, auditors, human rights commissions, central banks, anti-corruption offices, and so

Pandemic Response Hits New Low," *Morning Consult* (June 1, 2020), https://morning consult.com/2020/06/01/trump-pandemic-response-polling-low.
[22] H. Arendt, *On Revolution* (New York: Penguin, 1963), p. 143.

on.[23] Constitutions are practically a catalog of checks on executive overreach.

The Hungarian Constitution that Viktor Orbán inherited when he came to power a decade ago possessed abundant checks, including a powerful Constitutional Court and a wide variety of independent institutions meant to ensure accountability.[24] In addition, every Hungarian government after democratization in 1990 was a coalition government that further constrained the Prime Minister – until 2010, when Orbán won a mandate to govern alone. The constitution that Orbán wrote for himself in 2011 preserved many checking mechanisms in name only. By capturing the election machinery, the courts, the ombudsperson, the public prosecutor, the audit office, and more, Orbán neutralized all legal means that could potentially remove him from control.

By the time COVID-19 arrived, then, Hungary was an autocracy masquerading as a constitutional government. The checks that could have been brought to bear on Orbán's overreach were neutralized. As with the *Ancien Régime* that de Tocqueville eulogized, the old constitutional order could not have been toppled by a crisis if its core institutions had not already been weakened.[25] The Hungarian case, in which a pandemic has effectively resulted in a dictatorship, counsels sounding the alarm on the consolidation of unchecked power long before an emergency gives an autocrat the cover for a final power grab. Early corrections of assaults on checks and balances are crucial for staving off executive overreach down the line.

Arendt also identified a second principal function of constitutions, which helps us to think through underreach. Simply put, constitutions must constitute effective power. In diagnosing why the American Revolution succeeded in establishing a stable government while the French Revolution did not, Arendt argued that the French revolutionaries assumed that the people themselves were the source of continuing revolutionary power, whereas the American revolutionaries organized that power into a constitutional form that channeled it through ongoing institutions. In Arendt's account, reinforced in recent years by legal scholarship

[23] K. L. Scheppele, "Parliamentary Supplements (or Why Democracies Need More than Parliaments)," *Boston University Law Review*, 89 (2009), 795–826.

[24] M. Bánkuti, G. Halmai, and K. L. Scheppele, "From Separation of Powers to Government Without Checks: Hungary's Old and New Constitutions," in G. Tóth (ed.), *Constitution for a Disunited Nation: Hungary's Fundamental Law* (Budapest: Central European University Press, 2012), pp. 237–68.

[25] A. de Tocqueville, *The Ancien Régime and the French Revolution* (New York: Penguin Classics, 2008 [1856]).

highlighting the collective action problems that plagued the young nation under the Articles of Confederation,[26] the American framers were rightly concerned about the problem of underreach:

> What the founders were afraid of in practice was not power but impotence . . .. Clearly, the true objective of the American Constitution was not to limit power but to create more power, actually to establish and constitute an entirely new power centre, destined to compensate the confederate republic . . . for the power lost through the separation of the colonies from the English crown.[27]

How was this power to be created and harnessed for the public good? A happy equilibrium would emerge from a different sort of separation. Power would be tamed by giving each branch of government the ability to thwart the improper maneuvers of the other branches; as James Madison famously put it in *Federalist 51*, "Ambition must be made to counteract ambition."[28] But the division of power was also meant to encourage each branch to play its part proactively. "Prominent among [the framers'] reasons for embracing the separation of powers was the promotion of energetic and responsible governance in the common interest" – a goal that was seen as consistent with, not the inverse of, anti-tyranny.[29] To the extent that the US Constitution has succeeded in achieving this goal, one potential lesson is that it is crucial not to separate powers too cleanly. Some amount of overlap and duplication of powers not only may serve to limit overreaching by any given branch but also may provide a fallback for underreaching.

As one of us has argued about the current US predicament, Congress could at least theoretically fill many of the gaps left by President Trump's underreaching.[30] Because one chamber of Congress is controlled by the President's party, however, Congress has not done so. The "separation of parties"[31] has undermined the separation of powers in checking Trump's underreach and stimulating energetic and responsible governance. Courts in the United States, furthermore, take a long

---

[26] N. Siegel, "Collective Action Federalism and Its Discontents," *Texas Law Review*, 91 (2013), 1937–67.

[27] Arendt, *On Revolution*, pp. 153–4.

[28] J. Madison, "Federalist No. 51," in A. Hamilton, J. Madison, and J. Jay, *The Federalist Papers* (New York: Signet Classics, 2003 [1787]), pp. 317–22.

[29] D. Pozen, "Self-Help and the Separation of Powers," *Yale Law Journal*, 124 (2014), 2–90, 75.

[30] Gould and Pozen, "How to Force."

[31] D. Levinson and R. Pildes, "Separation of Parties, Not Powers," *Harvard Law Review*, 119 (2006), 2311–86.

time to act[32] – a luxury the pandemic does not permit – and treat claims of executive "inaction" as presumptively unreviewable.[33] Given the US Constitution's overwhelming focus on "negative" liberties to be spared state interference and its corresponding lack of "positive" rights to health or welfare, it is not clear that President Trump's underreach has violated anyone's constitutional rights, whether judicially enforceable or not. The US response to the pandemic has therefore largely been devolved to the states, where some governors have stepped in admirably but without the resources or authority to manage a problem of this scale.

In some constitutional systems, the other branches are better positioned to compensate for an underreaching executive. In Scotland, for example, an expansive view of equitable remedies permits courts to order others to act in place of the executive if necessary.[34] The Brazilian Constitution likewise creates positive duties that courts can require the state to fulfill. Of particular relevance, the Brazilian apex court has robustly interpreted constitutional rights to social security and health to require positive state action, which can be carried out by ministries without presidential direction. As the then-chief justice of the Brazilian Supreme Federal Court noted in 2011:

> The Brazilian Constitution of 1988 ... establish[es] what legislators and rulers must do and how and when they should act to implement ... constitutional guidelines and principles .... The constitutional court ... [has] taken upon [itself] the responsibility not only of functioning as negative regulators (as defined by Kelsen), but [it] also acquired an obligation to ensure the fulfillment of promises positively inscribed in the Constitution.[35]

Consistent with this vision, other government institutions became increasingly active as President Bolsonaro avoided dealing with the pandemic. As discussed above, state governors took the lead, while the national Parliament overrode some of Bolsonaro's actions

---

[32] J. Greene, "The Supreme Court as a Constitutional Court," *Harvard Law Review*, 128 (2014), 124–53.

[33] *Heckler* v. *Chaney*, 470 U.S. 821 (1985).

[34] S. Thomson, "Brexit, Boris Johnson and the Nobile Officium," *Journal of Civil Law Studies*, 12 (2019), 295–304.

[35] C. Peluso, "Constitution, Fundamental Rights and Democracy: The Role of the Supreme Court." Speech delivered in Washington, DC on May 12, 2011, www.stf. jus.br/repositorio/cms/portalStfInternacional/portalStfDestaque_en_us/anexo/ Cezar_Peluso__Constitution_Fundamental_Rights_and_Democracy.pdf.

regarding the distribution of relief funds. Still more dramatically, the judiciary invalidated some of Bolsonaro's executive orders designed to open the economy after the governors had shut it down. The Brazilian courts can be activated through *actio popularis* (popular action) petitions, which allow a faster and broader range of challenges to executive action than US courts permit. One court in Brasília went so far as to order Bolsonaro to wear a face mask in public or else face a daily fine.[36]

Yet despite this pushback and the differences in constitutional structure that have facilitated it, the pandemic response has been just as disastrous in Brazil as in the United States. The United States has 4 percent of the world's population and, as of mid-May, had more than 25 percent of the global deaths from the pandemic.[37] Brazil, with less than 3 percent of the world's population, has been on a trajectory to surpass the United States' COVID-19 death toll.[38] Even if constitutional mechanisms are necessary to counteract destructive forms of underreach – and could be strengthened in negative rights-oriented countries such as the United States through greater use of judicial "prods and pleas" that prompt or force the government to act[39] – the pandemic suggests that these mechanisms are apt to be insufficient when the stakes are high and time is of the essence.

Some commentators have identified a range of international law norms that arguably apply to the problem of government underreach in a global crisis.[40] Those norms, however, may be even harder to enforce against a recalcitrant head of state. If they have any effect at all, they are also likely to operate on a slower timeline than domestic constitutional devices.

---

[36] T. Phillips, "Brazilian Judge Tells Bolsonaro to Behave and Wear a Face Mask," *Guardian* (June 23, 2020), www.theguardian.com/world/2020/jun/23/brazilian-judge-tells-bolsonaro-to-behave-and-wear-a-face-mask. On *actio popularis* petitions, see L. C. P. da Silva, "Popular Action in Brazilian Law: From Its Source to Its Actual Inflection Points," *Quaestio Iuris*, 11 (2018), 548–58.

[37] J. Chamie, "United States Leads the World in COVID-19 Deaths," *InterPress Service* (May 18, 2020), www.ipsnews.net/2020/05/america-leads-world-covid-19-deaths.

[38] Z. Aleem, "Brazil Could Surpass the US as the Country Worse Hit by Coronavirus This Summer," *Vox* (June 20, 2020), www.vox.com/2020/6/20/21297786/brazil-coronavirus-cases-deaths-bolsonaro.

[39] B. Ewing and D. Kysar, "Prods and Pleas: Limited Government in an Era of Unlimited Harm," *Yale Law Journal*, 121 (2011), 350–424.

[40] See T. de Souza Dias and A. Coco, "Part III: Due Diligence and COVID-19: States' Duties to Prevent and Halt the Coronavirus Outbreak," *EJIL: Talk!* (March 25, 2020), www.ejiltalk.org/part-iii-due-diligence-and-covid-19-states-duties-to-prevent-and-halt-the-coronavirus-outbreak.

We suspect that more robust solutions may come from changes in legal culture rather than from formal legal tools. Because the problem of executive overreach is so familiar and so salient, human rights groups and other observers tend to be on the lookout for it as soon as a real or alleged emergency arises. As far as we can tell, all of the major civil society efforts to monitor government responses to COVID-19 have highlighted the risk of overreach while ignoring or deemphasizing the risk of under-reach. Consider, for example, the "COVID-19 Civic Freedom Tracker" and the numerous compilations of states of emergency.[41] By moving beyond the implicit negative-liberty paradigm for assessing government performance in emergencies – and in particular by naming and shaming executive underreach when it threatens severe harm to public safety, security, and other basic goods – nongovernmental organizations could help lay a foundation for more effective legal and political challenges.

None of this is to deny that executive overreach continues to demand vigilance. Relative to the United States and Brazil, Hungary apparently managed to contain the virus before it spread beyond control. Orbán will say that his plan worked. But Hungary shares in common with its neighbors a history of universal administration of the BCG vaccine as well as low rates of COVID-19, which may be linked.[42] No other country found it necessary to overthrow the last vestiges of its democracy to successfully fight the virus.

* * *

COVID-19 has created a terrible natural experiment in governance. Whether people live or die depends, in part, on the competence of the governments under which they live. While overreach remains a serious constitutional problem in emergencies, the underreach of national executives has had the worst public health effects in the pandemic. Constitutions need to do more than limit power; they must also help create state capacity and harness it toward public ends. If an executive

---

[41] International Center for Not-for-Profit Law et al., "COVID-19 Civic Freedom Tracker," www.icnl.org/covid19tracker (last accessed July 1, 2020); Center for Civil and Political Rights, "Tracking Tool – Impact of States of Emergencies on Civil and Political Rights" (April 1, 2020), http://ccprcentre.org/ccprpages/tracking-tool-impact-of-states-of-emergencies-on-civil-and-political-rights; Grogan, "States of Emergency."

[42] A. Miller et al., "Correlation Between Universal BCG Vaccination Policy and Reduced Morbidity and Mortality for COVID-19: An Epidemiological Study," *medRxiv* (March 28, 2020), https://doi.org/10.1101/2020.03.24.20042937.

fails to address a serious problem, other institutional actors must be given the authority and incentives to fill the void. Constitutional design can only do so much, though. It is also incumbent upon advocates and academics to devote greater attention to executive underreach and its myriad moral, practical, and democratic costs.

3

From Political Accountability to Criminal Liability: The Strange Case of French Penal Populism

OLIVIER BEAUD[*]

On May 20, 2020 the front-page splash of *L'Express*, one of France's leading weeklies, ran "Out for blood! Upping-the-ante in COVID-19 lawsuits" (*"Surenchère judiciaire autour du COVID-19. Cette soif de coupables"*). The headline flagged the spate of criminal complaints brought against ministers of Edouard Philippe's government. The latest count tops seventy! This chapter endeavors to explain why the declaration of a "health-related" state of emergency to address the COVID-19 epidemic – an out-of-the-ordinary event – produced this rash of criminal complaints in France.[1] Why are citizens frantically looking to hold ministers liable under criminal law? Or, more polemically, why this surge in "penal populism" by complainants "out for blood"?[2] This phenomenon is one indication, among many others, of the worrying state of democracy in France.

Inopportune Remarks Set the Wheels of Criminal Justice in Motion

The event that triggered this string of complaints was the publication of the "confessions" of the former Minister for Health, Ms. Agnès Buzyn. On February 16, 2020, she resigned her position in order to stand in, at

---

[*] Sincere thanks to my friend and colleague Jean-Marie Denquin for his close reading of the initial version of this chapter.

[1] For details, see O. Beaud and C. Guérin-Bargues, "L'état d'urgence sanitaire: était-il judicieux de créer un nouveau régime d'exception?" *Recueil Dalloz* (2020) 892–7.

[2] O. Beaud, "Si les gouvernants ont failli, la solution de la plainte pénale n'est pas la bonne," *Le Monde* (April 21, 2020), http://lirelactu.fr/source/le-monde/4aece89d-e09b-4154-bc5a -20cc2bc8075f. This chapter expands on the ideas set out in the newspaper commentary.

short notice, for Mr. Griveaux,[3] who was running for mayor of Paris. He was the leading candidate on the list of *La République en marche* (LREM, the party of President Macron). In the thick of the coronavirus crisis, she left the Ministry of Health – the ministry chiefly responsible for combating the epidemic – to spearhead the electoral campaign in Paris. Her resignation was more than a personal career choice: It signified the subordination of the managerial to the political.

Despite the local character of the electoral contest, her decision was of national significance. In France, local elections have national scope and therefore capture the attention of all political parties. This is especially true of the mayoral election in the capital city, because France is an ultra-centralized country. Hence, this seemingly ludicrous decision in terms of "managerial" reasoning: Just when the epidemic was exploding in France, Ms. Buzyn, who had been in office for close to three years, left the Ministry of Health to take up the banner of her political party.

She campaigned as best she could but without much success. She was heavily defeated in the first round of the election on March 15, 2020, leaving her with next to no chance of winning the second round. In the aftermath of that thrashing at the polls, she made a costly mistake of the sort only a political novice can make. She confided her thoughts – those of a politician beaten in the polls – to a reporter, who was all too eager to lend a listening ear. This was the sort of story for which the presses stop. She stated that holding the local elections in the middle of the health crisis was "farcical." Worse still, she acknowledged alerting both the President of the Republic and the Prime Minister to the gravity of the looming health crisis back in January.[4] In making these "unofficial" confessions, she blatantly contradicted her official statement of January 24: "the risk of propagation of coronavirus among the population is very slight." Ms. Buzyn's untimely comments sent shockwaves through public opinion, which her subsequent half-hearted denial failed to dampen. Public opinion was now convinced that the government "knew," as early as January 2020, of the serious risk of the pandemic spreading to France. The government allegedly put party political interests – winning local elections – before its citizens' health.

---

[3] He had to pull out of the mayoral race after featuring in a sex tape disclosed over social networks.

[4] "Les regrets de Mme Buzyn," *Le Monde* (March 17, 2020), www.lemonde.fr/politique/article/2020/03/17/entre-campagne-municipale-et-crise-du-coronavirus-le-chemin-de-croix-d-agnes-buzyn_6033395_823448.html.

On March 19, immediately after this scoop, a lawyer filed the first complaint against Ms. Buzyn and Prime Minister Edouard Philippe. He filed in the name of a collective of some 600 medical practitioners, who accused the government of not acting soon enough against the epidemic and of failing to take proper health measures (stockpiling masks and organizing systematic testing). The lawyer, tasked with characterizing these accusations in criminal law terms, tracked down the offense of "willful failure to counter harm" (Criminal Code, art. 223–7).

This first complaint was then echoed in a petition accusing the government of giving precedence to ordinary business over the extraordinary business of defending the nation's health. The petition targeted, in particular, the government's controversial effort to force a bill on retirement pensions through the National Assembly while the health crisis was developing. The petition gathered 200,000 signatures in a matter of days to "contribute to denouncing the lies, rank amateurism and mediocrity of our leaders that have led to the calamitous management of this health crisis and a national scandal." This aggressive language, common among many supporters of criminal complaints, illustrates the instrumentalization of criminal law for political ends – the hallmark of political justice, according to Otto Kirchheimer's judicious definition.[5]

Since then, complaints against several ministers have come thick and fast. They come mostly from private and public sector workers' unions. They target the ministers for Health (Mr. Véran replacing Ms. Buzyn), the Interior, Labor, Justice, and Education. Other criminal complaints have been filed – in the general courts of law – against senior civil servants; for example, against the Director General for Health. I shall spare readers the list of criminal offenses that ever-imaginative lawyers have produced. Suffice it to say that these offenses are "involuntary": The accused are criticized for failing to act. The standard offense is "endangering the lives of others" (Criminal Code, art. 223–1), an offense that is admirably vague and does little credit to French criminal legislation.

To round off this presentation of the facts, it should be added that (1) these criminal complaints against ministers are made possible by art. 68–1 of the constitution which provides for ministers to be held criminally liable for wrongdoing in their official capacity, and (2) that the complaints must be filed with the Court of Justice of the Republic and not with the general courts of law. This is a special politico-criminal court

[5] O. Kirchheimer, *Political Justice. The Use of Legal Procedure for Political Ends* (Princeton University Press, 1961).

for trying "members of the government" (Constitution, art. 68–1, para. 1). This ad hoc court was created by a revision effected by the constitutional amendment of July 27, 1993 to try members of the government in the "contaminated blood" case.[6] This court has not been successful and has, therefore, faced periodic threats of termination.[7]

Comparison with the Contaminated Blood Case

The contaminated blood case marked French political life throughout the 1990s. It began in 1991, when a journalist claimed that, at a time when the AIDS epidemic was rife (1983–1985), blood transfusion centers had distributed potentially contaminated blood products to hemophiliacs and blood transfusion recipients.[8] Following this revelation, criminal justice complaints led to a first trial in 1992 in the Paris Criminal Court. That trial resulted in the convictions of four "administrative" heads, including the former Director General for Health. Many thought that criminal accountability should extend to the highest political authorities, namely the Prime Minister (Mr. Fabius), the Minister for Social Affairs (Ms. Dufoix), and the Secretary of State for Health (Mr. Hervé) – who were all Socialists. After many twists and turns, in March 1999 the three members of the government were tried by the same Parisian court. Mr. Fabius and Mr. Hervé were acquitted; Mr. Hervé was found guilty but spared any sentence.

At first sight, there is a striking resemblance to the current wave of criminal complaints. We find three ingredients of the politico-criminal law scenario: First, a particularly serious epidemic; then, the challenge of decision-making under uncertainty; and finally, recurrent criticism of the government for not having taken adequate preventive measures. Both cases involve authorities confronting an outbreak of a new virus – AIDS or COVID-19 – about which nothing was known for sure and for which there is still no vaccine. Such uncertainty, illustrated by untold disagreements among scientific experts, renders decision-making

---

[6] It is a hybrid institution composed of fifteen members – six from the National Assembly, six from the Senate, and three judges from France's highest civil court, the *Cour de cassation*.

[7] For the reference work on its failings, see C. Bargues, *Faut-il juger les politiques? La Cour de justice de la République* (Paris: Dalloz, 2017). The two latest draft constitutional revisions under Presidents Hollande and Macron planned to abolish it.

[8] See O. Beaud, *Le sang contaminé. Essai critique sur la criminalisation de la responsabilité* (Paris: PUF, Behemoth, 1999).

haphazard and perilous. The would-be prosecutors benefit from the sure and certain knowledge born of hindsight about what *should have been done*, whereas the decisions taken had to be made in the heat of the moment.

The accusers erase any uncertainty and simplify an extremely complex reality. This cognitive bias of after-the-event omniscience was pretty much ubiquitous in the contaminated blood case. It prevails in the thinking of today's "prosecutors," voicing their opinions on the COVID-19 epidemic. They view Ms. Buzyn's shocking comments as an avowal: Ministers knew but did nothing. Obviously, they are wrong, but they have managed to convince some segments of public opinion.[9]

In 1999, I offered a critique of this turning toward criminal law in place of political accountability. I argued that when the state makes mistakes or is negligent in its management of affairs, standard practice in a parliamentary regime is to call the members of the government to account politically. Criminal law, especially when it is as invasive and illiberal as in France – as evidenced by the flourishing of these strict liability offenses – is not the right instrument for evaluating decision-makers' responsibility. My argument rests on the essential and far-reaching difference in kind between criminal liability and political accountability.[10]

My earlier critique of this turn to criminal law is wholly applicable in the case of the coronavirus crisis. Indeed, the critique is even stronger here. The specific circumstances of the contaminated blood affair included a gap between the acts and knowledge of the acts. The "scandal" came to light in 1991, several years after the events at issue (1983–1985). This meant that the ministers involved could no longer be held to account for their acts in Parliament, because they were no longer ministers. The road to pure political accountability was therefore barred. The Court of Justice of the Republic was created to address this situation; it was to serve as an institutional "stopgap." The criminal complaints regarding the new pandemic, however, were filed in March 2020 *as the crisis unfolded*. They operated in "real time," as it were.

With the exception of Ms. Buzyn, the government members against whom legal actions have been brought are *all serving ministers*. Under the

---

[9] To recall, in late January no one knew for certain whether the epidemic would take hold in France. The cases of contamination (of Chinese in Paris and Britons in the Alps in early February) had not caused any massive contagion.

[10] See the two significant chapters, "Responsabilité politique contre responsabilité pénale" and "La politisation de la responsabilité criminelle," in Beaud, *Le sang contaminé*, pp. 105–33.

cardinal rule of parliamentary government, they can be held to account in Parliament, which is the competent authority under the Fifth Republic for implementing political accountability.[11] Indeed, during the health emergency, Parliament has not been inactive. As early as mid-March, it set up an information mission in the National Assembly and a "supervision and monitoring mission" to examine measures relating to the COVID-19 epidemic. Those missions are to evolve into a parliamentary commission of enquiry at the end of June 2020. Plans have been made to hear from serving ministers, including the Prime Minister, as well as from former health ministers of previous governments. Commissions of each House are likely to want an explanation of the critical shortage of masks and respirators during the crisis.

To conclude. Every constitutional lawyer knows that the transition from politico-criminal liability – impeachment – to political accountability in the UK was concomitant with the advent of parliamentary government.[12] Conversely, the substitution of criminal liability for political accountability characteristic of the current position in France is a major step backward. The outbreak of "penal populism" is one sign, then, of the twilight of constitutionalism.[13]

A Diagnosis of the Worrying State of French Democracy

In characterizing this flood of criminal complaints as "penal populism," my aim is to point out a worrying phenomenon: The subordination of political accountability to criminal liability. The term "populism" is intended to denounce a demagogic political turn to criminal procedure. These criminal complaints have no real chance of leading to convictions, if the contaminated blood precedent is anything to go by. Criminal liability presupposes some very stringent conditions: The causal link is especially hard to prove, the provisions of the Criminal Code are – normally – narrowly construed, and the burden of proof lies with the plaintiff. Moreover, unlike ordinary criminal trials, proceedings in the

---

[11] Art. 24 Constitution: "Parliament ... oversees Government action." Articles 49 and 50 set out the mechanisms for political accountability that may lead to a vote on a censure motion. Article 51-2 provides for parliamentary commissions of enquiry to ensure this overseeing.

[12] An enlightening book on this point is D. Baranger, *La formation d'un Exécutif responsable en Angleterre* (Paris: PUF, 1999).

[13] This is an allusion to P. Dobner and M. Loughlin (eds.), *The Twilight of Constitutionalism* (Oxford University Press, 2010).

Court of Justice of the Republic are terribly slow, and because there is no confidentiality for matters *sub judice* in France (a national shame), the press will have a field day for years, keeping its readership on tenterhooks by "revealing" evidence portrayed as a scoop at every opportunity.

This brings us to the fundamental question: *Why this thirst for criminal responsibility in France, a thirst that emanates from civil society, represented essentially by the victims?* The reasons are both cultural and institutional. First, the cultural. For at least two decades, France has been experiencing an uncanny phenomenon that might be termed the "sanctification" of victims. Whenever any catastrophe of any kind occurs, the media and politicians go to town.[14] The victims' suffering becomes the nub of all discussion. Criminal trials seem the *only* way to soothe that suffering. This point can be illustrated by an anecdote that speaks volumes.

At the criminal trial after the crash of the *Concorde* passenger plane at Goussainville outside Paris in 2000, the prosecution service provided both an interpreter and a special room for the victims' families (all German apart from the French crew). To their stupefaction, not a single German family attended the opening of the trial at Pontoise on February 10, 2010. The German lawyer said in a BBC interview that his clients were unhappy about the fuss surrounding the trial because it needlessly opened up old wounds. The families, he noted, had promptly received appropriate compensation.[15] Apparently, that was enough for them, but not for the French.

In recent decades, a culture of dramatization "for the sake of remembrance" of victims of catastrophe has developed. The criminal trial is seen as means of cathartic release for the victims and at the same time "a way to build symbolic bonfires" on which to sacrifice the accused, who are modern-day scapegoats.[16] The victims demand a personal right to vengeance against those who had the misfortune to be at the helm of the state, local authorities, and government agencies. This is a dreadful step backward for criminal law and criminal procedure. Procedurally, it is possible because victims may, under French law, bring actions for

---

[14] See the superb film by P. Schoeller, *L'exercice de l'Etat* (The Minister), an object lesson for legal scholars.

[15] As reported by one of France's leading attorneys, Maître Soulez Larivière (email to the author, June 12, 2020).

[16] Maître Soulez Larivière, "Un moyen d'élever des bûchers symboliques," *Journal du Dimanche* (May 16, 2020), www.lejdd.fr/Societe/Justice/tribune-plaintes-visant-la-gestion-du-covid-19-un-moyen-moderne-delever-des-buchers-symboliques-3968715.

damages in criminal cases (with victims replacing the prosecution service). I made this point in 1999. The situation has grown worse over the last twenty years.

Alongside the shift in culture, there has been an institutional change. Political accountability has not worked in France for decades. Consequently, citizens turn by default to the criminal courts to hold those in power to account. They do this increasingly so that the courts can monitor and advertise their integrity.[17] More importantly, they do so to oversee their *actions*. This requires an explanation arising from constitutional law.

The Fifth Republic is a parliamentary regime. Certain provisions of the 1958 Constitution make the government accountable to Parliament. The government may put a question of confidence (art. 49) and members of Parliament may table a motion of censure (arts. 49–50). In practice, only one government has been censured since 1958: The Pompidou government in 1962, when President de Gaulle sought to change the constitution by way of a referendum rather than through parliamentary channels. As in many parliamentary regimes, the existence of a stable majority means that governments are not overturned.

Everything hangs, then, on the stability of the coalition in power, or the robustness of the majority in power, as was the case with Mr. Macron's presidency, whose party held an absolute majority in the National Assembly until very recently. The upshot is that the government is seldom turned out, marking a major change from the Fourth Republic under which ministerial instability was the rule. Moreover, there is nothing in the constitution of the Fifth Republic on the individual responsibility of ministers. To bring a particular minister down, the whole government must be toppled – not a realistic option. Above all, the head of government is not accountable to his own political party (as in the UK) because the president of the Republic is the party leader. In short, all ways out are stopped tight.

The most important institutional point is the strange two-headed character of the executive branch of government under the Fifth Republic, shared between the head of state (the president of the Republic) and the head of government (the prime minister). Practice, impelled by General de Gaulle between 1959 and 1969, meant that this diarchy was superseded by a monocracy dominated by the president of the Republic – the celebrated topic of "republican monarchy" (Maurice Duverger). This presidential rule

---

[17] See this magisterial essay: Alessandro Pizzorno, *Il potere dei giudici. Stato democratico e controllo della virtù* (Bari: Laterza, 1988).

under de Gaulle remained acceptable because he held himself politically accountable to the people. He did so in the 1965 presidential elections when he ran for office, and again in the plebiscites on self-determination for Algeria. Indeed, de Gaulle resigned on April 28, 1969 when the French public disapproved by referendum of his plan for institutional reform. Apart from three periods of cohabitation (1986–1988, 1993–1995, and 1997–2002), presidential rule has remained the chief legacy of the Gaullist interpretation of the constitution.[18] Yet no president since de Gaulle has put the question of their political accountability to the people. Rather, they have done their utmost to avoid doing so. The most prominent case is that of François Mitterrand, who clung to power despite two resounding electoral defeats for his (Socialist) party in the general elections of 1986 and 1993. Subsequently, the supposedly Gaullist President, Jacques Chirac, backed this policy of political unaccountability for the president of the Republic on two occasions: First, when, after losing the general elections of 1997 to an ill-advised dissolution, he did not see fit to resign; and second, after the referendum defeat of May 29, 2005 on the treaty to establish a European constitution.

In short, the president of the French Republic enjoys far wider powers than the president of the United States, but has become politically unaccountable. In addition, the president benefits from broad criminal immunity granted under the constitutional amendment of February 23, 2007 (art. 67C). To offset this extended immunity from prosecution, the act provided a "safety valve" with the possible removal from office of the president of the Republic in the event of a "failure to perform his duties manifestly incompatible with the holding of office" (art. 68 L.1). All the evidence, however, is that this provision is meant to apply only in highly exceptional circumstances.

A further quirk of the French system is that the president of the Republic, who is the highest political authority, is not accountable to Parliament in the ordinary forms of a classical parliamentary regime. The president has the right to decline to testify before a commission of enquiry, even when he or she is the leading protagonist in the matter under investigation. This privilege was granted by Mr. Mitterrand to his predecessor Mr. Giscard d'Estaing, when a commission of the National Assembly wanted to question him about a hoax concerning "sniffer

---

[18] "Cohabitation" is not a legal term. It is used to describe the fact that the president has lost his majority in Parliament, meaning that it is the prime minister (as in the cases of Chirac, Balladur, and Jospin) who actually governs while the president of the Republic plays a subordinate although not negligible part.

aircraft." The Socialist President therefore accepted that, for reasons of "republican tradition," the former head of state could not be forced to testify by a commission of enquiry. This privilege was even extended to the President's advisors, the staff of the Elysée. That practice, however, was recently reversed in the Benalla affair (July 2019), in which a bodyguard of President Macron conducted himself like a police officer although he was not one. The President of the Republic declared that his political opponents could "come and get him." In point of fact, the commission of enquiry could not hear testimony from him, but it did question close advisors to the Elysée. Thus, as things stand in France, the politically accountable authority (the prime minister) is not the one who makes the decisions, while the decision-making authority (the head of state) is not constitutionally accountable. Understandably, disgruntled citizens turn to criminal liability when up against this brick wall of unaccountability.

This French exceptionalism also raises its head when comparing constitutions. The COVID-19 crisis provides an interesting test case. Neighboring countries to France, also badly hit by the epidemic, are parliamentary regimes. None have seen a massive turn to criminalization of responsibility. No one is seeking, for example, to indict UK Prime Minister Boris Johnson for wasting precious days before taking steps to protect the population. In Italy, a lawyer and former member of Parliament for *Forza Italia* filed a complaint against the government, accusing it of a special offense of negligence in the face of an epidemic (*epidemia colposa*). In addition, a victims' collective in Bergamo – the epicenter of the epidemic in Lombardy – filed some fifty complaints against "a person unknown" on June 9, 2020. A few similar complaints have been filed in Spain,[19] while in Belgium a complaint has been filed by five doctors against the state for failure to render assistance to a person in danger. These complaints demonstrate the possibility of turning to criminal law in these countries, but nowhere has that possibility been

[19] On July 2, 2020, at the time of writing, it was reported that Spanish citizens had brought fifty-two actions (https://elpais.com/espana/2020-07-02/el-supremo-pide-opinion-a-la-fiscalia-sobre-51-querellas-y-denuncias-contra-el-gobierno-por-la-gestion-de-la-crisis-de-la-covid-19.html). Because of art. 102 of the Spanish Constitution, they will no doubt be held inadmissible – unlike in France where the Public Prosecutor (*Procureur Général à la Cour de cassation*) has decided to ask for the competent investigating judges – the *commission d'instruction de la C.J.R.* – to examine nine cases which were declared "admissible": *Le Monde* (July 5/6, 2020). The so-called "infernal [diabolic] machine" in France is launched.

seized as in France. *How can this difference between France and those other European countries be explained?*

Some political scientists point to the exceptional degree of mistrust of politicians in France and especially of Emmanuel Macron. It may be that angry citizens are bringing actions against government ministers in order to attack the head of state indirectly. The president of the Republic is now continually insulted on social networks by catchphrases, posters, or photos, even though there is no way to hold him directly accountable. This verbal and physical violence came to a head in 2019 with the Yellow Vests (*Gilets Jaunes*) protests which, at one point, threatened the Elysée from fairly close quarters. That rage continued in response to the plan to reform retirement pensions, which was also lambasted by part of the political class.

Mr. Macron's presidency has always had a weak electoral base. In May 2017, he won just 23 percent of the vote in the first round of the presidential election. He won in the second round because his rival, Marine Le Pen, represented a far-right party. Since the election, her party has sought to move toward the center by becoming the *Parti du Rassemblement National* (RN), instead of the *Front National* (FN). The fact of the matter is that two relatively extremist parties – the FN and *la France insoumise* on the left – won close to 40 percent of the vote in the first round of the presidential election. Together, they propagated a radical "anti-Establishment" stance that stoked violence in political debate in France. This is the political climate in which penal populism arises as a form of protest against those in government.

The objection will be raised that France is no worse off than Italy, which recently emerged from a government alliance between a populist party (the Five Star Movement) and a far-right party (Salvini's League). Why then are there so few criminal complaints against ministers in Italy? The reason is one of law and again underscores French exceptionalism. In other parliamentary regimes, ministers are members of parliament; they remain so when they join government, as was the case in France under the Fourth Republic. Consequently, a criminal complaint brought against them has to overcome the hurdle of parliamentary immunity. In Italy, for instance, the complaint from the lawyer for *Forza Italia* cannot go forward unless the chamber of parliament of which ministers are members removes their immunity.

In France, the 1958 constitution removed this procedural barrier. French ministers need not be members of Parliament. They are often senior civil servants or ministerial backroom staff. They may come from civil society, as in the case of Ms. Buzyn, who was previously a professor of medicine. Moreover, the 1958 constitution (art. 23C) was innovative in laying down the principle that ministerial and parliamentary functions are incompatible. A member of the National Assembly or the Senate who joins the government must resign from Parliament, thereby losing parliamentary immunity. Absent that immunity, the 1993 constitutional revision in its art. 68–1, para. 1 threw the gates wide open to criminal complaints. This put paid to any prior obstacles.

***

The spate of recent criminal complaints perfectly illustrate the *impurity of the parliamentary regime* and the *purity of exacerbated presidential rule* under which the exercise of power is uncoupled from political accountability. The frantic efforts to hold ministers criminally liable are nothing other than a consequence of this troubling state of affairs. Their proponents argue that these criminal complaints are better than nothing. To the contrary, they worsen the state of French democracy by promoting a new form of populism – penal populism.

4

Democracy and Emergency in Latin America

ROBERTO GARGARELLA

Introduction

In this chapter, I will present some reflections on the ways in which Latin American democracies have reacted to the COVID-19 crisis. I shall focus my analysis on some of the controversial institutional choices adopted during the emergency, and particularly on those choices that affect the bases of our constitutional democracies. I shall discuss the use of emergency powers; the decision to declare the "state of siege"; the value of democratic deliberation; the prevailing understanding of the principle of separation of powers; the problem of "democratic erosion"; and the threats posed by a growing economic crisis, which the COVID-19 emergency has seriously aggravated.

Emergency Powers, Discretion, and Democratic Procedures

Professor Stephen Holmes has properly emphasized the importance of respecting established democratic procedures in circumstances of emergency. During these critical circumstances, it is essential for political authorities to "tie their hands" to the mast of the law. Modern democracies choose to write down these procedural requirements, even in their constitutions, because they "minimize the risk of making fatal-but-avoidable mistakes" in the face of difficult circumstances.[1] Holmes's assertion does not rest on a prediction that, during the emergency, powerful presidents will tend to act irrationally, while more controlled presidents will tend to act reasonably. The point is rather about the risk of unchecked discretion. Our old systems of "checks and balances" minimize the risk of political authorities acting discretionally.

---

[1] S. Holmes, "In Case of Emergency: Misunderstanding Tradeoffs in the War on Terror," *California Law Review*, 97(2) (2019), 301.

Acting discretionally is not the same as acting irrationally. An executive acting with discretion may be motivated to make decisions only after considering their friends, advisors, or team of experts (for example, Alberto Fernández of Argentina or Iván Duque of Colombia, who have generally followed the advice offered by groups of experts), or they may be more inclined to act according to their capricious impulses (for example, Jair Bolsonaro of Brazil or Daniel Ortega of Nicaragua). Donald Trump's US administration offers a tragic example of the worst implications of unchecked discretion: Erratic, unfounded, and contradictory decisions. In Latin America, Brazil offers another dramatic illustration of the same phenomenon. President Bolsonaro has pursued capricious responses to the crisis, with catastrophic results. As an op-ed from the scientific magazine *The Lancet* put it, "perhaps the biggest threat to Brazil's COVID-19 response is its president, Jair Bolsonaro."[2] Mexico, where we also find an omnipresent and unreasonable executive which acts with discretion, offers another sad illustration of the implications of having a discretionary leader in times of emergency. There too, the President's acts have been characterized by lack of information, opacity, denial, and unfounded statistics, if not directly public lies.[3]

The point suggested by these examples is not simply that citizens should select a better leader in the next elections. Something more structural and less subjective is involved. In a democracy, policies should not depend on good luck or the good will of the decision-maker. When discretionary rule prevails, a good policy adopted on the first day of the emergency (say, confinement according to the dictates of science) may be reversed on the second day. A "science-based" response to the emergency should not itself be a matter of chance or good luck. Moreover, recognizing the proper place of expertise is not the only problem connected to acting with discretion: There is also the issue of democratic responsiveness. A decision relying on expert advice might turn out to be insufficiently democratic, improperly biased, or insensitive to the specific demands of those more in need. A democratic decision-making procedure needs to be informed and enriched by the viewpoints of "all those potentially affected."[4]

---

[2] "COVID-19 in Brazil: 'So What?'" *The Lancet* (May 9, 2020), www.thelancet.com/journals/lancet/article/PIIS0140-6736(20)31095-3/fulltext.

[3] For a critical note in this respect, see for instance this op-ed: "Hidden Toll: Mexico Ignores Wave of Coronavirus Deaths in Capital," *New York Times* (May 8, 2020), www.nytimes.com/2020/05/08/world/americas/mexico-coronavirus-count.html.

[4] J. Habermas, *Between Facts and Norms* (Cambridge, MA: The MIT Press, 1996).

Latin American constitutional systems have failed to ensure that which they were designed to guarantee: Proper institutional mechanisms for checking power. Contrary to this goal, our constitutions have allowed unreasonable leaders to make and enforce discretionary choices.[5] The results have frequently been frightening.[6] In fact, when we compare the deaths caused by the COVID-19 among Latin American countries, it is difficult to explain the significant differences observed without making reference to the outrageous character of certain presidential decisions.

Argentina and Brazil, for example, are two large, neighboring countries, quite similar in many respects (economic development; levels of inequality; political history). At this time, however, Argentina (a country with 44.5 million inhabitants) has had 1245 deaths due to COVID-19, while Brazil (a country with 210 million inhabitants) has had 58,314 deaths. The remarkably different results cannot be explained without making direct reference to the irrationality of Bolsonaro's responses to the pandemic – for example, he downplayed the severity of the pandemic, calling it a "little flu."[7] The fact that our democratic systems have allowed, in these extreme circumstances, outrageous responses to the crisis, while making it difficult for the people at large to control and sanction their political authorities, speaks less to the people's political incapacities and more to the deficiencies of constitutional structures.

An Undeclared "State of Siege"

In many Latin American countries, the emergency offered an excellent excuse for executive leaders to gain additional powers and also rule beyond the limits established by the constitution. Worse still, in numerous cases – including, notably, those of Argentina, Colombia, and Mexico – the emergency facilitated the imposition of an *undeclared "state of siege."* The state of siege (or "state of exception") is an extreme mechanism that appears in almost all Latin American constitutions (Argentina, Brazil, Bolivia, Colombia, Chile, Ecuador, Paraguay, Venezuela, Guatemala, El Salvador, Nicaragua, Honduras, and Panamá). It is also a constitutional

---

[5] B. Ackerman, *The Failure of the Founding Fathers: Jefferson, Marshall and the Rise of Presidential Democracy* (New York: Belknap Press, 2017); also B. Ackerman, *The Decline and Fall of the American Republic* (Cambridge, MA: Harvard University Press, 2010).

[6] www.statista.com/statistics/1103965/latin-america-caribbean-coronavirus-deaths/ (last accessed May 15, 2020).

[7] Tony Kirby, "South America Prepares for the Impact of COVID-19," *The Lancet* (April 29, 2020), www.thelancet.com/journals/lanres/article/PIIS2213-2600(20)30218-6/fulltext.

mechanism regulated through strict legal procedures and subject to severe controls. Unfortunately, in a majority of cases, those procedures have been ignored because of the practical and political difficulties of declaring a "state of siege." Presidents have preferred to declare the emergency through executive decrees.[8] They have made use of emergency powers which were originally designed for short, rapid deployment in the face of catastrophic circumstances that might make political deliberation impossible, such as responding to an earthquake or a military intrusion.

Presidents have been making use of these easily accessible emergency powers, as if a state of siege existed, but without a declaration by Congress. The presence of such a de facto state of siege lies in three fundamental elements: (1) Concentration of powers in the hands of the executive; (2) severe limitation of fundamental constitutional rights; and (3) militarization of the public space.

In numerous Latin American countries, the executive branch made all the relevant public decisions under the umbrella of the emergency.[9] Many of these decisions have restricted fundamental constitutional rights (i.e., the rights to free movements, reunion, or protest). In short, chief executives in most Latin American countries are acting to restrict fundamental rights in ways not authorized by their constitution. The silence of the vast majority of members of the legal community, who have not voiced objections to these restrictions, is both alarming and condemnable.

Epistemic Democracy and Deliberation
(Avoiding Biases and Partiality)

Many constitutional scholars insist on the importance of inclusive collective deliberations before defining public policies. They recognize the value of listening to the voices of "all those potentially affected." Decisions by a few (even a group of experts) maximize the chances of

---

[8] In Argentina, the main reason explaining the lack of desire of the Executive to establish the state of emergency through the proper legal channel (Congress) relates to the trauma caused by the most recent declaration of a state of siege, during the government of President De la Rúa. He declared the state of siege on December 19, 2001, and thus launched the most dramatic contemporary political crisis in the country (a crisis that was followed by a long period of political instability, with around forty people killed by the repressive forces of the State). So – in my view – the recently elected President Alberto Fernández decided to prevent the return of that collective memory or trauma, and thus established what represented, in fact, a state of siege, without formally declaring it.

[9] R. Uprimny, "La Cuarentena Constitucional," *El Espectador* (April 19, 2020), www .elespectador.com/opinion/la-cuarentena-constitucional-columna-915234.

losing relevant information and ignoring the demands and criticisms coming from all the rest – particularly claims coming from the most disadvantaged. An "epistemic" approach to democracy demands (always, and particularly when we face serious social and constitutional threats) that public decisions be adopted following an inclusive discussion (rather than in a rush and/or by a few). The idea is that under certain circumstances, a democratic procedure tends to "produce results which are closer to the requirements of impartiality than those produced by any other procedure."[10] In other words, "different people bring different perspectives on the issues under discussion."[11]

A few examples illustrate the relevance of taking into account the demands of "all those potentially affected." The first example concerns federalism, particularly in the case of large countries, such as the US, Brazil, and Mexico. In these countries, consultation with the different member states is crucial, not only in terms of ensuring political coordination among different sections of the country, but also in order to ground those decisions on adequate information. Without a permanent process of mutual consultation, the risk of adopting wrong, misinformed, or insufficiently impartial decisions is enormous. In Brazil, however, "the President has repeatedly and publicly clashed with state governors around Brazil for their strict implementation of social distancing measures, including the banning of public gatherings and the closure of schools. He has appeared regularly on television addressing the nation regarding the pandemic and has used phrases such as, 'get back to work' and 'people die, that's life.'"[12]

Another example illustrates the importance of making decisions only after taking into account "all the relevant voices" – particularly those of the most disadvantaged.[13] In Latin America, as in other areas of the world, the main medical advice offered by political authorities in the face of the COVID-19 crisis has typically been "wash your hands regularly and stay at home." Unfortunately, neither is feasible in the context of profound social and economic inequalities. In most Latin American countries, millions of people face serious difficulties in accessing clean water. In addition, in vast areas of the region, members of disadvantaged groups live in overcrowded conditions (perhaps between five and ten people in the same room). Facing these circumstances, it may be that the

[10] C. Nino, *The Ethics of Human Rights* (Oxford University Press, 1991), p. 249.
[11] J. Waldron, *Political Theory* (Cambridge, MA: Harvard University Press, 2016), p. 132.
[12] *The Lancet*, "COVID-19 in Brazil: 'So What?'"
[13] Habermas, *Between Facts and Norms*.

best medical advice would have been just the opposite to the one that was then offered – perhaps one simply like this: "Go out from your place and get some fresh air in a park." The point is that the (class) bias expressed by that crucial and dominant medical advice reflects a serious lack of information. This is also reflected in government orders "closing down" or "fencing out" poor neighborhoods that were affected by the virus. Even assuming good faith in trying to limit the transmission of the virus, there is a failure to consider or take into account the voices and points of view of those affected.

Separation of Powers and Constitutional Dialogue

In most Latin American countries, the division of powers is subject to old and unfortunate doctrinal readings, which generate serious problems in the working of our institutions. Two of these old approaches have had serious consequences for pandemic responses. The first concerns the notion of a "strict separation of powers,"[14] under which the different branches of government are understood as separated and unconnected powers. For this view, every attempt by members of one branch to take part in the affairs of the other branches is an unconstitutional invasion. A second and related approach sees the relationship between the branches through the logic of war, which presumes that each branch will always attempt to trespass and invade constitutional jurisdictions reserved to the other branches.

This approach to the constitutional organization of powers make it difficult to put into practice more democratic and cooperative readings of the institutional system: One, for example, in which the relationship between the branches is governed by a logic of mutual collaboration, rather than of suspicion and confrontation. In the end, and as a product of the dominant view, the relationship between the branches in times of COVID-19 tends still to respond to an unattractive binary dynamic: Either subordination (one branch dominates the others) or mutual confrontation (an institutionally channeled "war" between the branches).

We find examples of subordination in Mexico and Nicaragua, where the will of the president tends to be followed, in a silent and disciplined way, by the other branches. We find scenes of mutual confrontation between the branches in Brazil or Argentina. In Argentina, for example,

---

[14] M. J. C. Vile, *Constitutionalism and the Separation of Powers* (Indianapolis, IN: Liberty Fund, 1967).

the Supreme Court has recently received a formal consultation from the head of the Senate, who wanted to know whether the Court considered online legislative sessions to be constitutional. The Court declined the opportunity of engaging in a cooperative conversation with the legislative branch – a conversation related to the scope and meaning of the procedural rules established in the constitution. Instead, and through the invocation of the old, prevailing understanding of the division of powers (and also an impoverished reading of the doctrine of political questions), the Court maintained that there existed no "case" or "conflict" that justified its intervention.[15] In contrast, the Colombian Constitutional Court explored some different forms of more open ("crowdsourcing") intervention in the control of executive acts. By doing so, the Court demonstrated more promising alternatives to judicial review, which are still available even in the extreme circumstances of the pandemic.[16]

Political History and Democratic Erosion

In recent years, numerous scholars have begun to study what they describe as a novel phenomenon of "democratic erosion." In fact, with the coming to power of authoritarian leaders in the United States, Hungary, Poland, Turkey, etc., numerous authors began to call attention to the risks posed by situations of democratic erosion and "democratic backsliding."[17] The idea refers to "the risk of slow, but ultimately substantial unraveling along the margins of rule-of-law, democratic, and liberal rights."[18] More precisely, "democratic erosion" implies a "process of incremental but ultimately still substantial, decay in the three basic

---

[15] See CSJ 353/2020/CS1 "Fernández de Kirchner, Cristina en carácter de Presidenta del Honorable Senado de la Nación s/ acción declarativa de certeza," (April 24, 2020) www .cij.gov.ar/buscador.html?acc=search&search=cristina%20fern%E1ndez%20de%20kirch ner. See an op-ed on the matter in R. Gargarella, "Frente a la pandemia, respuestas viejas a emergencias nuevas," *Clarín* (May 12, 2020), www.clarin.com/opinion/frente-pandemia-respuestas-viejas-emergencias-nuevas_0_3gtQ1KYcs.html.

[16] See, for example, an attempt of promoting a "crowdsourcing" approach to judicial review, in www.corteconstitucional.gov.co/micrositios/decreto444/.

[17] N. Bermeo, "Democracy Backsliding," *Journal of Democracy*, 27(1) (January 2016), 5–19; T. Ginsburg and A. Huq, *How to Save a Constitutional Democracy* (The University of Chicago Press, 2018); M. Graber, S. Levinson, and M. Tushnet (eds.), *Constitutional Democracy in Crisis?* (Oxford University Press, 2018); D. Landau, "Abusive Constitutionalism," *UC Davis Law Review*, 47 (2013), 189; S. Levitsky and D. Ziblatt, *How Democracies Die* (New York: Viking, 2018); C. Sunstein (ed.), *Can It Happen Here? Authoritarianism in America* (New York: Library of Congress, 2018).

[18] Ginsburg and Huq, *How to Save*, p. 39.

predicates of democracy – competitive elections, liberal rights to speech and association and the rule of law, across different institutions, against a baseline of some ongoing level of democracy."[19]

This "new" phenomenon, which usually begins with the concentration of powers in the executive, followed by the gradual dismantling of the structure of controls ("from inside"), is actually an "old" and longstanding practice, in Latin America. Of course, a few decades ago, this "gradual erosion from inside" usually came together with violent and abrupt military coups.[20] For a variety of reasons, in the twenty-first century our politics have become less violent. However, this political change (namely, the passage from the abrupt to the gradual breakdown of democracy) should not make Latin Americans forget about the lessons learned from our difficult political and social history. Particularly at this time, we should not forget that Latin American countries have a long and tragic history of political abuses, curtailment of rights, violations of the constitution, and emergency powers quickly adopted in times of crisis but never relinquished by executive authorities. Just an example to bear in mind: In Argentina, President Néstor Kirchner asked Congress for emergency powers on January 6, 2002, in the face of a dramatic socioeconomic crisis, and he never resigned them. Those emergency powers (which were periodically renovated by a favorable Congress) continued in the hands of the executive even after the coming of the "boom of commodities," a few years later. The powers were only eliminated after sixteen years (January 6, 2018) when an opposition party came to power.

Latin America's long history of political authoritarianism suggests extreme caution before conceding additional powers to the president or restricting constitutional rights. We have a lot of information about how presidents – unequivocally – tend to use and abuse those powers; we should avoid repeating those traumas. Moreover, we know that when presidents manage to seize additional powers, they tend to retain them. Unfortunately, we see that already executive authorities are again – surreptitiously or not – taking advantage of the crisis to seize additional powers.

The pandemic has offered political leaders a wonderful opportunity to reaffirm or strengthen their own powers. For example, in Chile, President Sebastián Piñera's administration decided to defer the much-anticipated constitutional referendum scheduled for April. (At the end of 2019, President Piñera decreed a curfew and ordered the military to take to the

---

[19] Ibid., pp. 43–4.
[20] Ibid.

streets, following an unprecedented social crisis. Piñera's decision only exacerbated the situation of social stress and, as a result, the President accepted to call for a plebiscite. The plebiscite would precede the reform of the 1980 Constitution, which was drawn up by Augusto Pinochet's dictatorship.) COVID-19 offered a perfect excuse to postpone the popular consultation until the end of October.[21] A still more worrying scenario appears in Bolivia, where the seriously irregular interim government, led by Jeanine Anez, announced that it would postpone presidential elections originally slated for May 3 (the ballot was a rerun of a fraught 2019 election that "sparked widespread protests and violence").[22] Of course, in both these cases, there were good reasons to postpone the call for popular elections. Nevertheless, it is also apparent that the incumbent governments obtained what they had been unsuccessfully trying to obtain through other, politically less attractive means. Perhaps the preservation of our basic constitutional structures, in times of emergency, requires other responses from national authorities – more specifically, responses that enrich rather than restrict, still further, the functioning of our democracies.

Inequality, Economic Crisis, and Social Protests

My final comment relates to the profound economic crisis that is affecting Latin America. Latin America remains the most unequal region in the world – a situation that the COVID-19 pandemic has only aggravated.[23] Under these conditions, we need our institutions to be particularly open and sensitive to demands and criticisms coming from below. Unfortunately,

---

[21] See, for instance, "Chile to Postpone Referendum on New Constitution as Coronavirus Concerns Grow," Reuters (March 19, 2020), www.reuters.com/article/us-health-coronavirus-chile/chile-to-postpone-referendum-on-new-constitution-as-coronavirus-concerns-grow-idUSKBN2163TL. See also J. Contesse, "Chile's Constitutional Awakening," Open Global Rights (April 13, 2020), www.openglobalrights.org/chiles-constitutional-awakening/.

[22] See, for instance "Bolivia Election Body Proposes June-to-September Window for Coronavirus-Delayed Vote," Reuters (March 26, 2020), www.reuters.com/article/us-health-coronavirus-bolivia-election/bolivia-election-body-proposes-june-to-september-window-for-coronavirus-delayed-vote-idUSKBN21D39N; "Bolivia Postpones Elections, Announces Nationwide 14-day Quarantine to Stem Spread of Coronavirus," Reuters (March 26, 2020), www.reuters.com/article/us-health-coronavirus-bolivia/bolivia-announces-nationwide-14-day-quarantine-to-stem-spread-of-coronavirus-idUSKBN2180VG.

[23] F. Alvaredo and L. Gasparini, "Recent Trends in Inequality and Poverty in Developing Countries," in A. Atkinson and F. Bourguignon (eds.), Handbook of Income Distribution (Amsterdam: Elsevier, 2015), vol. 2, pp. 697–705.

I think that we are about to receive the crisis in the worst possible way, with limited constitutional rights and power concentrated in the hands of a few.

Beginning with Mexico's 1917 Constitution, Latin American countries have enacted robust constitutions including social, economic, and cultural rights. This trend toward the expansion of constitutional rights has only increased in recent years (particularly after the human rights crises of the 1970s). In fact, as expressed in a recent IDEA report,

> in a sample of 29 important reforms in this area of design from 1978 to 2012, 19 of them (65 per cent) added new rights to the classic list of civil rights. The same pattern, although less pronounced, is observed in the area of social and economic rights, where 15 reforms (52 per cent) increased the number and types of these rights. Innovations in community and group rights, in turn, have occurred in 10 (34 per cent) of the reforms.[24]

Poor people need fair opportunities to demand recognition and respect for their fundamental rights. They need the ability to present demands against the state, when it violates or does not properly satisfy their constitutional social rights.

Institutional conditions are, at this point, completely unprepared to advance these demands. The COVID crises has brought with it an economic crisis for the worst-off. As a director of the IMF declared to the *Financial Times*, the situation is "going to worsen the already unequal income distribution and poverty levels."[25] During the emergency period, the judicial system has not worked or has worked in slow motion; in Argentina, for example, the Supreme Court declared a continuation of the annual judicial leave period that usually ends in March, restricting access to justice.[26] Given both history and the depth of the crisis, there are no good reasons to think that the situation will improve in the foreseeable future. There is even less reason to assume that the judiciary will start pursuing an active role for the enforcement of social rights after the crisis reaches an end. These "warnings" have already been raised by the Due Process Legal Foundation. The list of their concerns included, among others, the following: (1) Lack of access to information; (2) failure to

---

[24] G. Negretto, "Constitution Building Processes in Latin America," IDEA, *International IDEA* discussion paper 3/2018 (2018), 32, www.idea.int/sites/default/files/publications/constitution-building-processes-in-latin-america.pdf.

[25] "Poverty and Populism Put Latin America at the Centre of Pandemic," *Financial Times* (June 13, 2020), www.ft.com/content/aa84f572-f7af-41a8-be41-e835bddbed5b.

[26] See Corte Suprema de Justicia de la Nación Argentina, Gobierno Abierto Judicial, www.csjn.gov.ar/sentencias-acordadas-y-resoluciones/acordadas-de-la-corte-suprema.

expand regular capacities to address the exceptional needs of access to justice for groups in a vulnerable situation (e.g., women exposed to situations of violence, persons deprived of liberty; migrants); (3) continuing ongoing fiscal reform, and the struggle against judicial corruption; (4) expanding the judicial processes to investigate and prosecute acts of corruption committed during the pandemic.[27]

Worse than the failure to protect social rights has been the efforts of some governments to establish even more severe restrictions and controls upon the claims and protests of the most disadvantaged. Latin Americans will not only rank worse in terms of the enforcement of social rights after the crisis, but they will also confront even more severe difficulties in demanding justice. Argentina offers an illustration: The Minister of Security, Sabina Frederic admitted (on April 9, 2020) that the forces under her control are developing tasks of internal security – such as "cyber-patrolling" the web – that were explicitly prohibited by a recent law regulating National Intelligence.[28] The Inter-American Commission of Human Rights has already shown its concerns about this situation. Other Latin American countries are adopting data and technology initiatives to monitor the location and contacts of citizens. "Some of these measures impose severe restrictions on individual freedoms, including to their privacy and other human rights. Unprecedented levels of surveillance, data exploitation, and misinformation are being tested across the world."[29]

In this brief chapter, I have examined six issues of public and institutional relevance, which may help us understand and critically evaluate the behavior of Latin America's state authorities at the time of the COVID-19 crisis.

---

[27] "También en pandemia, la justicia es un servicio esencial," DPLF, www.dplf.org/sites/default/files/infografia_justicia_y_pandemia_diagnostico_y_preocupaciones.pdf.

[28] Manuel Tarricone, "Qué es el ciberpatrullaje y qué relevancia toma durante la cuarentena," Chequeado (April 10, 2020), https://chequeado.com/el-explicador/que-es-el-ciberpatrullaje-y-que-relevancia-toma-durante-la-cuarentena/.

[29] "Tracking the Global Response to COVID-19," Privacy International, https://privacyinternational.org/examples/tracking-global-response-covid-19.

5

Apocalyptic Christianity, Democracy, and the Pandemic

STANLEY HAUERWAS

Trump and the Pandemic

"Barmen! We need something like the Barmen Declaration that challenged the German Christians' accommodation with Hitler."[1] That was my first thought on May 22, 2020, when I read US President Donald Trump's order for churches, synagogues, and mosques to open and welcome all those ready to respond to his desire that everyone to return to church. After prohibiting the gathering of diverse groups in the first weeks of response to the virus, Trump suddenly commanded Christians, Jews, and Muslims to open their places of worship as if the virus did not exist.

On reflection, I thought I was letting my dislike of Trump tempt me to overreact to his sudden call for religious people to attend church. Trump was urging Christians to return to church as a sign he had defeated or come close to defeating the virus. No doubt, I thought we needed something like Barmen because of my deep and profound dislike of Trump. Yet Hitler is one thing and Trump is quite something else. Trump is stupid, crass, self-absorbed, and shallow – the list could go on – but he is not Hitler.

Yet on further reflection, I think my original response was not without reason. Barmen was at the time the most significant response Christians had made against Hitler. It was written in 1936, primarily by that

---

[1] Arthur Cochrane, *The Church's Confession Under Hitler* (Philadelphia, PA: Westminster Press, 1962) remains one of the best accounts we have of Barmen and Karl Barth's role in writing the document. Those that gathered at Barmen represented a break from the classical Lutheran orders of creation/redemption doctrine that left the state free to do its will. Barth was Swiss but at the time held the chair at Bonn, which he soon lost because he refused to take an oath of loyalty to Hitler. The German Christian Church was founded by Hitler.

extraordinary theologian, Karl Barth. Barth had fomented a revolution in European theology by recovering the Christological center of Christian faith. In his famous commentary on the Book of Romans, Barth reclaimed the apocalyptic character of Christian convictions in a manner that challenged the accommodated and compromised form of mainstream Christianity. Barmen was the document that made these developments politically concrete.

How is a document like Barmen relevant to a pandemic and/or the confusing politics of a Trump? Hitler was evil. Trump at his worst is just mean. But then, the whole Trump presidency is inexplicable, if seen narrowly and only through the frame of his character. Something like a Barmen is required, if we are to lift our vision beyond the pathology of Trump the person, to the pathologies of democracy and contemporary Christianity. It is required particularly because without convictions like those of Barmen, Trump can claim to represent what Christianity looks like today. Even more troubling, his claim to represent Christianity is not without support, given the compromised character of American Christianity. We dare not forget that Billy Graham is Christianity for Americans.

Trump's presidency has been a crisis that has the feel of a drama associated with an apocalyptic time. And time is the "stuff" that makes an apocalyptic moment. Apocalyptic means there is no going back. To describe a time as apocalyptic is to mark a time that changes time. If Trump's view of Christianity is accepted by Christians, we may indeed be at the end times of the Christian faith.

Given the Establishment character of most forms of Christianity, it is hard to remember that Christianity is an apocalyptic faith. For Christians, all time has been reconfigured by the crucifixion of a Palestinian Jew. Barth was the theologian who saw that this claim meant that Christians could not make peace with worldly peace. Jesus has already made time, our time, apocalyptic. The result is the creation of a politics that is a challenge to all politics based on violence. It is the burden of this chapter to show the difference that makes.

Theology in Times of Pandemic

It may well be that only a theologian would think something like the Barmen Declaration to be important in response to Trump's attempt to use the pandemic to insure his reelection. But then I am a theologian. It is my job to try to show the difference God makes. Trump may not be a Hitler, but that does not mean he is not dangerous. He is dangerous for no other reason than he is a liar. Democracies cannot be sustained unless a people exist who will tell one another the truth. Neither can Christian faith be sustained, if it fails to tell its own truth. Christians are called to speak truth to politics. Accordingly, Trump is a threat both to politics and to Christianity.

We need Christians who can recognize idolatry when they see it. Barth was able to recognize the threat Hitler represented because, as he wrote in the second article of Barmen, "We reject the false doctrine that there are spheres of life to which we belong not to Jesus Christ but to other masters, realms where we do not need to be justified and sanctified by him."[2] That claim followed from the first article of the Barmen Declaration, which concluded with a stark declaration condemning the false doctrine that there is a source of the church's proclamation apart from the Word of God found in God's revelation in Christ.[3] From Barth's perspective, that means the church knows what the state must be better than the state can know on its own. Trump fundamentally contests this position, by claiming to know better than the church what faith is.

The theologian's role is to contest Trump's claim for the sake of a politics of redemption. Democratic politics is a competition of narratives that go to the meaning and so to the possibilities of politics. Those meanings are very much at issue in our collective response to the pandemic. To enter the contest with Trump, however, Christians must have a hold of our own narrative.

One may well wonder if I am not making a major mistake by calling attention to Barmen in a book of essays meant to assess the effect of the pandemic on democracy. Barth supported democracy, but he was also quite aware that often some forms of democratic liberalism can result in making strong convictions questionable. "Jesus is Lord" was not a political opinion for Barth. "Jesus is Lord" is the claim that gives the church the task of keeping any political form modest because it is judged by such a Lord. Trump's politics are anything but modest. Yet he claims, with some evidence, Christian support.

For some, Barmen was too Christian and for others it was not Christian enough. But then part of the case I want to make is that the Christian support of Trump has not been subject to the kind of critique required by the Gospel. As a result, a politics has not developed that is

---

[2] Ibid., p. 172.
[3] For the full text of Barmen see ibid., pp. 172–8.

capable of calling into question the faith Trump and his followers claim to be driving their response to the pandemic. I have held this critical attitude toward American politics for many years; it has earned for me some rather negative attributions. Nevertheless, I have maintained that the subject of theology and ethics in America has always been America.[4]

The Politics of the Pandemic

I may well seem to be writing a chapter on Donald Trump rather than the virus. There is something to that but I see no alternative. There can be no discussion of this virus by itself. Politics has been present from the origins of the virus in China, to the attempt to limit the spread of the disease in the United States. Absent a consensus about how to account for the existence of the virus, competing narratives arise to tell the story of the pandemic and how difficult it is to control its spread. The choice among these competing narratives is a political decision.

In that regard, it is quite fascinating to consider appeals to science as crucial for legitimating different strategies of control. It is as if science has become a self-validating abstraction – thus, the constant claim by political figures that they are simply following the dictates of science. That is an appeal to authority that is meant to depoliticize the response to the pandemic. Seldom is the political more political than when it denies it is political.

Yet, the difficulty of understanding the virus as well as the complex policies developed to try to limit its spread has frustrated many. Some have tried to understand the pandemic theologically by comparing it with the Black Death. Indeed, as I will suggest below, like the Black Death the current pandemic is a reminder that we are death-destined creatures. Yet those that died of the Black Death died with some confidence that they would be properly buried. They also shared what we do not, that is, a common way of life.

Trump's declaration that Christians should return to church was no doubt calculated to play to his supporters on the religious right. Not to be missed, however, is how his call for religious groups to fill up the churches on Sunday reflects his view of Christianity in particular and his understanding of religion in general. For example, he seems to have

---

[4] See my previous writings, for example in Rom Coles and Stanley Hauerwas, *Christianity, Democracy, and the Radical Ordinary: Conversations between a Radical Democrat and a Christian* (Eugene, OR: Cascade, 2008).

forgotten that Jews have a quite different way to mark time than Christians.

When it comes to religion, Trump manifests all the marks of a good Protestant liberal. He vaguely believes in a vague god who is vaguely found in all religious traditions. What is important is not what you believe but that you believe. Accordingly, the different faiths can be lumped under the general description of "religion," because the various traditions are assumed to be the same.[5] Each, in its particular way, is celebrated to the extent that it serves to sustain Trump's understanding of what makes America – and thus Trump – great.

Trump made a brief but fascinating suggestion of what he thinks people get from going to church – it is where they are comforted. He never quite says it explicitly, but he seems to imply that religions provide a way to go on in the face of death. One suspects Trump does not feel he ever needs such comfort, but for the weak such comfort is not without its uses. To relegate the church to providing care of the soul is to imagine a church that is incapable of producing a Barmen Declaration.

Interestingly, Trump seems to assume that the comforting role of faith explains why faith has a role in sustaining democracies. Trump, like many Americans, thinks of religion as a generalized attitude of reverence that makes democratic politics work. While in practice he is an authoritarian, he nonetheless purports to represent the religious convictions of the American evangelical right. That faith community assumes that the political task of the church is to support the subjectivity of religious believers.

Which brings me finally to say why I thought of Barmen in response to Trump's call for the churches to fill the pews – so much for the six-feet rule. That I responded so critically has less to do with Trump than with my worry about the character of the church that Trump has tried to call into existence. He presumes, not without some support, that Christians will do that which he asks of them. How could that have happened? How could followers of Christ, when faced with a pandemic, end up as followers of Donald Trump? The answer is straightforward and clear – they are Americans first and Christians second.

Here is the critical point. The basic political reality of the pandemic is that it has legitimated Trump's assumption that he can speak as a Christian and

---

[5] For this understanding of Protestant liberalism, see George Lindbeck, *The Nature of Doctrine: Religion and Theology in a Post-Liberal Age* (Philadelphia, PA: Westminster Press, 1984).

for Christians. That he is able to assume such a position is made possible by the fact that, although the church has not been legally established through most of America's national life, it has been socially established.

To be sure, the status of Christianity in America is changing and that change is more radical than Trump and his supporters can comprehend. His call for Christians to fill up the churches assumes that the churches in America are not on the road to being empty buildings. Christianity may still be the civil religion of America but that may be true only because Christians remain more American than Christian.

Trump's May 22 declaration that Christians should fill the churches should be taken seriously as an indication that Christians have lost control of what makes them Christian. When Trump quotes Romans 13, he thinks he is legitimating his rule as a strongman. It does not occur to him to read Romans 12, in which Christians are commanded not to repay evil with evil. Trump is without a doubt ignorant of the substance of Christianity, but that is why he is so dangerous. He has become the pope of evangelical Christianity presiding over a civil religion that bears the name "Christianity." That faith, however, is a pale reflection of a people whose identity is determined by a crucified messiah. Few developments could be more debilitating for Christians than to accept Trump's response to the pandemic as an expression of the meaning of their faith.

It is tempting not to take seriously Trump's call to fill up the churches. His appeal seems to be but another of his spontaneous ejaculations that have little long-term significance. Whether or not he was sincere – whatever it might mean for Trump to be sincere – he clearly had the impending election in view. That Trump's religious appeal was just Trump's politics as usual does not make it less significant and dangerous for us.

Trump deploys religion to inspire his followers. Doing so, he assumes he understands better than most why religion is so important. For him, the meaning of Christianity is that of the civil religion in which he was formed. That was the prosperity gospel of Norman Vincent Peale. It was a gospel designed to make late capitalism a legitimate form of life for American Christians. Donald Trump's life indicates he drank deeply at that well.

On Fear and Death

The truth of the matter is that Christians were generally ill-prepared to know how to respond constructively to the pandemic in general, or to Trump's declaration that Christians should return to church in particular. Like most people, Christians found they had no idea what to do or why they should do one thing rather than another. The fear of death, no doubt, was their first reaction to the reality of the virus. As a result, the pandemic left Christians, as it did most people, basically out of control. To be out of control is to live in fear, and fear makes one vulnerable to those who promise safety.

Christians were quite docile, doing what they were told to do. They had followed orders to cancel worship services, because they listened to warnings against gathering in large groups. Interestingly, this often involved an order from some representative of the state directed specifically at churches. It is not clear to me why churches could not be included under the general prohibition of large gatherings.

Of course, such gatherings were prohibited in the hope of limiting the spread of the virus. While it is really quite remarkable how much we still do not know about the virus, we do know that large groups can act as breeding grounds for the virus. The six-feet rule seems arbitrary, but it turns out that it and the face mask are the most effective preventive measures we have to control the virus.

But how were churches to observe that social-distancing rule? Indeed, the whole strategy of isolation seemed to run counter to one of the central practices of the church, that is, the gathering of people from the world to worship God. For Christians, to be isolated from one another in the interest of avoiding the virus seems to contradict one of the things that makes Christianity what it is. Christians, whose faith is founded on the sacrifice of the martyrs, seemed to let the public health concerns of the government dictate their response to the virus. Moreover, by accepting the strategy of public health, the church seemed to underwrite the presumption that any response to the pandemic is to be based on the fear of death.

Such fear, I have argued elsewhere, is at the heart of democratic liberalism. That is why Thomas Hobbes is the central figure in explanations of the basic structure of American politics. The task of government, on this view, is to insure the longest life possible. Thus, the legitimacy of American politics is secured by promising better health care. Not surprisingly, our largest political battles in the last ten years have been over the creation of national health insurance. Yet, to the extent that Christians accepted this understanding of the war on the virus, it was not clear whether they too thought the good of the democratic process to be nothing other than survival.

There was, however, another alternative, at least for Christians. The Christian response to the pandemic could be one grounded in acts of neighborly love. By assuming a stance that protects others from being infected, Christians can be understood as enacting an ethic of mutual care for themselves and their neighbors. Such an ethic might be subject to sentimentalities about which Trump is a master, but that does not mean we must accept his narration of the challenge the virus presents. Christians must give their own account; they must offer a compelling and competitive narrative. Such a narrative must speak to the role of love for those whose lives are destined to death.

No one knows how long the pandemic will last. Most people, and I include myself, assume that before long life will be back to normal. But we have little reason for calling the life we led prior to the virus "normal." The pandemic is our opportunity to reclaim a Christian imagination that refuses to let the way things are be the limit of a life well lived. Such a view, however, means our first task is to recognize that we are a people scattered around the world. Our task is to be a people who reflect the greatness of God. We do not need to make God great. That was done on a cross.

In 1933, Hitler began his rule with wide support in the German population. He had that support, in part, because he appeared to be friendly toward Christians. It was not long, however, before he sought to create a nationalistic church with its own Reich head. Barth, in service to the formation of the Confessing Church, wrote the stirring words of the Barmen Declaration. They are apocalyptic words asserting that a new world was created by the crucifixion of a Palestinian Jew two thousand years ago. That apocalyptic stance created a politics called "church" which is constituted by a people who refuse to be ruled by a politics of death. That is the challenge for Christians on this side of the pandemic. It is not a new challenge for those people who follow Jesus.

PART II

Knowledge

Introduction

The COVID-19 pandemic was the crisis of modernity that had long been anticipated. Globalization of commerce and movement was responsible for the rapid spread around the world. Globalization of information was the only hope for an effective response. Those information flows included forms of public health response as well as unprecedented cooperation among scientists. Nations learn from success and failure in other countries, as do scientists.

Best practices emerged, as did worst practices. Transparency became a watchword in order to keep open the possibility of learning and preserve accountability, in a context where policies are in constant change. Pandemic response created a global school in public health, which nations could not afford to ignore even if, paradoxically, it simultaneously challenged the legitimacy of the only genuinely global multilateral health organization (the WHO).

Global information flows also included the science that everyone looked to for a long-term answer. The pandemic has initiated the most concentrated and integrated global scientific effort ever. We will have to see if that is followed by an equally cooperative effort to make globally available the results of that scientific effort.

Both of these developments point to a unique feature of the pandemic response. It has put at issue the relationship between political leadership and expert knowledge. A necessary role of government is to facilitate the development of the knowledge needed to respond. Yet, an early lesson of the pandemic is that experts do not speak with a single voice. Even worse, they can change their minds as new information becomes available. Political leadership is dependent upon expert knowledge, but it cannot leave it to the scientists to decide what must be done. To make matters even more complicated, virology and epidemiology are not the only

85

forms of expert knowledge relevant to the crisis. There is also economics, for the virus is destroying livelihoods right alongside the destruction of health.

The crisis, therefore, has been a vast experiment in integrating democratic accountability with expert knowledge. In this respect too, the crisis is the emergency added to a long-term reconsideration of the relationship of expertise to democratic governance. Populist movements around the world had been challenging the role of experts, and even the trustworthiness of science. The visible expression of this has been the anti-vaccine movement, which may make it difficult to eradicate the disease even after the experts invent a vaccine.

In politics, knowledge claims are always related to the development of public opinion. Indeed, we can think of public opinion as that which the public "knows." From an expert point of view, that may not be knowledge at all. But from a political point of view, it may be the only knowledge that counts in a democracy. One role of political leadership is to try to manage the development of public opinion in such a way that it is open to expert knowledge. But one cannot ignore the temptations of political leadership to manipulate expert knowledge to advance a partisan public opinion. The "knowledge" upon which our collective will is formed is, today, impacted by the substantial flow of misinformation on both new and old media. This raises fundamental questions on the use of government power to regulate information.

The chapters in Part II address fundamental issues concerning the relationship of democracy to knowledge, information, and opinion. Against the background of the pandemic, they highlight democracy's need for knowledge and discuss how knowledge is or ought to be developed.

Michael Ignatieff addresses political leadership, in times of crisis, by focusing on how citizens do and ought to exercise democratic scrutiny. The answer to this question is located at the intersection of moral perfectionism, which demands our leaders to behave better than us, and the competitive advantage of politics, whose administrative apparatus, intelligence services, and access to expertise allow for better foresight. Ultimately, Ignatieff suggests that we face a reckoning with ourselves. A reckoning that starts with realizing that our institutions have failed to protect the weakest among us, and that can turn this awareness into the political will necessary to address inequalities and redress a liberal democratic order with moral legitimacy.

Contrary to Ignatieff, Samuel Moyn believes that the transformative potential of the pandemic is highly over-estimated. In his thought-provoking contribution, he provides an entirely different perspective on the COVID-19 pandemic. Drawing upon historical records of the great flu epidemic of 1918–1919, he argues that pandemics rarely leave long-lasting marks in history or deeply transform societies. He suggests that, despite the many claims that everything will change after the coronavirus, this pandemic is no exception.

Moshe Habertal's chapter investigates emergency response in societies. He argues that emergencies are diagnostic tools, exposing societies' systemic weaknesses. The effectiveness of a society and its institutions to respond to threats can be measured against three main dimensions: Institutional reorganization, public emotional reaction, and the exercise of power by political leaders. The pandemic has exposed serious shortcomings on all of them, highlighting the current fragilities of our political institutions and public discourse. It calls for a recentering of our public debate around a realm of values and knowledge free from the grip of politics.

According to Daniel Innerarity, the fundamental political issue is that of learning from the crisis. Crises notoriously present learning opportunities, but we can fail to take advantage of the situation. The real challenge of this crisis is to learn to think in terms of systemic complexity. Early responses did not rise to the challenge, instead taking a linear approach, as if the pandemic developed on a single causal chain rather than as a complex system of interconnected risks and dynamics. While this lesson of complexity must be learned by governments everywhere, pluralistic democracies have, Innerarity believes, advantages over authoritarian regimes precisely because of their openness to diverse approaches, insights, and claims.

6

The Reckoning: Evaluating Democratic Leadership

MICHAEL IGNATIEFF

The pandemic is still upon us, but the reckoning with its political conse-quences in Europe has already begun. A commission of inquiry will be set up in the UK to explain why COVID-19 has claimed more than 50,000 lives in a country that once prided itself on its public administration and its health service; public prosecutors in Italy are interviewing the Prime Minister to see whether there was dereliction of duty in the Bergamo region, where the epidemic had a savage impact; in Spain, grieving families are suing politicians for failing to order quarantine early enough.[1] Elsewhere, the daily plebiscite that is democracy is in full swing: Opinion research companies are tabulating how citizens feel their leaders "performed" and the opinion formers on social media are assessing leaders' records, often according to their own ideological pre-dilections. Future elections will be referenda, in whole or in part, on leadership performance in the pandemic.

The key question in all these reckonings is: Did leaders anticipate consequences and act in time? The flood of judgments in the press suggests people think this is an easy question to answer. In fact, it's anything but easy. What data, for example, should we use, and what data should we trust? Can leaders be praised or condemned, simply on

---

[1] I am indebted to Niall Ferguson for sharing with me "The Coronavirus Pandemic in the Light of History and Network Science," unpublished, Stanford University, June 2020. Michael Buchanan and Judith Burns, "Coronavirus: 'Start Public Inquiry Now to Prevent More Deaths,'" bbc.com (June 12, 2020), www.bbc.com/news/uk-53009946; Alasdair Sandford, "Coronavirus: Italy Prosecutors Question PM Giuseppe Conte over lockdown 'delay,'" euro-news (June 12, 2020), www.euronews.com/2020/06/12/coronavirus-italy-prosecutors-ques tion-pm-giuseppe-conte-over-lockdown-delay; Brian McGleenon, "Spain's Prime Minister Sued by Thousands of Furious Coronavirus Victims' Families' Relatives," *Daily Express* (May 12, 2020), www.express.co.uk/news/world/1281302/spain-coronavirus-prime-minister-pedro-sanchez-sued-coronavirus-death-toll-supreme-court.

the basis of death rates and infection rates? Can country performances be compared at all? Should the record of New Zealand, an island nation in the South Pacific, be compared to, say, Belgium, a country with high population densities in crowded northwestern Europe? These important questions will occupy social science for a decade.[2]

While we wait for that, we can ask a preliminary question: What expectations about political leadership are legitimate for citizens to have in a crisis? What can we reasonably expect political leaders to have known and done? What we know now about the virus – how it spreads, whom it impacts and whom it spares, how it can be prevented – is not what we knew before it struck. In order for evaluation to be fair, we need to retrace our steps back to the point at which we knew, all of us, so much less.

Once we compare this epidemic with other crises in the past, it appears that citizens have long understood there is a problem evaluating political foresight. This may be why they have often tended to be more forgiving of failures of anticipation than of execution. Franklin Roosevelt did not pay a political price for failing to anticipate the bombings of Pearl Harbor. George W. Bush won reelection in 2004 despite 9/11, even after subsequent inquiry discovered that the warning lights on the national security dashboard were blinking red before the attack.[3] Failures to anticipate, in these two instances, were at least partially forgiven thanks to subsequent performance. Roosevelt was forgiven thanks to titanic leadership through the next four years. George W. Bush pivoted from questions about his failure to anticipate 9/11, by insisting that his administration prevented subsequent attacks on the US mainland. This pivot may not have saved the historical reputation of his presidency, but it helped him to complete two terms as president.

Our resigned tolerance for the failures of leaders follows from what we know about ourselves. We are prone to panic at threats that prove harmless, only to be blind-sided by events we should have foreseen. When it comes to prediction, politicians aren't much better than the rest of us.

---

[2] Gavin Lee, "Coronavirus: Why So Many People are Dying in Belgium," bbc.com (May 2, 2020), www.bbc.com/news/world-europe-52491210; Konstantin Richter, "How New Zealand Beat the Coronavirus," Politico (May 14, 2020), www.politico.eu/article/kiwis-vs-coronavirus-new-zealand-covid19-restrictions-rules/.

[3] "The 9/11 Commission Report: Final Report of the National Commission on Terrorist Attacks on the United States," (n.d.) https://govinfo.library.unt.edu/911/report/911Report_Exec.pdf.

We also know that political leadership is exceptionally hard. Every president or prime minister who has ever lived complains about having to make decisions in a hurry, under pressure, with limited information. In modern conditions, the problem is not too little information but too much, but either way, failures of anticipation and execution are routine. The experience of the pandemic will certainly increase disillusion with political leadership – and some initial studies of European public opinion confirm this – but the real issue may be: What *can* be expected of agents as fallible as we all are?[4]

It is a mercy – as well as a stabilizing factor in democracy – that there is any portion of forgiveness in citizen's reckoning with their leaders. There cannot be continuity in leadership if leaders are "spilled" – as they say in Australia – every time they make a mistake. Some citizens at least understand that accountability needs balancing with empathy, for a citizen's reckoning with a leader is always, at least indirectly, a reckoning with themselves. The least elevating but most truthful meaning of democracy – "government of the people, by the people, and for the people" – is that we are governed by people no better than we are.

Indeed, one of the dangers to democracy is moral perfectionism, the demand that leaders behave better than the rest of us, display more foresight than most of us are capable of, and protect us when we fail to protect ourselves. Perfectionists of this kind think of themselves as disappointed friends of democracy: It is in the name of high ideals that they lament, if only our leaders could "inspire" us, "rise to the occasion," "fulfill our dreams" and in extremis, protect us from harm. In reality, perfectionism of this sort is an ally of cynicism and disengagement. To demand such high standards of foresight and wisdom from leaders is to set the bar beyond reality, and to reinforce the disillusion and easy despair about politics and democracy that is the standard fare of sophisticated discussion in far too many dinner tables and back garden barbecues.

At the same time, "to understand is to forgive" would be to give some culpably negligent politicians a free pass. Some rough justice toward leaders' failures is already overdue. Any leader who recommends taking bleach, even as a joke; or who promotes the effectiveness of an anti-malarial agent, without proper medical evidence; or who counsels

---

[4] Ivan Krastev and Mark Leonard, "Europe's Pandemic Politics: How the Virus Has Changed The Public's World-View," ECFR (June 24, 2020), www.ecfr.eu/publications/summary/europes_pandemic_politics_how_the_virus_has_changed_the_publics_worldview.

wearing masks and then fails to wear one; or who orders lockdown and then breaks their own lockdown rules; or who exploits the pandemic to permanently abridge constitutional freedoms, deserves censure.[5] But these cases are easy. The more difficult ones occur where leaders did their best but were unable to prevent high death tolls. Quebec might be such a case, or Belgium, where well-led governments struggled with high death rates.[6] Here is where citizen evaluation may prove difficult, at the next election or beyond, when leaders' historical reputations will be made.

While politicians are fashioned, just like the rest of us, from what Immanuel Kant called "the crooked timber of humanity," they *are* better informed and should be held to a higher standard of foresight. Any democratically elected leader has a staff, a bureaucracy, an intelligence service, diplomats overseas, scientific advisors, and the convening power to seek information from business, industry, and academia. The staff who surround a democratic leader are supposed to funnel this information into actionable intelligence, to be their leader's eyes and ears, to put out brush fires before they become blazes, to silence the dogs so they don't bark, and to reproduce the impression that their leaders are never nonplussed by the course of events. This simulacrum of mastery may be an illusion, but it is the key to the performance art that is politics. Tony Blair liked to say that being prime minister meant conveying the impression that you were floating along on the tide, serenely in charge, at least from the waist up, while below, you were furiously pedaling to keep afloat.[7] Harold Macmillan's famous reply to the question about what was most challenging about being prime minister – "Events dear boy, events" – is wise because it acknowledged how frequently the vast apparatus of institutional foresight at a prime minister's command breaks down.[8]

The inquiries that are likely to follow, in those countries such as the UK where a sense of failure is palpable, will have to explain why the vast apparatus of foresight failed the Prime Minister when he needed it. Did

[5] Elizabeth Zerofsky, "How Viktor Orbán Used the Coronavirus to Seize More Power," *New Yorker* (April 7, 2020), www.newyorker.com/news/letter-from-europe/how-viktor-orban-used-the-coronavirus-to-seize-more-power.

[6] Government of Quebec, "Situation of the Coronavirus in Quebec," www.quebec.ca/en/health/health-issues/a-z/2019-coronavirus/situation-coronavirus-in-quebec/ (accessed August 1, 2020).

[7] Tony Blair, *A Journey: My Political Life* (London: Vintage, 2011).

[8] It is possible he never said it. Elizabeth M. Knowles, *What They Didn't Say: A Book of Misquotations* (Oxford University Press, 2006), pp. vi, 33.

the intelligence services grasp the seriousness of the outbreak in China? Were the scientific advisors aligned or at odds? When were decisions actually taken, and were critical opportunities for early action missed? Questions such as these will lay bare how science, politics, and information interacted, and we can only hope that the results of any inquiry will improve the operations of government next time.

These official inquiries will be of interest chiefly to insiders, to the professionals who manage foresight in advanced democracies. For the rest of us who have to pronounce rough and ready judgment on leaders at the next election, the question remains: To what standard should we hold our elected officials?

A citizen never creates these standards alone. In any crisis, standards emerge in a chaotic public debate that leaders vainly seek to control, as a country careens into chaos. These standards – set by journalists, social media exchanges among citizens, experts, real and self-appointed – then become a kind of common sense that stabilizes, at least for a time, the terms of a public's reckoning with a leader's performance. These standards are unstable and because they are contested, they may change over the course of a crisis. They may only command the embattled center of debate, not its margins to the left and right. It is a fallacy to suppose that consensus reigns, around which frightened citizens can find a secure basis for judgment. For leaders and led alike, a crisis is a crisis precisely because the whole evaluation frame for democratic leadership is placed into question.

In order to examine the battle over standards of estimation more carefully, we should look at what came, at least for a time, to be regarded as political common sense, in the center of democratic debate in most European countries. There were four elements of conventional wisdom that came to frame the assessment standards that many citizens used when judging their leaders:

1. "Go early and go hard." The earlier and more thorough the lockdown, the lower the eventual death toll.
2. "Follow the science." Base public policy decisions on the best available epidemiological advice.
3. "Be transparent." Tell the public what they need to know, even if they don't want to know it.
4. "Do what it takes." Use all the powers of government to restart the economy.

While these four elements constituted the "conventional wisdom," both citizens who were judging their leaders and leaders who were struggling to control the pandemic soon discovered how difficult these standards were to comply with in practice. The complexity of evaluation is such that any definitive answer will be left to historians and academics, and since that is the case, reputations in the here and now, where careers of politicians are decided, will depend less on evidence of performance, according to these criteria, than on the Machiavellian skills they display in taking credit and avoiding blame.

"Go Early and Go Hard"

In May, when the Italian pandemic had passed its apex and death and infection rates were beginning to decline, the BBC interviewed the Italian Prime Minister and asked him whether he should have imposed quarantine restrictions in the north several weeks earlier, given that the seriousness of the epidemic in China was already apparent. The Prime Minister replied: "When I had no fatalities?" He went on, "People would have thought I was crazy."[9]

When President Donald Trump was asked why, having closed down travel from China and Europe, he did not impose national quarantine measures for the month of February, he replied – like the Italian Prime Minister – that it would have been impossible to justify locking down the whole country when there were, as yet, so few fatalities.[10]

These are politicians putting the best face on failure, but they are raising in their defense an age-old dilemma of democratic leadership. How far ahead of their electorate can leaders afford to be? How can they secure consent if they act before there is demonstrable evidence of a threat? "Better safe than sorry" is hard to sell and may make a politician look skittish and weak. Even if the Italian Prime Minister's advisors were warning him about the likely consequences of the epidemic, he still faced the unenviable task of justifying restrictive measures in the absence of direct consequences that his fellow citizens could measure and assess for themselves.

Because Italy was the first to face the consequences of failing to act in time, that unhappy country's experience solved the problem of democratic consent for every other leader in Europe. Once the deadly

[9] "The Coronavirus Pandemic: An Interview with Italy's Prime Minister," BBC News (April 12, 2020), www.bbc.co.uk/programmes/m000hp4v.

[10] Oliver Milman, "How Trump's Missteps Undermined the US Recovery from Pandemic," *Guardian* (June 17, 2020), www.theguardian.com/us-news/2020/jun/17/trump-coronavirus-pandemic-recovery-missed-chance.

consequences became apparent in Italy, leaders in other countries – Germany, the Netherlands, Denmark, Austria – introduced measures of quarantine and gained political credit for "going early and going hard." In fact, these leaders simply profited from Italian mistakes. In evaluating their leaders' decisions, therefore, citizens needed to know where their countries or regions were in the epidemic cycle between January and June of 2020. Europe as a whole, and its political class, ought to have reaped the benefit of coming after East Asia in the infection cycle, but in practice they failed to heed warnings from Korea, Taiwan, Hong Kong, Singapore, and Vietnam.[11]

Timing is everything in leadership, and leaders are forgiven many a failing if they get their timing right. A good leader cannot afford to get too far ahead of their electorates, but they must be quick to catch up if they get behind. They must also be quick to learn from other leaders' mistakes. In twenty-first-century conditions, they must be looking over their garden fence all the time to see what other leaders are doing. Under conditions of modern globalization, where near simultaneity of events and impact have become the rule, epidemics prove that the old adage – all politics is local – no longer applies.

Evaluating leaders then became a matter of judging whether they got their timing right. In Europe, a leader whose country was hit early in the cycle – Italy – was more easily forgiven than one, like the UK, which was attacked by the virus later. It is possible that the UK achieved the worst of all worlds: By acting late, by as much as two weeks, its leaders then had to come down hard, with the result that it has had both a very high death rate and the most serious long-term economic impact among Organisation for Economic Co-operation and Development (OECD) countries.[12]

Elsewhere, as in New Zealand, leaders who took rigorous measures early reaped compounding benefits, plus credit for an early exit. Facing a virus, without a vaccine, means, however, that no political leader, not even those who went in early and went hard, can be sure that they will

---

[11] "Coronavirus: US and Europe Told to Learn From Past Asian Pandemics to Beat Virus," *Independent* (March 19, 2020), www.independent.co.uk/news/world/americas/corona virus-testing-us-europe-asia-sars-mers-a9410481.html; James Traub, "The Future is Asian—but not Chinese," *Foreign Policy* (April 27, 2020), https://foreignpolicy.com /2020/04/27/the-future-is-asian-but-not-chinese-coronavirus-pandemic-china-korea-singapore-taiwan/.

[12] Andrew Walker, "Coronavirus: UK Economy Could Be Among the Worst Hit of Leading Nations says OECD," bbc.com (June 10, 2020), www.bbc.com/news/business-52991913.

escape a later spike. Hence, premature victory laps are risky. Wise leaders know that in politics, all victories are provisional, and in the case of an epidemic without a vaccine, a succession of temporary truces with the virus may be the best any leader can hope to achieve.

"Follow the Science"

To "follow the science" meant, in effect, to use epidemiology to legitimize a massive, if temporary, reduction of human freedom. This in turn was regarded, at least in the center of the democratic political spectrum, as a scientifically validated necessity. In reality, while political leaders claimed that they followed the science, not the politics, the line between a "political" and a "scientific" rationale for action was never clear.

Scientists promoted their scientific authority as an arbiter above politics, but their authority had been politicized long before the pandemic. Populist political leaders – Trump and Jair Bolsonaro, for example – went into the pandemic having made political capital pandering to popular suspicion of expertise.[13] When the pandemic hit, they had to choose whether to double-down or backtrack. Bolsonaro seems to have doubled down, while Trump first signed an uneasy truce with experts, only to decide, as the evidence of economic havoc became clear, to distance himself and pass the responsibility for the crisis to state governors. Having failed to act in time, he decided that the political course most likely to aid his reelection chances was not to act at all.

It's an easy business to despise a leader who ducks, but in any democracy there is a competing understanding, at once resigned and cynical, shared by citizens and politicians alike, that it can be more profitable to duck responsibility than to shoulder it. We do not know whether Americans will allow the President to get away with this. They might forgive if they believe he did his best, but they are unlikely to forget if they feel he left them to their fate.

Evidence from polling data in Europe suggests that a large number of citizens, even in countries like Germany, where leaders acted early, ended

[13] Lisa Friedman and Brad Plumer, "Trump's Response to Virus Reflects a Long Disregard for Science," *New York Times* (April 28, 2020), www.nytimes.com/2020/04/28/climate/trump-coronavirus-climate-science.html; Barbara Fraser, "How Anti-Scientific Attitudes Have Impacted the Coronavirus Pandemic in Brazil," *Scientific American* (May 27, 2020), www.scientificamerican.com/article/how-anti-science-attitudes-have-impacted-the-coronavirus-pandemic-in-brazil/.

up thinking that they were left alone with their fate.[14] As lockdowns end and citizens have to decide how much risk to take when returning to their jobs and to public spaces, it is likely that this feeling of having been abandoned, to face existential decisions alone, will only grow.

In the US and Brazil, both Trump and Bolsonaro made a virtue out of inconsistency, encouraging quarantine measures, then signaling support for the libertarian protests against quarantine.[15] They did so to flip the question of securing citizen consent from how to attract support across the electoral spectrum to the more agreeable question of how best to pander to their own electoral base. Trump and Bolsonaro understood the pandemic, to the degree that they understood it at all, within the habits of mind that define populism itself, i.e. as an opportunity not to unite but to rule by exploiting division.

These exercises in populist positioning were repellent to many citizens, but they did gain their leaders traction in remote and rural parts of the country where the low incidence of the pandemic made it plausible to believe that too much liberty had been sacrificed for too little benefit.[16] Not coincidentally, these regions were right-wing strongholds. In progressive regions of the country, by contrast, governors understood that there was an immense political opportunity in displaying leadership that "followed the science."

Pandemics were framed, initially, as moments demanding that leaders rise above partisanship, but evaluations of leadership were framed through partisan spectacles everywhere, especially in the United States. The particularly American strength of libertarian arguments against quarantine suggests, in turn, that political culture, the ruling assumptions of a nation's political discourse, plays a central role in determining how

---

[14] Krastev and Leonard, "Europe's Pandemic Politics."

[15] Sean Illing, "Is America Too Libertarian To Deal with the Coronavirus?" Vox (May 24, 2020), www.vox.com/policy-and-politics/2020/5/22/21256151/coronavirus-pandemic-american-culture-keith-humphreys; Andy Craig, "Libertarianism and the Coronavirus Pandemic," Cato Institute (March 25, 2020), www.cato.org/blog/libertarianism-coronavirus-pandemic; Jim Epstein, "Libertarians Forged An Alliance with Brazilian President Jair Bolsonaro. Was it a Deal with the Devil?" *Reason* (July 2019), https://reason.com/2019/06/01/deal-with-the-devil/.

[16] Tara C. Smith, "The Pandemic Will Soon Test Rural America: COVID-19 Meets Poor Health and Collapsing Hospitals," *Foreign Affairs* (May 6, 2020), www.foreignaffairs.com/articles/united-states/2020-05-06/pandemic-will-soon-test-rural-america; Jack Healy et al., "Coronavirus Was Slow to Spread to Rural America. Not Anymore," *New York Times* (April 8, 2020), www.nytimes.com/interactive/2020/04/08/us/coronavirus-rural-america-cases.html.

citizens evaluate leadership. For partisan Americans, the evaluation question became: Did they tell me what I wanted to hear?

Even in other democratic societies – UK, France, Canada – where the authority of science went unchallenged, the science on offer was never just technical advice. It provided legitimacy for political decisions so momentous, in terms of their impact on freedom, that they could not be justified on the usual probabilistic or utilitarian grounds. Scientists kept silent when "political" questions were in play, but their very presence provided politicians with the stamp of a higher authority.[17]

It would be perfectionist to think it could have been otherwise. In a pandemic, a strict separation of the purely scientific and political aspects is impossible. Scientists could advocate social-distancing regimes and quarantine, but they couldn't predict whether populations would follow their recommendations. This was at its core, a political, not a scientific calculation. Scientists themselves were keenly aware that their advice had to take into account what the public would accept. The UK government's scientific advisors apparently did not recommend a quarantine style lockdown in the UK in February because they thought it would be politically unthinkable to bring the entire economy to a standstill.[18] Two weeks that might have saved lives were wasted until the death toll turned the unthinkable into the unavoidable.

While the core scientific advice in the pandemic did not vary – social distancing, lockdown, "test, trace, and quarantine" – on other issues, science had no clear answers. Was asymptomatic transmission of the virus possible? Did those who survived the illness acquire immunity, and for how long?[19] Was two meters necessary for social distancing, or would one meter suffice? Did masks reduce spread of infection? Politicians had to decide on these questions in the absence of scientific consensus.

---

[17] John Dupre, "'Following the Science' in the COVID-19 Pandemic," Nuffield Council on Bioethics (April 29, 2020), www.nuffieldbioethics.org/blog/following-the-science-in-the-covid-19-pandemic; Venki Ramakrishnan, "Following the Science," Royal Society (May 18, 2020), https://royalsociety.org/blog/2020/05/following-the-science/.

[18] Ian Sample et al., "Sage Minutes Reveal How UK Advisers Reacted to Coronavirus Crisis," *Guardian* (May 29, 2020), www.theguardian.com/world/2020/may/29/sage-minutes-reveal-how-uk-advisers-reacted-to-coronavirus-crisis; Jana Bacevic, "There's No Such Thing as 'Just Following the Science': Coronavirus Advice is Political," *Guardian* (April 28, 2020), www.theguardian.com/commentisfree/2020/apr/28/theres-no-such-thing-just-following-the-science-coronavirus-advice-political.

[19] Matt Apuzzo et al., "How the World Missed COVID-19's Silent Spread," *New York Times* (June 27, 2020), www.nytimes.com/2020/06/27/world/europe/coronavirus-spread-asymptomatic.html.

Anyone in the public who was following the "scientific" debate that raged in the press quickly understood that "following the science" could leave a politician with more questions than answers. This helps to explain why, when citizens come to their rough and ready evaluations of their leaders, few will end up caring, or even being sure, whether their leaders "followed the science." Voters will praise those who got good results, no matter what complex alchemy of science, politics, and sheer luck went into the result, and what counts as "good results" will depend on the cunning and skill with which politicians manage to take the credit.

"Be Transparent"

The pandemic was, from a politician's point of view, a nightmarish problem of political communication: Striving to reassure, when the news was anything but reassuring, conveying mastery of the situation, when it seemed out of control, conveying hope when, in the absence of a vaccine, hope was in critically short supply. From the citizen's point of view, the pandemic was a nightmare of uncertainty: Whom to believe?

It would have been easier for leaders and their public if there had been a global commons in public information, presided over by an authoritative international organization. But this turned out to be just another unrequited longing of the diminishing band of liberal internationalists. Organizations, such as the WHO, which could have performed this role were sidelined and discredited by their failure to challenge the Chinese narrative about the outbreak.[20] For their part, the Chinese hoarded or concealed information, making it harder for leaders in their regions and elsewhere to act in time. Courageous Chinese doctors did their level best to spread the truth on social media and it is thanks to them that information began to percolate in mid-January, but by then, global air travel was spreading the virus from Wuhan through the airports of Asia and from there to Europe and North America. Transparent information-sharing is possible only where there is a global commons and a widely accepted gold standard of reliable data, but this time, both the commons and the gold standard fell prey to state capture.

In a twenty-first-century social media universe, it is doubtful that a global commons is actually possible. Information is contested, revised,

---

[20] Hinnerk Feldwisch-Drentrup, "How WHO Became China's Coronavirus Accomplice," *Foreign Policy* (April 2, 2020), https://foreignpolicy.com/2020/04/02/china-coronavirus-who-health-soft-power/.

superseded, replaced, tampered with, in an incessant cycle that leaves any responsible citizen or politician forced to make their own judgments about whom or what to believe. The politicians' role was to decide which epidemiological model, which set of data, to accord the stamp of political authority. The citizen's role was then to decide whether to accept the politician's decision on this matter. Neither enjoyed their role, and for neither of them was "transparency" much of a guide. Citizens both demanded transparency, i.e. free debate on risks, on modeling, on social distancing, but they also cried out for the opposite – decisive, debate-ending leadership. They wanted reassurance more than they wanted transparency and so the political task – being transparent while also being decisive – was excruciatingly difficult. It is no wonder, therefore, that few political leaders escaped the crisis with their prestige enhanced.

Chancellor Angela Merkel was much praised for bluntly telling the German public in March that 70 percent of her population might be infected.[21] Plain speaking of this sort epitomizes the virtues of transparency, yet, the Chancellor was actually taking a gamble on the efficiency of German municipal and state government. If they had failed her, her transparent bluntness would have done her no good at all. She had a "good pandemic" not primarily because she treated citizens like adults, but because Germany is an efficient administrative state.[22] Elsewhere in France, the UK, and the United States the pandemic ripped open an ill-kept secret: The advanced decay and administrative incapacity of their welfare states.

In any crisis, leaders want to pull their people together. At the beginning of the crisis entire populations did pull together around a shared sense of vulnerability, but unity dissipated as soon as the public realized that this was an illness that discriminated between old and young, black, white and Hispanic, rich and poor. It was an illness that traveled along the preexisting fault lines of our societies, compounding the already considerable difficulty that political leaders always have in holding their national community together.[23] Transparency is good, but here was

---

[21] "Coronavirus: Up to 70% of Germany Could Become Infected – Merkel," bbc.com (March 11, 2020), www.bbc.com/news/world-us-canada-51835856.

[22] Brian Pancevski and Bertrand Benoit, "Local, Practical, Apolitical: Inside Germany's Successful Coronavirus Strategy," *Wall Street Journal* (May 1, 2020), www.wsj.com/art icles/local-practical-apolitical-inside-germanys-successful-coronavirus-strategy -11588325403.

[23] "Coronavirus Disease 2019: Health Equity Considerations and Racial and Ethnic Minority Groups," Center for Disease Control (July 24, 2020), www.cdc.gov/corona virus/2019-ncov/need-extra-precautions/racial-ethnic-minorities.html.

a case where the information that emerged had a deeply divisive effect, revealing fissures that neither leaders nor led wanted to face.

Presidents and prime ministers tried to "shape the narrative" of the pandemic, but the illness kept escaping their reassuring frames. It shone an unsparing light on leaders and government, but also on long-hidden realities. Once the pandemic laid bare these realities, then the evaluation question for a citizen ceased to be: Did you see this coming? It became, more menacingly: Why did you fail me?

"Do What It Takes"

Political leaders legitimized lockdown with the promise that once it was over, they would "do what it takes" to restart the economy.[24] Political parties that had been locked in static trench warfare on the role of the state in the modern economy temporarily aligned on a massive state takeover of market economies. Within weeks, governments that once lived by the mantras of neoliberal deregulation were providing wages to substantial portions of the workforce and bailing out the balance sheets of gigantic corporations. This strategy bought time for politicians to figure out how to manage the damage, but eventually a reckoning will come due. The costs of emergency relief will take years to pay off: In effect the future of entire economies has been mortgaged in order to survive the present.[25] The need to scale back the assistance will trigger resistance and bitterness. Furlough schemes will be cancelled, and it is anybody's guess whether the labor market will revive sufficiently to provide wages for those released back into the economy. If the recession turns into a depression, the politicians who were praised for foresight, early in the crisis, may be punished later for making promises they couldn't keep. If

---

[24] "Report on the Comprehensive Policy Response to the COVID-19 Pandemic," European Council of the European Union (April 9, 2020), www.consilium.europa.eu/en/press/press-releases/2020/04/09/report-on-the-comprehensive-economic-policy-response-to-the-covid-19-pandemic/; "Coronavirus: Congress Passes $484 billion Economic Relief Bill," bbc.com (April 24, 2020), www.bbc.com/news/world-us-canada-52398980; James Politi et al., "Why the US Pandemic Response Risks Widening the Economic Divide," *Financial Times* (June 18, 2020), www.ft.com/content/d211f044-ecf9-4531-91aa-b6f7815a98e3.

[25] Chris Miller, "The Effect of COVID-19 on Government Debt, Borrowing and Spending," Foreign Policy Research Institute (April 29, 2020), www.fpri.org/article/2020/04/the-effect-of-covid-19-on-government-debt-borrowing-and-spending/; "COVID-19 and Sovereign Debt," UN Department of Economic and Social Affairs, UN/Deca Brief #72 (May 14, 2020), www.un.org/development/desa/dpad/publication/un-desa-policy-brief-72-covid-19-and-sovereign-debt/.

moreover, state aid is seen to be siphoned off by the most powerful at the expense of the most vulnerable, leaders who allowed this to happen may be swept from power.[26]

The reckoning with the political consequences of the pandemic, in other words, has just begun. It may take years before all of its effects work through the political system, and it may be years before the political leaders currently in power face the judgment of their citizens. But it is not just politicians who have been faced with a reckoning.

As citizens, we too face a reckoning, this time with ourselves. Any white middle-class professional who went into lockdown experienced it as a rude awakening to realities that were at the edge of their moral awareness: The astounding differential in mortality rates by race and class, the terrifying vulnerability of the elderly in care homes, and the staggering lack of capacity in the institutions that they took for granted to maintain the frayed decencies of a liberal order. To say that these issues were at the edge of their moral awareness is not to say that they were not discussed. Inequality and ritualized concern about the fragility of the welfare state were the banal common currency of all politically correct discourse at dinner tables, seminars, conferences, and social media long before the pandemic. What we – and I speak of myself – hadn't grasped, and what hadn't become a truly insupportable fact requiring action, was that our institutions failed to protect so many of our fellow citizens and these failures cost them their lives.[27]

So the reckoning to come will be whether this new awakening to brutal facts will create a politics to go with it.

There is no lack of feverish activity in "civil society." The pandemic and its aftermath have stirred everyone. Young people are demonstrating. "Black Lives Matter." "We can't breathe." No question, some of our fellow human beings are choking. But any serious reckoning, anything

---

[26] "Government Support and the COVID-19 Pandemic," OECD (April 14, 2020), www .oecd.org/coronavirus/policy-responses/government-support-and-the-covid-19-pandemic-cb8ca170/; Abi Adams-Prassl, "The Impact of COVID-19 on Economic Inequality and Employment Progression," Oxford University, Department of Economics (April 24, 2020), www.economics.ox.ac.uk/news/the-impact-of-covid-19-on-economic-inequality-and-employment-progression; Enrico Bergamini, "How COVID-19 is Laying Bare Inequality," Bruegel (March 31, 2020), www.bruegel.org/2020/03/how-covid-19-is-laying-bare-inequality/.

[27] A. B. Atkinson, *Inequality: What Can Be Done* (Cambridge, MA: Harvard University Press, 2015); R. Wilkinson and K. Pickett, *Spirit Level: Why Great Equality Makes Societies Stronger* (New York: Bloomsbury, 2011); Angus Deaton and Anne Case, *Deaths of Despair and the Future of Capitalism* (Princeton University Press, 2020).

that goes beyond slogans, means long years of hard political work to correct inequalities that inflict premature death on those born black and poor. It is anyone's guess, pious hopes aside, that this time, at last, something will be done, for example, to ensure that care homes are regulated, that health workers are paid decently and have the protective equipment they need, that police learn how to regain the tacit support of the people they are supposed to protect, and that through progressive taxation, redistribution, and regulation of the Leviathan, we use the power of markets and government to claw our way back to a liberal democratic order that regains sufficient moral legitimacy to survive.

Recovering legitimacy for liberal democracy is a political problem, and it needs to be fixed with political action: Electoral campaigns to elect good people, fights to prevent voter suppression and enhance political inclusion and participation, battles that achieve small victories and then bigger ones, long struggles that will last for years, undertaken by people smart enough to know that "movements" only win when they acquire the sinews of institutional power and clear leadership. Any politics with staying power needs more than passion. It needs people who are willing to make compromises, to work with those we distrust, dislike, or even fear simply because there is no other way to get the result we both want.

It remains an open question whether the passionate activity we have witnessed in the streets is a prelude to such a politics or a substitute for it. Since the pandemic, there has been identity-signaling in abundance, but so far it is steam escaping from a kettle, not the energy powering an engine of change. There is nothing wrong with identity politics, provided it actually results in a politics, that is, an activity that assembles coalitions, interests, and the pressure needed to make corporations and governments change.

Citizens will fail this moment of reckoning if, instead of politics, we get more signaling. The moment that has arrived is a reckoning not with our virtues or with our identities, but with our willingness to sustain a politics with the strangers we need as allies, across the racial and class divide. The moment we are living is a test not of our good intentions nor our feelings, but of our political will, our commitment to ensure that this time, at last, change does come. Only if we reckon with ourselves, after all, will our leaders be forced to reckon with themselves.

7

The Irrelevance of the Pandemic

SAMUEL MOYN[*]

Why did you have to go back, go back
to that awful time, upstream, scavenging
the human wreckage, what happened or what we did
or failed to do? Why drag us back to the ditch?
Have you no regard for oblivion?

History is organic, a great tree,
along the starched corduroy of its bark
the healed scars, the seasonal losses
so asymmetrical, so common – why should you set out to count?

Don't you people have sufficient woe?

Ellen Bryant Voigt[1]

Somewhere between 17 and 22 million soldiers and civilians perished in
the Great War between 1914 and 1918. At least 20 million people, and
perhaps as many as 50 million, died in the great influenza of 1918–1919.
But somehow the deadliest twentieth-century pandemic has seemed
uninteresting, as if it was acceptably forgotten, or as if there were little
to say about it.

Tens of thousands of books about the Great War have been written in
English, but fewer than fifty about the great influenza of 1918–1919.
Appropriately, one of the best of those few books is entitled *America's
Forgotten Pandemic*. About the experience of most of the world beyond
America and Europe in the most renowned global plague before our own
moment, even less was retained. Will our months entering and exiting
lockdown amid so much death due to COVID-19 – nearly half a million

---

[*] Thanks to Paul Kahn and Aaron Shakow.
[1] "[Why did you have to go back, go back]," from KYRIE by Ellen Bryant Voigt. Copyright ©
1995 by Ellen Bryant Voigt. Used by permission of W. W. Norton & Company, Inc.

worldwide at the time of writing – suffer a similar oblivion, justified or not?

It is not just the number of books or pages. Pandemics have also been analytically and artistically slighted. Where most blame the Great War for the rise of Adolf Hitler and the global wars that followed – it was, in historian Fritz Stern's dictum, "the first calamity of the twentieth century, the calamity from which all other calamities sprang"[2] – the 1918–1919 morbidity remains entirely unintegrated in major accounts of the twentieth century, whether in national or global histories. Even those who dutifully cover it in their textbooks assign the great pandemic of 1918–1919 little significance. The death of an individual is meaningful, at least to those who love that person, and man-made mass death too; it would seem that, when it is a microbe's fault, everything changes.

No one has written on "the great flu and modern memory," an analogy of Paul Fussell's celebrated account *The Great War and Modern Memory*, which chronicles how years of fruitless gore transformed aesthetics and sensibility. The artistic canon misses the great pandemic, a couple of lesser-known works (such as Katherine Anne Porter's *Pale Horse, Pale Rider*) to one side. Even then, they joined the tradition of older plague fiction dating back to the 1830s cholera epidemics, if not before. In this tradition, disease becomes the setting for human interaction of dramatic and special poignancy, posing yet another obstacle to fulfillment. And while there is a long tradition of person versus nature in fiction, somehow invisible microbes – in spite of causing more death than fish and whales, perfect storms, and unscalable mountains – have never incarnated evil as easily. Albert Camus's *The Plague* (1947) become a bestseller again in spring 2020. Few registered the irony that it dramatized an outbreak not because disease is interesting in itself but as a (highly problematic) analogy for political evil.

It is not obvious, then, that our current pandemic will be regarded as pivotal, when a mortality total at least forty times and (more plausibly) one hundred times higher a century ago was consigned to be forgotten. You might reply that, precisely because it came at the end of a real war, the early-twentieth-century experience was cast in the shadows or lost in the shuffle, where our twenty-first century pandemic will not be. But one reason for the original disparity is that viruses are not demonic enemies easily converted into contestants in the kind of titanic struggles that make

---

[2] Cited in C. Clark, *Sleepwalkers: How Europe Went to War in 1914* (London: Allen Lane, 2012), p. xxi.

war meaningful to participants and observers. The difficulty of making mass death by plague significant might hold, even when something we have entirely done to one another does not eclipse the experience of disease.

Some, of course, have tried to frame our current attempt to limit the damage of COVID-19 as a "war," but an equal or greater number have pushed back, on various grounds. But the main reason for the disanalogy is that illness, even on a global scale, could not hold the attention of enough people for long enough – unlike the all-encompassing efforts that transformed economic and social relations during wartime and left a conscious legacy. No wonder that one way in which people have tried to grapple with the virus is to observe how it illustrates the toll of our earlier and ongoing choices about how to organize our communities – such as how elder care is organized, or how class and race are lived. But this just proves the point. The temptation to find *something else* to make sense of meaningless loss is a temptation even when it leads us to truths about meaningful human choices before or during the crisis. That certainly applies to this virus: If it is remembered, it is going to be because of the human failures of response, and above all those of leaders.

Whether or not the pandemic will change much in fact, even if it is forgotten, is a different matter. Just because people leave memories behind, and fail to assign importance to events, hardly means that those events are not transformative in fact. But amid widespread claims that COVID-19 is epoch-making, the oblivion of a much worse disease is startling. It forces us to consider other possibilities. It could even suggest that – like all crises – such episodes merely interrupt or else intensify existing trends.

That is apparently what happened a century ago, and provides one reason to explain why the experience wasn't preserved in memory or history. "The status quo was really powerfully reinforced during the pandemic," one of the great scholars of 1918–1919 responded, when asked for an explanation for forgetting the plague. There was no public memory of its ravages because "the pandemic didn't transform the society." It ratified preexisting relations, and for that very reason the wave of death was easily figured as part of the nature of things, a personal tragedy for those affected, with some potential consequences for improving readiness in public health for comparable events, but no more.[3]

[3] N. Bristow (with E. Della Zazzera), "From Private Lives to Public Memory," *Lapham's Quarterly* (April 27, 2020).

And in fact, it is beginning to look like the experience of COVID-19, too. It is much less a matter of caesura than one of continuation.

***

Will our pandemic transfer more power to experts, in recognition that their knowledge and leadership matter, in medicine, public health, and beyond? It was widely speculated that it would, but that prediction has proved wildly premature. One reason may be that expertise had faced limits to its technocratic inroads before disease hit, and was eliciting pushback already. But the deeper causes of the limitations of expertise that the pandemic revealed concern the built-in features of expertise itself. The attempt to manage the pandemic proved that expert rule, ascendant until recently, has been left with about as much authority as before, and perhaps less.

It was essential to this outcome that the pandemic hit amid the greatest crisis of expertise in living memory. The election of populists across the Atlantic and around the world already suggested that people were weary of guardianship that failed in domain after domain even before epidemiologists took their turn. Among the experts challenged now that the entire era since 1989 looks increasingly like a false dawn of excessively optimistic promises, domains such as economic governance and national security had led the way. The global war on terror delegitimized Cold War Atlanticism long before US President Donald Trump began to fret about America's role in the North Atlantic Treaty Organization. And the financial crisis of 2008–2009 suggested that economists had a lot to learn and little to teach. Under the circumstances, it was going to prove impossible to insulate public health expertise from the fact that other claims to authority based on credentials and training have taken a massive hit in the past decades. If there was a chance of doing so, it was missed.

For one thing, public health experts are people too. That experts prove almost as subject to popular delusions and the madness of crowds as everyone else places a hard limit on the feasibility of technocracy – quite apart from its desirability. Precisely because earlier policies such as economic neoliberalism and endless war had been so mainstream at the time of their adoption, and Trump stood for their repudiation (at least in part), experts were already on trial for their own faddishness. As a result, many suspected that, in their policy advice, public health experts were not only understandably beset by the uncertainties of the situation, but also voicing the popular consensus about the disease formed by the chattering classes. As the US President himself vacillated about whether or not to follow his own public health staff, his support did not erode.

And experts come in the plural, as a "they" rather than an "it," meaning that technocracy is always divided against itself to some greater or lesser extent. Predictably in retrospect, in the early phases of the pandemic, experts disagreed about what to do. Once consensus emerged, the disagreement descended to newer and smaller issues. That process is normal in the workings of expertise. Experts are captured by different theories, rewarded for going their own way and not just hewing to truth, and responding to genuine alternatives that no amount of technocracy ever banishes. That experts were atop national bureaucracies and politicians deferred to them in the crisis meant real-time experiments – the abortive British and longer-lasting Swedish pursuit of "herd immunity" most notably – in expert variation and its consequences. As a more or less educated public followed expert variation, individuals took sides, generalizing that variation across whole populations: Every person became their own epidemiologist. That effect demonstrated both the appeal of technocracy and its limits.

Finally, the course of the pandemic has revealed that expertise cannot provide the enduring conditions for its own ongoing application. It was natural for early policy to be based on guesswork. But the consensus (Sweden aside) to lock down society made it extremely difficult to rein in control of the process of opening up. At the time of writing, almost all states in America have begun to reopen, even as the global death toll continues to rise, and sometimes in those very states. While a few experts began to acknowledge a phase of overzealous quarantine at the start of the international policy-making, almost none of them conceded that exerting authority in an atmosphere of uncertainty had made it easy to squander that authority later. People just stopped listening, not only because they are fickle, but also because experts did not seem perfectly reliable in the window when they had most authority. Thus, expert rule is difficult to sustain. Getting the first dose of technocracy completely right is almost unimaginable. But getting it wrong undermines the likelihood of its later application, precisely when it could be calibrated with more evidence.

Nor was this merely because the disease was unknown. Variations in response illustrated the workings of expertise, not a bug in this pandemic but a feature of expert response. All told, the appeal of deference to public

THE IRRELEVANCE OF THE PANDEMIC

health experts at the beginning and at various points of the pandemic was undeniable. But it was also limited and self-limiting. It portended no radical shift in the ongoing contest between democracy and technocracy – which, of course, remains highly fraught and open, just as it had been in the halcyon days before anyone had ever heard of COVID-19.

***

Will the pandemic strengthen the hand of the state? The mobilization of expertise was only part of this question, for when the disease hit it was widely anticipated that it would empower public authority, eroded for decades in a "neoliberal" age. Criticism of the retreat of the state had already been rising on left and right; the main issue was how far the pandemic would reverse it. Once again, it quickly appeared that the claim that the pandemic would mark an immediate turning point was rather premature.

The biggest reason was that the declining competence of states – as well as the intergovernmental organizations they have built – had long since caused public confidence to hemorrhage. It is true that, like experts, states benefited from early compliance from people, especially those who had the means not to work for months or work from home. But this compliance was essentially negative, not signaling transfer of authority to states beyond the command to pause. And as with experts, the very visibility of state leaders and representatives during the early phase of the crisis was self-undermining.

Perhaps these generalizations only apply to the Anglo-American governments – not coincidentally those that initiated a global neoliberal turn. But if so, it was because states elsewhere, having retained more competence and trust, elicited enough compliance during the pandemic to minimize the incidence of disease. Even then, one of the most famous social welfare states on earth, Sweden, bet on the strategy of developing herd immunity, before eventually deciding it wasn't working. It was not clear that states regarded highly for their competence and enjoying the trust of the citizenry gained even more trust due to the crisis – and in fact may have lost some. And in Anglo-America, the buffoonery of Boris Johnson and Donald Trump practically guaranteed that, ill-prepared for national crisis, some states lost even more credibility, an astonishing achievement given how poorly they were regarded at the start.

The clearest counterexample to the crisis of the state under pandemic conditions occurred in East Asia, where a combination of factors led to outcomes that humbled states elsewhere on the globe. Even Vietnam,

poor and ill-equipped compared to richer states to its north such as
China, Japan, or Taiwan, escaped almost scot-free from the death-
dealing. Perhaps such states will gain in deference and trust from their
citizens, but only a little, on the basis of the high levels they enjoyed
before the pandemic.

The American story at the opposite pole illustrates not just the impact
of neoliberalism but the much longer-term dynamics of devolution and
federalism. With deep roots in history, and after an early- to mid-
twentieth century of nationalization and state empowerment, the dynamics of devolution have since gone far. So far in fact, over the neoliberal
decades of the minimization and starvation of the national government,
that now it is not so much states as cities that must shoulder an increasingly ambitious agenda of governance, to fill the neoliberal void. From
the first days of the crisis, states such as California and an array of cities
were celebrated for "stepping up" in the place of the abstention and
dithering of Trump's federal government.

The international institutions that states create above them hardly came
off better than America's federal government. Most notably, the WHO – at
the pinnacle of disease control and with some past successes behind it
(such as the elimination of smallpox) – lost authority from the earliest
days. One reason was that any claim to answers amid the uncertainty of
this plague quickly rang hollow, but there were also specific shortfalls of
governmental credibility beyond the more general crisis of expertise.
Trump's abusive treatment of the organization appalled internationalists,
but one factor in the decline of the WHO's reputation was that it had been
chronically underfunded and unprepared by decades of the negligence of
states to create functioning global institutions for problems of collective
action. And the impression that international institutions, far from soaring
above states, were under the thumb of the most powerful of them was
graphic – most notably when it came to China, which remained in, rather
than the United States, which made efforts to withdraw.

All things considered, chroniclers of the state will associate its pandemic response with its recent history, which that response confirmed
and ratified. "The sole aim," as Alexis de Tocqueville wrote of the apparent toppling of the *Ancien Régime*, "appeared to be to make a clean sweep
of the past. [But t]he Revolution made far fewer changes than is generally
supposed."[4] Our case, however, was also the inversion of Tocqueville's

---

[4] A. de Tocqueville, *The Old Regime and the French Revolution* (New York: Anchor, 1983),
pp. x, 20.

position, who famously proposed that the events of 1789 intensified the administrative centralization and governmental empowerment that the absolutist state had already begun. What the pandemic of 2020 extended and ratified, in contrast, was the erosion of state authority and capacity alike. If there are attempts in the future to counteract these tendencies, it will be because neoliberalism was long since open to criticism – even as it survives crisis after crisis, including apparently the current one.

***

Will the pandemic "end globalization" and promote nationalist autarky, from an economic or political perspective? That is a related but slightly different question than the one I have been considering, if only because it looks at neoliberalism from a different perspective. And the fate of globalization is not settled by whether the pandemic helps challenge the erosion of state authority and capacity. For the trust in and powers of states could stay the same or weaken, even as the progress of neoliberal globalization reversed. At the outset of the pandemic, many anticipated or proclaimed that it would do so. It was foreseen that states would compete with each other, not merely over masks and ventilators in the emergency and vaccines once available, but across the board. And after years of intensifying ties with each other, they would sever relations. But much early evidence undermined this expectation.

Thomas Friedman, leading guru of neoliberal globalization, provided inadvertent testimony to how impervious people were to the costs of globalization and unready to reimagine its inherited terms. There were certainly things to learn, Friedman conceded. "If recent weeks have taught us anything," he reported in his *New York Times* column in late May, "it's that the world is not just flat. It's fragile." And if the pandemic confirmed the dark sides and limits of globalization – at least, globalization on neoliberal terms – it was not as a novel event. For Friedman, the events of 2001 and 2008–2009 already showed that the end of history was not nigh. The pandemic merely elevated what he had dismissed before as flies in the ointment into the superbugs they really were. But while others had long since criticized the theory of beneficent and inevitable globalization conjured up by Friedman and others, for Friedman a reality check led only to offsetting its beneficent inevitability with more observance of the golden rule. "Technically speaking, globalization is inevitable," he still concluded. "How we shape it is not."[5]

---

[5] T. Friedman, "How We Broke the World," *New York Times* (May 30, 2020), www .nytimes.com/2020/05/30/opinion/sunday/coronavirus-globalization.html.

It was a good example of learning almost nothing in the guise of claiming to register novelty. And that complacency may seem extraordinary. How could we forsake a teachable moment like the one the pandemic brought? But the truth is that Friedman epitomized a general commitment to stay the course on globalization in its familiar form, in spite of the interruption. If correcting the course was in order, it was for the sake of the old globalization, following the recommendation of the Prince of Lampedusa in his novel, *The Leopard*: If things are going to remain the same, they have to change.

As the economy crashed during the pandemic, there was state aid, but no nationalization of industry, as in the last Great Depression, and no reform of trade, even though politicians such as Trump had promised it. After disrupting the global economy, China's relatively quick, state-managed return as principal site of global manufacturing meant that consumption-driven economies in America and Europe would not have to rearrange their supply chains better for the future. (It remained to be seen if they will protect those chains from the threat of comparable disruptions.) The crisis in China never got bad enough for anyone to propose restoring manufacturing to the global North, where the toll of the disease got bad enough to make doing so implausible. And while it is, of course, true that states everywhere took acts unprecedented since the 1930s to avoid disaster for their citizens, it was with the endgame of restoring the globalized economy much as it was before. One is forced to conclude that not even the pandemic led to significant moves to overturn neoliberal globalization, even though it had led to the populist disruption.

And the most successful challengers to the moral aspects of globalization – right-wing populists – did not exploit the crisis to seize power. Cries that Trump is a fascist, awaiting his Reichstag fire, were embarrassed by the fact that he plumped before the camera when he thought it would help his polls, while avoiding responsibility and deferring from his existing powers – seizing no new ones – when the crisis came. Hungarian strongman Viktor Orbán seized the powers of emergency rule, allowing him to sidestep the Hungarian Parliament even more than he was already doing – and then ended the state of emergency, demanding an apology for accusations that had rained down on him of aggressively disrupting liberal norms. This isn't to trivialize the danger of such politicians, only to accept the sane conclusion that the pandemic did not unduly empower them to shake the foundations of the cosmopolitan consensus since 1989 more than they already had. Economic turmoil and migration pressure thus proved far more threatening to the liberal moral consensus of the era of globalization than the pandemic did.

Globalization had been an American project, first and foremost, with many global collaborators. China had been its greatest unexpected beneficiary economically, along with the global rich it was intended to help most. But in the service of protecting their regime, and lacking missionary ideologies, there was little evidence that the Chinese now wanted to challenge America or the West generally for "global leadership." That meant that, in spite of its dithering and failures, a declining America looked set to be default hegemon as much after as before the pandemic. "The United States leads no matter what it does," American foreign policy advisor Samantha Power remarked along the way, couching her criticisms of Trump's shambolic regime in an affirmation of her country's eternal indispensability.[6] Once again, it is not that such beliefs have lacked their critics. But if American hegemony in an era of neoliberal globalization has an expiration date, it does not appear to be one meaningfully hastened by this crisis.

***

The normalization of the pandemic and the swift ratification and resumption of earlier outlooks suggests that prior tendencies outlasted their interruption. Much evidence suggests that the pandemic was not only easily normalized, but was also easily ousted by new events (in America, most obviously, the police slaying of George Floyd in May that led millions of cabined people into the streets).

This is hardly to say that pandemics never transform existing arrangements. From examples before modern times such as the Black Death to the Columbian exchange, we know they do – sometimes profoundly. But it does not follow that outbreaks of disease unfailingly make a difference. And perhaps this one is leaving things mostly the way they were before, only more so, with grief among the survivors who knew a victim, and perhaps a bit of guilt for those who feel it.

French writer Emmanuel Carrère opens his beautiful memoir *Lives Other Than My Own* with an account of the December 2004 Indian Ocean tsunami, which he happened to witness on a trip to Sri Lanka with his family. Staying at a hotel on a cliff, he and his loved ones are completely unaffected. The rich and well-off tend to be unaffected even

[6] S. Power, "This Won't End for Anyone Until It Ends for Everyone," *New York Times* (April 7, 2020), www.nytimes.com/2020/04/07/opinion/coronavirus-united-states-leadership.html?searchResultPosition=9.

when others suffer dire straits. Of course, Carrère's narrative makes clear that anyone who happens to be at the wrong place at the wrong time can die, like the child of some friends washed out to sea. As in our pandemic, no one is by definition safe from the tsunami. But mostly, the patterns of death track preexisting facts about society.

Afterwards Carrère descends into the nearest village, where he visits the local clinic, except that it is "more like a fish market than a hospital lobby." Corpses are piled everywhere, "bloated and grayish," and numberless too. In an experience that became familiar again in the pandemic, many of the bodies go unclaimed, either because logistics forbid it or because some families were wiped out completely. "We are still together," Carrère reflects of his own family, "our clothes are clean, and we aren't searching for anyone in particular." What he adds explains the attitude of so many to look – and look away – from mass death, before resuming life as it was, even if that is something mainly the lucky (and privileged) get to do: "After our visit to hell, we will return to our hotel, where lunch will be served to us. We'll swim in the pool, we'll kiss our children and think, We came so close. ... A guilty conscience is pointless, I know, but mine torments me anyway and I'm ready to move on."[7]

E. Carrère, *Lives Other Than My Own* (New York: Picador, 2011), pp. 16, 18.

8

Emergency, Democracy, and Public Discourse

MOSHE HALBERTAL

Not all emergencies pose a surprise. Hurricanes, though devastating, are common and predictable. The bombing of Aleppo by Russian and President Assad's forces caused a grave emergency to its inhabitants, but given the past brutal conduct of the Syrian Civil War, it came as no surprise. Not all emergencies evoke menacing uncertainty; in many of them, we have a clear sense of what they entail. The nature of the threat, its duration, and its impact are more or less predictable. The COVID-19 pandemic caught us unprepared; it appeared as a surprise (though we should have known better), and its future ruinous path is unknown to us. The conjunction of emergency, surprise, and uncertainty formed a perfect, unsettling, ominous storm. Unprepared and uncertain, we seek ways of responding to the pandemic. The effectiveness of our response to the threat and our capacity to weather its devastating impact rest on the strength of our public institutions and the quality of our political discourse.

Emergency Response in Three Levels

In exploring the ways in which societies confront emergencies and the relation between emergency and democracy, three different levels of response ought to be carefully distinguished. These three modes of response differ from each other in the degree of their severity and the depth of transformation that each calls for.

The first and most elemental level is reflected in the way in which emergency impacts the allocation of attention, resources, and effort, all directed toward the newly emerging threat. Ordinary activities are put on hold, reduced to minimal maintenance mode; resources are marshaled; and capabilities are recruited and concentrated to confront the impending disaster. In the case of an epidemic that threatens to spiral out of control, hospitals for example defer elective surgeries and routine medical procedures, while diverting staff and equipment to deal with the emergency. As the crisis grows, industrial production and economic activity might be constrained so that the limited resources at hand can be directed and focused toward the threat. The degree of strength and preparedness of societies can be measured by the extent to which the emergency forces a disruption of ordinary and routine life. Countries that took the SARS outbreak in 2003 seriously and had testing capacities ready were able to provide a greater continuity of ordinary life when the coronavirus appeared. Strong health care systems that were well staffed and had plenty of beds available were not forced to deplete the rest of their resources and suspend routine care.

At the same time, it is important to note that the absence of an emergency's impact on economic and social life can also reflect a society's crippling weakness. In these cases, societies are helpless in deploying any means to deal with the emergency; life goes on and the devastating consequences of the emergency are fatalistically normalized. A dramatic increase in mortality and uncontrolled spread of illness is taken as yet another misfortune to endure, part of life's unmanageable burden.

The application of this first level of response to emergency in the mobilization of the public confronting the coronavirus pandemic has been dramatically different to what usually happens in emergencies. In the attempt to control the spread of the virus, people were called upon to isolate and withdraw in order minimize social contact and friction. This form of passive public effort is in striking contrast to most emergencies, which call for a deliberate concentration of bodies and equipment. Emergency response usually entails a coming together in a heightened sense of activity and solidarity. In the response to the coronavirus, people were deprived of the comfort of standing together and of the calming effect of heightened action. Such common modes of response were replaced by the desolate public sphere and the loneliness of encapsulated people. Resignation, as the order of the day, cast people in the role of spectators, a stance that magnified the eerie and ominous nature of the threat.

The second level in responding to emergency involves violations of protocol as a necessary means of short-circuiting what are determined to be obstacles to swift engagement. In a military emergency, troops are rushed to the front without adequate training and equipment, violating every rule in the manual for preparing troops for war, and the draft age is extended to younger and older cohorts. The protocol dictating that long-distance movement of armored vehicles must be done with the aid of trailers is breached, and tanks are hurried to the war zone, traveling along their own chains. Similarly, careful tests and procedures that screen the production and approval of new medications or vaccines are bypassed in cases of pandemic, tacitly assuming the risks that might occur as a result.

The most extreme examples of this type of breach of protocol appear in emergencies that have caused such a level of devastation that the institutions responsible for channeling coordinated activity are reduced to ruin. In such cases, the order of the day is to each their own; do not expect help from any quarter. Military units on the verge of complete defeat might issue the following retreat command to their soldiers: Now everyone must strive to survive alone moving across enemy lines, sometimes creating small new formations.

There is a difference between cases where a large explosion floods the hospital with wounded civilians and the hospital shifts to emergency mode, and when the hospital itself has been bombed. These are two types of emergency and their impact on protocol might be dramatically different, even though both forms of response belong to what I have called "level two."

The third level of response to emergency is the formation of a state of exception. In such a state, the norms that constitute the very basic structures of political community are suspended. Such a suspension of basic structures is far greater than the breach of a specific protocol, which aims solely to be effective when the time and care needed to follow protocol are perceived as unaffordable luxuries. Emergency powers in a state of exception do not pertain to the breach of this or that particular rule, but to the transformation of the mechanism of rule-making altogether. In such cases, the executive is granted the power to issue orders that may override or disregard legislative and judicial bodies, thus abolishing the democratic separation of powers. Elections, too, might be delayed, so as not to interfere with the all-encompassing struggle with disaster.

In addition to the transformation of the very structures of rule-making, in such states of exception the rules that are enacted breach basic constitutional rights and protections. Freedom of speech is limited, organized political opposition is banned, privacy is infringed, and due process of law is dismantled through the use of such mechanisms as administrative detentions.

States of exception ought to be approached with great suspicion; they might offer short-term relief and produce long-term horror. They are deployed by authoritarian rulers or those aspiring to seize power in order to facilitate the suspension of the basic democratic and liberal structures of society. One condition that enables such a deterioration of democratic norms is the breakdown of the discourse of truth. When there is no sense of independent facts and truth, the public is seized by what is called in medieval philosophy the imaginative faculty. It is the faculty that leads us to believe that everything is possible, without any of the constraints of causal necessity. Since everything is possible, people become particularly vulnerable to promises and threats, which are the instruments employed by a false authority to grab control. The attack on independent measures of fact-finding and truth is essential to authoritarian leaders, whose grip on power depends greatly on shaping a culture of terror and dread that would make emergency and the state of exception a permanent feature of political and social life.

The Political Psychology of Emergency Response

The emotional response that defines our reaction to danger appears as a political and social disposition in various shades – fear, panic, hysteria, terror, and dread. These emotional shades have to be carefully disentangled, since each of them constitutes a radically and uniquely different stance. Fear is a healthy emotional reaction to danger; it has an alarming, alerting, and directing quality. It calls for mobilization of attention and effort; it has a concentrating effect. It is the motivating force behind the first level of responding to emergency.

When fear turns to panic, response to danger becomes misdirected. Panic is marked by thoughtless frenzy, and when panic escalates to hysteria it gains an infectious quality. Hysteria is the pandemic of panic. Courage is the personal agency that is left after fear is experienced, and enables composure under pressure that allows us to realize and assess possibilities for actions while our mental field is not completely captivated by the source of danger. Panic marks a complete loss of composure. The desertion of protocol becomes risky when it is motivated by panic; it results in misdirected overreaction defined by erratic shifts of response. Sometimes the reliance on protocol is the best way to deal with states of emergency, especially when such protocol reflects the accumulated wisdom gained from years of experience. Protocol is the wall that blocks the deterioration from fear to panic.

Terror constitutes another shade of the emotional confrontation with danger. While in states of panic the danger is identified but the response to it is thoroughly misguided, in terror the danger itself becomes elusive.

The strategy of terrorist activity is to create the conditions of war of all against all and everywhere. These are the conditions under which the public moves from fear to terror. With widespread terror, the threat is perceived as lurking all the time and in all places; it cannot be pinned down. For this reason, a war on terror is a war with no front. Bus stations, airplanes, restaurants, crowded streets can suddenly turn into locations of carnage. The proper response to terrorism involves the attempt to define and locate the source of the threat, and to shift the population back from terror to fear.

If terror does not turn back into fear, dread might follow it. Unlike panic, dread is not defined by hyperactivity but by utter passivity. It signifies a far-reaching meltdown. Dread has a crushing quality, destroying agency altogether through an emotional paralysis. It can produce a paralyzed public that easily falls into the grip of a strong leader who promises salvation. In a condition of paralyzing dread, people are reduced to a state of anticipation. Some unconsciously wish for the threat to strike them if only to be freed from the excruciating burden of uncertainty. Some wish to become invisible, as if paralysis and avoidance of action affords greater protection since it manages to minimize the exposed surface. Dread is, thus, a mental parallel to the instinctive shrinking of bodies when confronting danger.

Whether societies respond to emergencies with healthy fear and concern while concentrating resources and efforts on dealing with the threat, or with panic and hysteria while violating careful protocols in a frenzy of misdirected action, or in terror and dread while suspending basic rights and shifting to authoritarianism, reflects to a great degree their past political culture and the strength of their public institutions. For this reason, emergencies have the diagnostic power of an x-ray; they lay bare the cracks and systemic areas of neglect – systems that were marginalized, disregarded, or denied, prior to the emergency. For example, the disproportionate impact of the coronavirus on people of color in the USA and other countries exposed, among other things, the racial disparities in access to medical care and in well-being throughout the developed Western countries. It is no wonder that the term *apocalypse* in its Greek origin means unveiling or revelation.

The Limits of Politics in an Emergency

There is yet another, more elusive though no less crucial, dimension of the response to emergency that depends on past political culture. In order to clarify this dimension, a larger malady of political life must be presented.

At the heart of political life reside two reversals that create a structural vulnerability of sovereign bodies. The first reversal is that of means to ends, and the second one is that of ends to means. For the subjects of a state, power is a mean to an end; it serves as a necessary instrument for security and protection. In contrast, for some political actors, power becomes an end in itself. Political power is, then, reversed from a means to an end. The second reversal, that of ends to means, follows the first reversal. Since power becomes a dominating end, political actors tend to instrumentalize valuable ends and turn them into means for maintaining or gaining power. Friends are exploited to gain power, promises are broken, rivals are destroyed through false accusations, allies are betrayed, and moral banners are hypocritically waved as routine practices in political maneuvers. The most extreme form of instrumentalization is the initiation of military operations in order to galvanize public support. Political leaders are well aware that at least in the initial phases of war, public support for the regime is enhanced. The use of war as a political tool involves the cynical manipulation of the lives of soldiers in order to gain some political advantage. At this extreme, the reversal of ends to means reaches its most corrosive and ugliest form.

Political leaders merit our respect when they manage to constrain the impact of these two reversals on their political lives. In the path of such leaders, we detect core convictions that motivate them beyond the exclusive aim to seize power. Even as they take part in political give and take, we trust such leaders to reserve some area of decision-making as a sacred protected realm, immune from instrumentalization. We assume that in essential matters such as welfare policy, major legislative initiatives, and war and peace, such leaders will be guided by their genuine commitment to the common good. Respect for these figures is independent from actually agreeing with their policies; it is based on the assumption that they have extracted themselves from the corrosive impact of the double reversal that pervades political life.

In times of emergency, when stakes are extremely high and where the physical, psychological, and economic well-being of the population is threatened, there is an expectation of transcendence. In the same way in which ordinary life is suspended, we expect that the leaders in charge will transcend their ordinary and routine political maneuvers and concentrate on the common good. There might be a genuine disagreement on how to respond to the emergency, such as the deep debate between those who put a priority on the preservation of life and those who put first protection of the economy. Controversies might also emerge in relation to the assessment of data and interpreting its meaning. However, in some countries, and especially in the USA, we have witnessed a total breakdown of public discourse, a breakdown that is marked by the politicization of the nature of the response. Political partisans act as if the spread of a virus and its devastating impact were not a matter of fact, but only another item in the ongoing political and cultural war.

In its revelatory power, the pandemic has exposed serious shortcomings of our societies. It has sounded an alarm that calls for a reevaluation of our public institutions and social order. Among the shortcomings is the deterioration of public discourse and the loss of a sense of transcendence. With such a loss, the very condition of trust that enables us to shape our response to an emergency has been gravely undermined. A worthwhile political struggle and debate depends on a realm of value and knowledge that is free from the grip of politics. Political life is destroyed when it becomes political through and through.

9

Understanding, Deciding, and Learning: The Key Political Challenges in Times of Pandemic

DANIEL INNERARITY

The main democratic challenges raised by the COVID-19 crisis can be divided into three groups, according to a time sequence: There are challenges raised before, during, and after the crisis. These different moments in time correspond to questions of understanding, deciding, and learning. The first set of questions concern whether or not we were prepared for a crisis on this scale, and whether we have been able to understand it correctly. At the heart of the crisis, what was in play was our ability to decide and to do so without damaging the values of justice and democracy. After the crisis, the most significant question is what needs to be learned, by whom, and in what way.

The Complexity of a Pandemic

At times of crisis, emergencies put the spotlight on practical people, those who organize, decide, and take on risks that might overwhelm anybody else. However, although theirs is not the most important voice in an emergency, it is important also to listen to those who have a different role, such as interpreting what is happening to us. Even at these times of health prioritization and triage, a theory of the crisis is not meaningless. We need to know and describe the nature of the crisis properly in order to take the best decisions. Let us remember that behind many erroneous decisions there was more ignorance than lack of resolution: Describing the crisis as a war, calling it a foreign virus, confusing the role of experts in a crisis, not to mention our collective lack of attention to reality when it comes to long-term latent issues. If many of our practical errors stem from theoretical failures, then we cannot consider theory as a waste of time, even at times like these.

When we begin to verify the depth of the crisis, we are confronted by questions that reference a theory of society behind the coronavirus:

Everything we have theorized until now about democracy and politics, about the relationship between public and private, the meaning of nations, and the justification for Europe or, even more importantly, about the nature of the world in which we live, requires a new interrogation. It is possible that things will not change as much as we might fear or desire, or it might be that they will change beyond anything we can imagine. In any case, the ability to know is increasingly less about learning a list of glorious achievements from the past and has to do, instead, with learning. In other words, with knowledge about and for the future. In dynamic and volatile civilizations, wisdom based on experience must inevitably begin to be complemented by processes that could be characterized as learning about the future: Prediction, prevention, anticipation, precaution . . .

One of the concerns I have had for years is that we should think in terms of systemic complexity. This requires transforming our institutions to govern complex systems and their dynamics, especially when we are confronting connected risks; in other words, when multiple things can go wrong together. At this point, it is clear that the crisis has not been addressed with this perspective in mind in all of its stages. At the beginning of the crisis, many political actors and analysts viewed the virus as something like a seasonal flu, localized in one region of a distant country, and they advised us that the only thing we needed to fear was the overreaction of panic. They saw numbers of infections and deaths that suggested an issue of limited scope, without realizing that numbers barely allow us to calculate risk in a complex system. The numbers should be understood in the context of a general system that includes the consideration of the ways an epidemic affects health care infrastructure, as well as the reverberation of those impacts. If we do not think systemically, if data points are considered independently, rates of infection and mortality may not seem alarming. Whereas, from a systemic perspective, even small numbers indicate a possible disaster. It is true that the flu kills many people every year, but that is not the comparison. The problem was what would happen if a coronavirus pandemic was added to the seasonal flu at its most critical point and the extent to which that could collapse the entire health system.

The theory of complex systems distinguishes between linear interactions and nonlinear or complex interactions. In the former, we can simply add quantities to predict their combined impact. Since we are handling predictable events that correspond to our expectations and infrastructures, we can make preventive predictions. Nonlinear dynamics, on the other hand, are those in which one thing is not simply added to another; they generate cascade effects where small changes can lead to massive transformations. The coronavirus falls into this second category. Why?

Our health care systems have a limited capacity: They cannot treat more than a particular number of people at any one time, and specialized units (such as intensive care units (ICUs)) act as bottlenecks. An unexpected viral illness that coincides with the seasonal flu is not simply twice as tragic as the flu, but potentially catastrophic. The characteristics of the coronavirus reveal that patients need especially costly resources. What was relevant to understand the gravity of the pandemic was not its rate of infection but that, if the coronavirus overwhelmed the ICUs, there would then be more deaths from other causes – from heart attacks to traffic accidents to strokes; in other words, from everything that requires an immediate response in order to guarantee survival, but that could not be addressed as it should be if the system was overrun.

The expression "flatten the curve" is an example of systemic thought. The lockdown and distancing that were decreed by the authorities are not due to the risk that each of us runs individually but instead serve to avoid a massive contagion that would overwhelm the hospitals. In order to identify and understand this type of measure, we must think systemically. The indecisiveness of the first moments of the crisis reveals, instead, that our dominant thought tends to be linear, and the way we describe our institutions (warning, management, medical attention, logistics, communication, and so on) is still indebted to a very simple way of thinking that struggles to respond to complex phenomena.

Lessons are never certain, and some are never learned. There will be various types of practical lessons, but also theoretical ones. Among them, I dare to point out that complex thinking is one of the most important for us not to miss. The coronavirus crisis is one example of an event that cannot be understood or even managed without complex thought, but there are many others that require us to engage in a new way of thinking about reality.

Our world is characterized by there being, in addition to gradual or predictable changes, ever greater numbers of what are called discontinuous, sudden, or nonanticipated changes, and these events may modify societies in a catastrophic fashion. A pandemic is a typical example of this type of event. The difficulty with predicting these outbreaks is not only about when they are going to take place but even about their nature. We neither know exactly when and if they will happen nor what is going to happen (or, once it happens, what is going to change afterward). This territory is unfamiliar for us, even for those who are tasked with managing it, experts and politicians. For that reason, decisions to confront the crisis feel somewhat improvised and experimental. Errors are common, especially when the nature of the problem has not been well identified. Most of the practical errors stem from a lack of knowledge, either because there has not been enough relevant effort to develop such knowledge (the creation of expert knowledge, collective deliberation, prediction and strategy), or because the very nature of these phenomena place them outside the scope of our knowledge.

The final question that unsettles me is the extent to which human beings learn from crises. Paul Nizan said that "when we fall, it's not always downward," to note that we can fall up. In other words, we can be ruined by success or be unhappy in prosperity. We can turn the sentence on its head and affirm that human beings do not necessarily learn from failures. Falling is not always followed by rising. Crises only teach those who are prepared to learn, and I am afraid that our societies – despite the repeated warnings we have received from the history of this twenty-first century, so peppered by diverse crises (terrorism, climate change, economic crisis, European disintegration) – have revealed our lack of motivation to understand the teachings of each of these crises and to act consequentially by undertaking the necessary institutional building. I do not mean to suggest that the teachings of history are unequivocal as if there were a type of signs of the times to which we need only surrender. Human learning takes place in confusing environments amid social pluralism, through institutions that channel the controversies in which we live, from science to the political institutions. The big question that should concern us is whether that "intelligence of democracy" (Lindblom)[1] that was capable of giving an answer to the conflicts of the nineteenth and twentieth centuries will appear when we try to address the global risks of the twenty-first century.

Democracy in Times of Pandemic

We say that this health crisis will put many things to the test and that some of them will never be what they once were, including democracy. An intense debate has already arisen between those who think that this crisis will be a wake-up call that will knock down capitalism and those

---

[1] Charles Edward Lindblom, *The Intelligence of Democracy: Decision Making Through Mutual Adjustment* (New York: The Free Press, 1965).

who predict a system of control that will consolidate the authoritarian tendencies inscribed in what we call illiberal democracies. The state of emergency has led to the adoption of exceptional measures that can establish dangerous precedents or consolidate preexisting authoritarian turns. This is more likely in a context where limiting liberties is more likely to be accepted by frightened populations. There are already "corona-dictatorships," such as Hungary, that are taking advantage of this emergency to accentuate its illiberal profiles.

At the same time, the long list of collective failures reaped by our democracies make the promise of effectiveness at the cost of democratic formalities especially tempting. Democracy, which has survived many challenges and changes in format, now finds itself at an unprecedented crossroads. The survival of democracy is conditioned on it being able to act effectively in the current contexts of complexity, juggling the expectations of effectiveness with the requirements of legitimacy.

The debate between philosophers and social scientists about democracy after the coronavirus has had epic, prophetic, and melancholic tones; the only thing it has not had is modesty. There are those who announce a new wave of authoritarianism, such as Giorgio Agamben[2] or Naomi Klein,[3] those who exalt Chinese efficiency and present it as a seductive model (Byung-Chul Han),[4] or those who warn us about the totalitarian surveillance of biometric monitoring (Yuval Harari).[5] We also cannot forget Slavoj Žižek,[6] who promises, once again, that this will be the (definitive) downfall of capitalism. In spite of the maximalist tone and the minimal scientific basis of their predictions, all of these thinkers present us with at least three problems that reappear regularly in democracy: The problem of exception, of effectiveness, and of social change.

Let us begin with the first of these problems, the one that presents democracy with the logic of exception. This issue has been, for a long

[2] Giorgio Agamben, "The State of Exception Provoked by an Unmotivated Emergency," Positions Politics (February 26, 2020), http://positionswebsite.org/giorgio-agamben-the-state-of-exception-provoked-by-an-unmotivated-emergency/.

[3] Naomi Klein, "Coronavirus Is the Perfect Disaster for 'Disaster Capitalism,'" Donestech (March 18, 2020), https://donestech.net/noticia/coronavirus-perfect-disaster-disaster-capitalism.

[4] Byung-Chul Han, "Asia is Working with Data and Masks," Reading the China Dream (n. d.), www.readingthechinadream.com/byung-chul-han-coronavirus.html.

[5] Yuval Noah Harari, "The World After Coronavirus," Financial Times (March 20, 2020), www.ft.com/content/19d90308-6858-11ea-a3c9-1fe6fedcca75.

[6] Slavoj Žižek, Pandemic!: COVID-19 Shakes the World (New York and London: OR Books, 2020).

time, Giorgio Agamben's preferred topic. He is now talking about "the invention of an epidemic" as an excuse to establish a state of exception.[7] It must be very difficult to survive the success of a metaphor and resist the temptation to apply it to any situation. Contradicting the evidence that if a state of exception is proclaimed at this point it is because there was not one earlier, Agamben maintains that "the epidemic clearly shows that the state of exception has become the normal condition for democracy." Thus, because of this "virocracy," we could finally realize that the logic of exception is the very logic of democracy . . . without exception.

Much would be gained in lucidity if there was a little more study of comparative politics, even at the expense of the impact of some theories. It would be possible to verify that the constitutions of democratic countries allow exceptions at the same time as they limit exceptions to specific topics and specific timeframes. If someone receives exceptional power, it is because that person does not have it before or after that moment. Another philosopher who sometimes prefers a brilliant metaphor to a good argument, Peter Sloterdijk, prophesies "the subjugation of a medical-collectivist dictatorship," in such a way that "the Western system will reveal itself to be as authoritarian as the Chinese system."[8] Neither Agamben nor Sloterdijk seems to have realized that the emergencies decreed by the European governments are conditioned on the fight against COVID-19, limited in time, and do not establish new crimes, three conditions lacking from the exceptionalism decreed by the government of Hungary. I compare, therefore I think.

States of exception do not suspend democracy or its deliberative and polemic dimension. Pluralism continues intact and normal social disagreement continues to exist, even if its expression is conditioned to facilitate the main objective of the health emergency. Any limitation on freedom is always regrettable and can only be justified as a temporary measure. Carl Schmitt, whom everyone now seems to have canonized, was a decisionist, but few people realize that understanding politics as a decision implies recognizing that it is exercised in a context of contingency, without overwhelming reasons, not even amid the emergencies of exception. Contingency means that decisions are debatable even if the

[7] Giorgio Agamben, "The Invention of an Epidemic," *The European Journal of Psychoanalysis* (February 26, 2020), www.journal-psychoanalysis.eu/coronavirus-and-philosophers/.

[8] Josef Joffe, "Die Corona-Krise offenbart auch eine Krise der Meinungsmacher: Ihnen fällt nicht allzu viel Kluges ein," *Neue Zürcher Zeitung* (April 11, 2020), www.nzz.ch/feuilleton/die-corona-krise-ist-auch-eine-krise-der-intellektuellen-ld.1551336?reduced=true.

conditions that implicitly regulate the way of governing and the way of being in opposition have been modified.

Any measure presented as if there were no alternative and as if it was scientifically unquestionable would be unacceptable. Virologists have powerful arguments, of course, but when politicians take decisions upon the basis of their advice, they are making politics. It is a particular exercise of politics, needless to say, but that does not preclude it from having that element of contingency that also characterizes politics in exceptional circumstances.

There are different arguments about how to confront this crisis, particularly regarding the balance to be made between the health emergency and the economic costs resulting from the measures necessary to address that emergency. Being in a state of emergency does not mean renouncing the exercise of reason and depriving oneself of the benefits of composed and trustworthy deliberation, and neither does it require the relinquishing of political pluralism, as the necessary coordination between institutions does not imply submission to that which is decreed by a single chain of command. Democracy, even at times of alarm, needs contradiction and demands justification. Pluralism is not only a normative demand but also a principle of rationality: A democracy owes its critics as much as it owes those who govern. If a context of minimal trust is generated, distributed knowledge and decentralized power are not an impediment for taking decisions but are procedures to minimizing errors. Emergency situations do not suspend pluralism but only its competitive dimension. It would be an error if the urgencies of the moment would lead us to give away pluralism and checks and balance. At moments like this, anyone who confuses having control with being right may always be tempted to forget that distinction. Another reason to constantly remember it.

Democracies were not created for states of exception but for normality. A democratic society would not support even the mere suspicion that rights will not return. This explains – and to a certain extent excuses – the reticence of governments to adopt drastic measures at the beginning of crises. Citizens are reluctant to accept limitations on their liberties when the seriousness of the situation is not obvious.

The decisive question is how long the justification for the exceptional measures lasts. A constitutional democracy institutionalizes distrust toward any extension of the prerogatives of power; we know from historical memory that governments tend to be irresistibly tempted to hold onto it. It is always easier to concede new powers to those who are responsible for our security than to take them back. The experience of the struggle against terrorism has taught us much in this regard. The very history of the word "quarantine" reveals in its origins an example of that type of extension of power. When the plague was spreading through Europe in 1348, the authorities in Venice closed the city port to ships coming from infected areas, and they forced travelers into thirty days of isolation ... which they then extended to forty (*quaranta* in Italian). One of the characteristics of democracies is that they handle any delegation of power carefully and condition any granting of exceptional power to a plan, objectives, and a timeframe to return to normality.

The second problem of democracies seems to be their effectiveness at resolving urgent problems, when time and authority are dramatically limited resources. Compared with our slow pace when it comes to taking decisions, the weakness of our social control, and our reluctance to invade the privacy of people, totalitarian systems seem better equipped for that type of situation. And given that turmoil and crises are going to be the new normal, the temptation to bypass or reduce democratic "formalisms" and rights becomes very powerful.

This relation between authority and effectiveness is at the heart of both the seduction and the fear of China. I find Fukuyama's judgment[9] more accurate than Harari's or Han's: Democratic governments are often plagued by inefficiencies, but it is not true that these issues stem from having to respect the popular will and legal procedures. Neither is it the case that autocracies are a model of efficiency.

We must keep in mind that debate on this topic is affected by a battle to define reputations amid a gigantic manipulation of information. The authority of the Chinese government is not a model for anything. Other countries and localities have realized lockdowns without sacrificing democratic values. In China, radical isolation, enforced through repression and censorship, was ruthless. It may be the case that the West was slow to realize the cruelty that was taking place in the enclosed space of Wuhan and, in general, to know the true data about the pandemic in China.

This is the true heart of the question: The relationship between power and information. Authoritarian regimes have a problem with information in both directions, toward the outside and toward the inside. The first of these is obvious, and we are all paying the price for it. It would have been

---

[9] "Francis Fukuyama on Coronavirus and the Crisis of Trust," *Financial Times*, podcast (April 16, 2020), www.ft.com/content/a42ba47c-2433-410f-8c5d-1753d4728570.

better if they had supplied true information at the beginning rather than masks later on. At some point, we will have to activate the limited global procedures to bring demands regarding the causes and extension of the pandemic.

Their second problem with information is internal, and reveals that repressing information is not a sign of strength but a foreshadowing of future weakness. The authoritarianism of the regime, the absence of freedom of expression, and obstacles to the circulation of information create the conditions to ensure that mistakes will be made when it comes to managing the crisis. It also ensures that less will be learned and, as consequence, new crises will be more likely. Inherent dysfunctions in the Chinese Leninist system impede the efficient circulation of information among local administrative bodies and the central government. The controls that the central government imposed on local administrations mean that the only information reaching Beijing is either good news or well-disguised bad news. This is why the measures against the epidemic have been chaotic and counterproductive, especially when the police in Wuhan preferred to arrest and repress doctors who had issued alerts rather than listening to warnings and guarding against the epidemic risk.

When I talk about the free flow of information, I am not referring to the mere flow of data (which the regime could compensate with the totalitarian monitorization of its systems of data collection and intelligent processing) but to the type of quality information that gives us real insight into a country's situation so that we can make accurate decisions. This is information that is only generated in places – such as consolidated democracies – where two fundamental values are respected: Tolerance for criticism and trust. A regime can have all the information that big data can provide and still have bad information. If there's no scrutiny of such information and no trust from those that can provide information, you will never obtain good information. We should remember that the Chinese authorities adopted spectacular measures only when the political regime's structural dysfunctionalities became a true threat to its own survival. As Marta Peirano has reminded us, totalitarian efficiency, if such a thing exists, never has the protection of the citizens as an objective but the survival of the regime.[10]

---

[10] Marta Peirano, "El coronavirus ha sido la tormenta perfecta para el control social," Publico (June 8, 2020), www.publico.es/entrevistas/marta-peirano-coronavirus-control-social-nuevas-tecnologias-aplicaciones-manifestaciones-derechos.html.

Democratic systems would distance us from the temptation of totalitarianism in the name of efficiency if we placed a higher value on the results without compromising the procedures. Efficiency is not a value that is on the upswing in our democracies, especially on the left, if we compare it with the prestige of values such as equality or participation. As long as we are still failing on so many issues, we should not be surprised that a large part of society is beginning to believe that these failures are caused by democratic formalities that we could do without. Instead, they should be viewing them as the reason behind many of our successes and why our errors are not even larger.

Democracies have a third serious challenge, regarding the intentional production of social transformations, whether they are called reforms or transitions. We live in democracies where little changes. It is this that explains why, when a catastrophe arrives, those who were least hopeful about the possibility of changing society through ordinary political will end up being the most hopeful that nature will put things right.

Now that there is no longer reform or revolution, all bets focus on something akin to an unexpected transformational change, a catastrophe, an accident of history in the form of a health or environmental crisis, that would fortunately turn us in the right direction. It is no longer only a question of hope disconnected from any sense of reality, but a curious expectation about the way we will move toward the new desired situation – the great transformational dream that failure will mechanically produce its opposite. It is a sacrificial vision of political history that has nothing to do with how change happens and should happen in democracies. In a democracy, change is simultaneously conflictive and agreed upon, between gradual and brusque, but always within the parameters of the intentionality of the actors. Those who encourage us to look at these natural, sudden events as the true moments of political change seem to be telling the natural history of plagues and not history as led by human beings.

Catastrophes provide evidence of the damage, but not of the cure. The idea that sacrifice leads to emancipation is as incredible as insisting that this commotion is going to benefit those who most need it. This expectation contains at least two assumptions that are difficult to believe: That negative events necessarily produce positive results, and that this new positivity is going to be evenly distributed. Ruins do not necessarily bring about the new order, and change can be for the worse. Times of crisis can lead to certain forms of destabilization that represent an opportunity for authoritarianisms and illiberal populisms.

Our social and political reality has very little to do with the type of changes from other time periods, the time of classic revolutions, the collapse of regimes or civilizations, uprisings, or coups. Liberal democracies are political spaces in which the expectations for change are balanced – at times, poorly balanced – by the resistance to change and where the will for transformation is channeled in an incremental fashion. There is no "natural" event that is going to save us from the work of transformation. This is not an argument against change, because there is nothing less transformative than the nostalgia for something completely other.

If the slow democratic learning process has taught us anything, it is that we should not exonerate ourselves from the guarantees and limitations that democracy has imposed to resist changes that can be for the worse. And the most important part of it, even at exceptional times, is to protect pluralism. This regards both measures taken to overcome the crisis and the transition we should undergo afterward. Of course, there are some ways out of this crisis that seem more reasonable than others, and even some decisions that verge on the indisputable. But we should not forget that there is a plurality of opinions about what is desirable and that the only way to decide which direction is best for the emphatic change that is being proclaimed everywhere is democratic debate. Even when something collapses it is not always clear what should be replaced, and democratic debate should be put into motion whenever there is something that is not fully clear. No one should be excluded from that debate, not even the conservative skeptics, if nothing else because there are certain things that should be maintained, and there is an optimism that results from assuring people that most things will continue on as they have been.

Karl Marx's argument that "Mankind thus inevitably sets itself only such tasks as it is able to solve"[11] has often been monopolized by those who confuse humanity with a concrete "us" (a group, some experts, a political party, an ideology), which is put forward as particularly capable of resolving those problems. If there is any solution to this, it will be resolved by humanity as a whole, not by those who want to flaunt the privilege of representing them.

Learning from the Crisis

A large biological crisis in the age of AI amid debates about transhumanism forces us to try to protect our corporeal condition. Ecological

---

[11] Karl Marx, *A Contribution to the Critique of Political Economy* (Moscow: Progress Publishers, 1977), Preface.

reflection has already taught us that we cannot understand each other without any type of inclusion in a natural context. This crisis places even more emphasis on our common fragility and the limits to our self-sufficiency; it reveals our dependence both on other human beings and regarding the nonhuman world.

The problem is that we have made ourselves more vulnerable to global risks without developing the corresponding protection procedures. Things that protected us (distance, the intervention of the state, predicting the future, classical defense procedures) have been weakened for different reasons and now barely afford us sufficient protection. The organizations that seem to return (like the state) no longer effectively protect us, and the ones to which we could appeal (such as the EU) do not sufficiently protect us from these risks because they were not designed for it.

It is within this context that we need to think about new measures for protection. For the moment, the EU's weak ability to respond to such crises and the states' inability to collectively coordinate a continental response have favored withdrawal to the national borders. The closing of borders would have been unnecessary had there been a coordinated response to the crisis. But additionally, the lockdown cannot be a permanent solution: It generates distrust, paralyzes the economy, and will affect us personally and socially. The question is how to protect people when the old instruments have lost much of their effectiveness. How do we do it without compromising liberties? Without simply offering placebos? And how to do it at a time when authoritarianism is gaining adherents?

In the face of these challenges, we should begin by recognizing that we do not know what to do in a crisis with these characteristics. In fact, we do not even know how to describe it. It feels like those who are going to learn the least from this crisis are the ones who already think they understand everything.

I do not mean to suggest that we have not learned anything from previous crises. Today something like the invasion of Iraq would be unthinkable. There continue to be advances, even if they are insufficient, in our policies against climate change. Europe is now better prepared to face and address asymmetric economic shocks. The Basel Accords have given us greater financial stability than we had at the end of the Bretton Woods system. But the happy determinism with which some claim that crises are opportunities is contradicted by the fact that the learning processes we undertake are unbearably slow and certainly insufficient.

And our analysis is not carried out with the profundity required by the seriousness and depth of the societal problems exposed by this century's crises. What is most revealing, in this regard, is that these crises continue to surprise us. The present works like a gigantic distraction – we focus obsessive attention on that which is immediate, the centrality of the competitive element in our democracies, our scant capacity for strategy and prediction. It may end up being easier to find a vaccine than to learn from a crisis like this one.

The self-help books repeat that we should not waste a good crisis, which are moments of opportunity. All the rhetoric of European integration has been understood as a succession of responses to its continual crises. In fact, paradoxically, the success of European integration seems to be constructed on the foundations of crises. These, however, are moments of change for the same reasons that they can be moments of preservation or regression. Our choice to move forward or backward or stay in place is not taught by any book but depends on the decisions we make.

How can we explain the fact that, even though the climate crisis is more serious than the coronavirus pandemic, it is the latter that makes us modify our conduct more extensively, that we accept the lockdown better than the modification of our consumption to halt climate change, that states more easily and quickly come to an agreement regarding a virus than in the rounds of negotiations about the climate crisis? The answer has to do with the fact that one crisis feels hypothetical and distant to us, while the other is immediate. The more distant, in time or space, we feel the consequences of changing or not our behavior will be, the less likely we are to modify it. This different reaction tells us a lot about the type of society we have constructed, a society that functions on the basis of incentives and pressures, that pays attention to that which is urgent, that which makes noise and is more visible, but does not pay attention to changes that are latent and silent, even though they can be much more decisive than the immediate dangers. The pandemic crisis threatens older people more than the young, while the climate crisis puts young people more at risk; this is another reason that explains the greater reaction in an older society, where defending the interests of the young has less electoral benefits than paying attention to the interests of those who are older.

Nothing assures us that this crisis will lead to a learning process. One world could come to an end, and we could continue to think of it with the categories from another time and treat it as if nothing had changed. The human species owes its survival to an intelligence that is adaptive, compatible with the fact that, in many aspects, we continue to cling instinctively to what has worked until now. In that case, we could wander about like zombies amid serious warnings that we would continue not to take seriously enough. It will be as if humans' natural situation was distraction, and as if society were the place where that enormous collective distraction is carried out.

PART III

Citizens

Introduction

The pandemic has not only been a test of leaders and experts. It has, above everything else, been a test of citizens. Unless and until there is a vaccine, successful response to the pandemic depends entirely upon the willingness of citizens radically to change their behavior. They have been asked – in some cases, compelled – to stop what they have been doing and to change how they have been behaving. Their leaders sent them indoors and into isolation. Schools have closed, as have places of employment. Households may be places of relative safety, but they are also places for the multiple mini-crises of everyday life as parents deal with childcare and work responsibilities. In many places, this lockdown regime was ordered even without a substantial public safety-net in place. If the virus was an invader, citizens everywhere were asked to join a silent army of resistance. One fights this virus in the loneliest of fashions: Stay home and stay away from others.

The pandemic posed questions of trust in leadership, but it imposed equally questions of how much we can and should trust each other. Would our fellow citizens change their behavior sufficiently to protect others? Could we trust them and could they trust us? The pandemic recalls our duties as citizens to each other, and through that, to the res publica that holds our democracy.

This question became more pressing as it became clear that different populations face radically different risks from the spread of the virus. Those risks were partly matters of health, but partly matters of economic survival. These issues played out differently in different regions. Everywhere, there were questions of what low-risk population groups would do for those at higher risk. In particular, would the young act to protect the elderly? In many places, however, the more pressing question was what the impoverished or disadvantaged could do to protect themselves and others. Orders to stay home had no purchase in regions in which homes were crowded and did not have even running water. The obligations of citizenship look different in Milan than they do in Lima. The same differences can appear across neighborhoods in New York or Lisbon.

Because the public health response to the pandemic primarily involved social distancing, the disease seemed at first an anti-political moment. Democratic politics may have a lively online appearance, but it stands on a deep tradition of popular mobilization in the streets. Accountability to the people would seem difficult, when the people could not gather in protest. There was, then, genuine surprise when in the middle of the pandemic popular politics broke out in the United States, after the police shooting of George Floyd in Minneapolis. Those protests were, then, copied in cities around the world. What had been an anti-political moment became just the opposite as citizens mobilized to protest structural inequalities resting on a history of racism, for which the bill had not yet been paid.

Scholars, in this section, try to understand the possibilities for citizen participation in politics during and after the pandemic. They confront this puzzle of political mobilization in an anti-political environment. They also address the question of the impact of the pandemic on the ethos of citizenship.

J. H. H. Weiler uses the pandemic to reflect on problems of democracy that predate and will outlive the pandemic. Using European states and the European Union as elements of a case study, he argues that problems in contemporary democracies have their root cause in a failed concept of citizenship. Citizenship has been reduced in a culture of rights; it has been deprived of a sound conception of collective values. In response, he argues that we need to develop a modern progressive narrative to support what he calls the Unholy Trinities of values. A liberal conception of patriotism, a coupling of rights with duties, and a healthy self-respect for one's collective identity and culture that is neither atavistic nor chauvinist.

Susan Neiman offers one of the more optimistic outlooks on the transformative social potential of the corona experience. She argues that as the crisis unfolded, it shook the conceptual framework within which we were living: The belief that we are only moved by self-interest, that human action can be reduced to a desire to maximize our own interest, and that we cannot change this. Neiman argues that "the tyranny of self-interest" has dominated public discourse for over a century. The response to the pandemic allows us to see that this attitude is not built on fact but on ideology. It is not natural, but historical, and thus contingent. By revealing self-interest to be only a contingent framework, the pandemic offers us the chance to reject this attitude and become a more caring society.

Kalypso Nicolaidis offers another optimistic perspective. She turns things upside down: The pandemic might have required social distancing, but it also makes clear our relational nature and mutual sharing and dependence. Politicians and scientists cannot guarantee our safety. Instead, they generate feelings of powerlessness to which we can respond with a new realization that we (as we) are in control. Instead of fear or despair, she expects a creative reimagining of democracy through a true exercise of self-government by a more horizontal, informal, and decentralized form of collective organization. She notes that we are experiencing a collective learning process out of which more creative forms of political action may emerge.

Shalini Randeria, Deval Desai, and Christine Lutringer argue that the pandemic has offered an opportunity for significant transformation of democracies through changes in the state's fiscal arrangements and political economy. They use case studies from India and Italy, involving special-purpose social welfare funds intended for the most vulnerable. They show how these funds are being captured and used for other social purposes. The state is able to recast the social contract in this way because of the weak political leverage of the marginalized beneficiaries, as well as because of deficient mechanisms of political and legal accountability. The capture of these funds further entrenches and institutionalizes these two political trends.

Paul W. Kahn reflects on the meaning of political decision-making across domains of justice and care. According to Kahn, majorities do not have a license to do whatever they want, even within the conditions of justice. Beyond justice, politics must satisfy the obligations of care toward community members. Kahn argues that care beyond justice is the ultimate standard of legitimate political decision-making during emergencies. The most admirable moments of the response to the pandemic have materialized when entire societies locked themselves down to protect the weakest and the health care workers, affirming their care for each other regardless of calculations of cost. These acts of sacrifice affirm that politics is not only about making reasonable choices, but also about sustaining a transcendent meaning that binds citizens together.

10

COVID, Europe, and the Self-Asphyxiation
of Democracy

J. H. H. WEILER

It's the People, Stupid!

I have no crystal ball with which to assess or predict the long-term impact of COVID on our democracies; long experience has taught me to avoid punditry – I always get it wrong. But the current circumstance has been helpful in highlighting and accentuating longstanding problems of democracy in and of Europe (Member States and the EU itself) which predate the pandemic and are likely to outlive it. And though the focus of this chapter is on Europe, the underlying issues are, I believe, relevant far more widely.

Let me start with the particular, the much commented upon instrumentalization of the pandemic by authoritarian regimes, within and without Europe to tighten their grip on the levers of power. It came as no big surprise, to give but one example, that Viktor Orbán has used the pandemic to dismantle further the checks and balances that are an integral part of any functioning democracy. On March 30, 2020, with the authorization of the Hungarian Parliament (in which the government has a large majority), an Act was passed,[1] which effectively gave the government sweeping powers to rule by decree. It is not unusual in times of emergency for the executive branch to revert to extraordinary measures, though in this case they have an Hungarian twist: The new law is of indeterminate duration (though Parliament can end it when it sees fit – in the case of Hungary de facto when the executive sees fit) and, in fact, the powers granted exceed those necessary to deal with COVID-19.

More ominously, alongside that enabling law, the Penal Code was amended, permanently, to introduce two new crimes – punishable by up

---

[1] See "Translation Of Draft Law 'On Protecting Against The Coronavirus,'" *Hungarian Spectrum* (March 21, 2020), https://hungarianspectrum.org/2020/03/21/translation-of-draft-law-on-protecting-against-the-coronavirus.

to five years' imprisonment – for any activity that interferes with the government in the discharge of its emergency responsibility and for any publication "distorting the truth" that might alarm a large number of persons, which I imagine could mean any publication that contradicts the government narrative. I consider this part of the package far, far more pernicious.

Hungary has deepened further its "illiberal democracy" – a juicy oxymoron.

Not unexpectedly, the social networks were full of (justified) fire and brimstone, though the official reaction of the EU by the President of the Commission was, in the eyes of many, rather "gentle." (The Christian Democrat EU family, which in this case strikes me as neither Christian nor Democrat, really needs to do some soul-searching.)

But a characteristic of the popular social network was, again not unexpectedly, like a commercial jingle: Orbán here, Orbán there, Orbán, Orbán everywhere.

And herein lies what I consider a real problem, both in analyzing the problem and reacting to it. In the name of democracy, we forget the basics of the democratic ontology.

By saying again and again Orbán, Orbán, Orbán (and make no mistake, he deserves every form of reproach), we fall into the trap that reflects a widespread malaise in our general democratic discourse – the "deresponsibilizing" of the People, the nation, the electorate. Orbán has been clear and transparent – he declares openly, *Urbi et Orbi*, to the world and his electorate, that he wants an "illiberal democracy." He, and those to his right, were elected with a significant majority and, hugely significantly, were reelected even after the reality of his regime was there to be seen by all and sundry. We call him a dictator. That is, paradoxically, comforting; the classical image that Dictator and Dictatorship conjures is one of 10 million Hungarians suffering under a repressive regime with all the attendant paraphernalia: The knock on the door in the middle of the night, disappearances, torture, gulags, etc. But this is not the case in Hungary. By my lights, in some deep ways, what is going on there is worse – not of course in terms of human suffering, but in the deeper and long-term damage to how we think of our democracies.

It is precisely because he is no Franco, he is no Pol Pot, he is no Ceaușescu; this is not the Greek colonels or the Argentinian generals who ruled by terror, disappearances, and the like; there is no Securitate or Tonton Macoute, which makes the new phenomenon, in the heart of Europe, in the EU, so pernicious, and so demoralizing.

This is not a regime about which it can be said that the free will of "the people" has been repressed. Even though the information, media, and deliberative processes have been perverted, and there were various shenanigans in who could and could not vote, the overwhelming electoral win is evidence that Orbán and those to his right enjoy widespread and deep support from a significant majority of the electorate. The Parliament, with his constitutional majority, is a more or less accurate and true reflection of the popular will. The majority of MPs who voted for these and previous acts, and the President who signed them, are expressing the collective will of a majority of the Hungarian people.

All the attempts to avoid this uncomfortable truth – they don't understand, they were fed fake news, etc. etc. – falls into the trap of that otiose Marxist trope of False Consciousness, a trope that expresses both arrogance and disrespect. Arrogance since it posits that we are smart enough to understand but they are not. And disrespect, but we treat them as children who are not to be held responsible for their actions. Those among the Hungarian people who voted for him – a substantial majority – understand perfectly well, just as you and I do, what he is about, what his worldview is, and they approve of it.

We all know, or should know, the difference between individual guilt, which is indeed individual, and collective responsibility that a society has to assume, admirably articulated in the May 8 speech by the President of Germany.[2] Laudably and with utmost integrity, like several of his predecessors, he did not resort to the "Hitler, not us the Germans" obfuscation. And yes, there was a not insignificant minority that voted against Orbán. And one should do everything in one's power to support them. But democracy also means collective responsibility. I observed the same with US President George Bush over the Iraq war. Bush, Bush, Bush. But it was not simply Bush, it was the American people who voted for him (twice – thus retroactively approving of his policies) and a Congress that also overwhelmingly approved his actions, ex ante and ex post. Responsibility for Iraq rests as much with the American people as it does with Bush. There are endless similar examples – choose your favorite.

---

[2] "75th Anniversary of the End of the 2nd World War," Der Bundespräsident (May 8, 2020), www.bundespraesident.de/SharedDocs/Reden/EN/Frank-Walter-Steinmeier/Reden/2020/05/200508-75th-anniversary-World-War-II.html.

Me? It's Never Us!

Why, then, is it all the time Orbán, Orbán, Orbán, and why the reluctance to point the finger at those also responsible for Orbán? Why do we refuse to acknowledge that Orbán enjoys majoritarian legitimacy, albeit in a state that has ceased to conform to our normal notions of liberal democracy? And we do the same with the likes of Salvini, Le Pen, the AfD, and all fellow travelers.

There are several possible answers to this question.

The first is that we operate under the false assumption that if it is democratic it is okay. It is good. How false. If it is not democratic it is certainly bad. As a technology of governance obviously, with all its flaws, we consider democracy indispensable. But the opposite is not necessarily true. A democracy of evil people will be an evil democracy. A democracy of (socially) unjust or uncaring or indecent people will be a socially unjust, uncaring, and indecent democracy. To point the finger and condemn those who, if we believe in democracy, should be the first and last to be held responsible – those who elected and reelected Orbán – is not to show disrespect to democracy; it is the opposite, it is to show respect for democracy. If we do not, we actually disrespect democracy.

But there are other reasons. Personalization is a self-exculpatory device, too.

The two principal sins of the "populists" – both leaders and electorate – is a growing Euroskepticism and a disillusionment with the fundamentals of the liberal democratic order. By personalizing the problem in this way and casting the likes of Orbán as dictators, we avoid asking the more difficult question of how has it come about that so many millions of Europeans, north and south, east and west, have turned their back on liberal democracy. It is a self-exculpatory device since it obviates the need to engage in some serious self-critique and soul-searching as regards our liberal democracies and the EU. If those people have fallen into the hands of a ruthless dictator, we are absolved of this kind of introspection.

I hope my credentials are such that my lifelong commitment to the European construct will not be called into question, nor my old-fashioned liberal commitment. But those commitments should not be an excuse for avoiding what I consider painful truths.

When it comes to Europe, we cannot turn a blind eye to some major fault lines in the construct which contradict its most cherished values. Despite the full empowerment of the European Parliament, European democracy remains deeply flawed. The two most primitive features of democracy, which cut across the rich variety of specific arrangements in what used to be called Western liberal democracies, are the ability of the electorate, through parliamentary elections (in this case elections to the European Parliament) to determine, or have a decisive weight in deciding, by whom they will be governed, and, at least in a broad way, what will be the ideological and policy direction by which they will be governed. It is not comfortable to admit, but European democracy fails on both grounds. The first point was painfully visible in relation to electing the current incumbent heading the Commission (like her predecessor I think she is an impressive incumbent, but this is beside the point); and over the years we have come to realize that voter preference in the outcome of such elections has had a tenuous connection to the policies of the Union. Our system does not allow European citizens to feel, even in relation to these two primitive parameters, that they have any appreciable impact on the governance of the polity.

What kind of democracy is it when the electorate has so limited impact on who governs them and how they will be governed? It should surprise no one that the slogan, iterated in different forms by Euroskeptics, "Taking back control," had and has so much resonance. The resulting alienation is not simply understandable but in no small measure justified. And since, regrettably the only alternative "game in town" is the so-called populist movement, since our mainstream parties have had their head in the sand on this issue for decades, it should not surprise us that it garners support and becomes popular.

And this points to another major fault line in the European construct – the total failure of the European citizenship project, introduced with much fanfare almost thirty years ago.

The issue of citizenship is profoundly and inextricably linked to that of democracy. There has always been to my mind a black hole in democratic theory from John Locke onwards. Why should the minority be bound by decisions of the majority? It seems so axiomatic as not to require justification. But, after all, the majority may be fools, the majority may be wrong, the majority might be evil. Be that as it may, and whatever justification you may find convincing, there is one commonly accepted understanding: The majoritarian discipline only applies for and within the demos of the polity – accepting that demos might be understood and experienced differently in different polities. Imagine an Anschluss between, say, Canada and the USA, or Denmark and Germany – where all citizens would have equal democratic rights. The Danes and the Canadians are likely to say: Thank you, but no thank you. We do not want to be ruled by Germans or Americans, respectively. The "demo" in the word democracy is not lexical; it is ontological. No demos, No democracy.

This failure of the European citizenship project is thus central to the democratic deficit of the Union and has come into very sharp relief, and, indeed, been accentuated by the COVID-19 crisis.

There has been much strife regarding the extent to which the Union would engage in offering help to the Member States sanitarily and economically hit the hardest by the pandemic. By the time this book is published some solution will have been found, one that is too little for some and too much for others – a typical European compromise. Since the Union's own resources are pitiful, this would involve, one way or another, a transfer of resources from north to south. Merkel, before her change of heart, and the leaders of the Netherlands, Austria, Denmark, and Sweden were roundly criticized by some for their lack of solidarity in their trenchant initial refusal to provide the Union with the necessary means to provide meaningful financial support to the countries most afflicted by COVID-19. Without taking sides in this debate, two things stand out clearly in my view: The leaders of these states were giving expression to a broad sentiment in their respective societies. One did not see even the semblance of the kind of solidarity which one associates with the citizenry of a polity, a segment of which have fallen on hard times. It was a discourse about the Dutch and Spaniards, of the Danes and the Italians – not a discourse among fellow European citizens. And even among those who supported this or that aid package, a dominant reason was utilitarian and enlightened self-interest, a far cry from citizen solidarity.

Why the citizenship project failed is beyond the scope of this chapter. But COVID-19 has brought it out in the open as nothing before. The failure of citizen solidarity at the level of the Union, the spectacle of a retreat to national identities at a moment of deep crisis, is but another manifestation of EU democracy in crisis.

There is however one COVID-19 marker which is worth elaborating. As mentioned above, the pandemic with its severe economic consequences, especially in southern Europe, made painful the absence of meaningful EU own resources. The reason for this is simple: The absence of any meaningful taxation power, not least direct taxation of European citizens, by the Union. The thought itself is anathema. We hear again and again about the economic disequilibrium created by the asymmetry between European monetary capacity and fiscal incapacity.

But I wish to highlight the socio-political dimension of this asymmetry since it so directly relates to the above-mentioned twin issues of democratic accountability and citizenship. Direct taxation is, I would argue, as essential to, or impactful on, democracy as voting, and is one visible marker of citizen solidarity. "What are you doing with my money" is the bread and butter of democratic discourse, creating an accountability imperative difficult otherwise to replicate. In just about all federal states, the norm is that bulk of direct taxation is federal: People are principally taxed in their quality as American, Canadian, German, or Australians and not as Texans, Bavarians, Nova Scotians, or Tasmanians. And it is not only about accountability. It is an essential republican feature. Each and every citizen, through direct and indirect taxation, is a stakeholder, one of the gardeners of the national patch.

In the US there might be fierce debates about austerity and growth, about the virtues and vices of bailouts and the like. But we rarely hear plaints as to why "we Californians should be helping West Virginians." It is American money, not Californian money. One is helping fellow citizens, not others. And the same goes for borrowing and indebtedness. Sovereign debt is principally, in federations, a federal debt, owed by all citizens, not that of the units of the federation.

COVID-19 has highlighted as never before not only the economic problems of derisory own-resources but the socio-political underlying pathology. The problem of Europe, in this respect, is not one of taxation without representation, but of representation without taxation.

This issue of limited fiscal capacity is not new, but the proposals for remedy are telling: They are all schemes that would tax all and sundry except European citizens as such. One notable proposal, taxing financial transactions, would surely be important in somewhat filling the coffers of the Union, but if one is worried about democracy and citizenship, there is no substitute for direct taxation of individuals in their capacity as citizens of the Union.

Not on Bread Alone Doth Man Liveth . . .

What of the deeper issue – the turning of the back on liberal democracy by so many Europeans?

Those who believe that the answer can be found entirely in the realm of the material – unemployment, the uneven distribution of the deserts of globalism – are mistaken. These economic factors are important but they do not explain the appeal of populists in countries and strata of society which cannot be included in a discontent that stems from economic dissatisfaction alone. It is also an explanation that laughably reduces the human person to their material needs only. The issues of values and the spiritual well-being of the person are no less important in understanding this weighty puzzle.

I want to postulate – i.e., I do not propose to give proof – that the human condition is such that each of us consciously or subconsciously seeks to satisfy not only material needs but metaphysical ones too and among them, first and foremost, the wish or need to give significance and meaning to our short lives, a significance and a meaning that goes beyond that which serves our own self-interests. Values play a role in satisfying that primordial drive. And it is here that we find another deficit in the ways we have articulated and come to understand the "values of Europe."

What are these European values? Again and again we face the Holy Trinity: Democracy, human rights, rule of law. Yes, Europe does stand for these. And yes, we should never accept to live in a society which does not respect and honor these. And the metaphor of the Holy Trinity is more than an irony: Like the real Holy Trinity they are three which are one – indivisible. You cannot have democracy without fundamental rights – that would simply be a return to the tyranny of the majority. Hitler and Mussolini were hugely popular at their time and came to power "democratically." And you cannot have human rights without the rule of law. So that, for example, the idea of an illiberal democracy is ontologically an impossibility, an oxymoron.

But there is an aspect of the Holy Trinity of these values which is rarely discussed. Fundamental rights guarantee our liberties – but give us no guidance on how to act under the canopy of such. Democracy is a technology of governance, indispensable. But that does not tell us how to exercise democratic powers. As mentioned, a democracy of evil people will be evil, even if democratic. And this is true for liberties and obviously for the rule of law. There can be pretty nasty laws, which do not perhaps violate fundamental rights, but are nasty nonetheless.

The Holy Trinity of values provides the conditions for action, individual and collective, but not its content. They are a necessary but not a sufficient condition to satisfy the primordial quest for meaning and significance.

Let me then mention three of the classical values which have disappeared from our public life that in the past catered just to that. The connecting thread among the three is the jettisoning of individual duty and responsibility toward the polity, a fundamental of republican democracy. We may wish to call them the Unholy Trinity of values. They are to be found in three processes which began as reactions to the Second World War and have evolved over the last decades.

The demise of patriotism as a discipline of love is the first such process. For reasons that are quite understandable, the very word "patriotism" became "unprintable" after the war, notably in western Europe. By abusing the word and concept, Fascist regimes (among others) had "burned" it from our collective consciousness. And in many ways this has been a positive thing. But we also pay a high price for having banished this word – and the sentiment it expresses – from our psycho-political vocabulary as patriotism also has a noble side: The discipline of love, the duty to take care of our homeland, people, and neighbor; of accepting our civic responsibility toward the community in which we live. In reality, true patriotism is the opposite of fascism: "We do not belong to the state, it's the state that belongs to us," and we are responsible for it and what happens to it.

This kind of patriotism is an integral and indispensable part of the republican form of democracy. Today, we may call ourselves the Italian or French or Bundesrepublik "Republics," but our democracies are no longer truly republican. There is the state, there is the government, and then there is "us."

We have become like shareholders of an enterprise. If the director-ate of the enterprise called "the Republic" does not produce political and material dividends, we change managers with a vote during a meeting of shareholders called "elections." If there is anything that does not work in our society, we go to the "directors" – as we do, for example, when our internet connection isn't working: "We paid (our taxes), and look at the terrible service they're giving us." The state is always the one responsible. Never us. It's a clientelistic democracy that not only takes away our responsibility toward our society, toward our country, but also removes responsibility from our very human condi-tion. The lousy Schumpeterian understanding of democracy is the reality we live.

The culture of rights and the rule and role of law is the second process which helps explain the current circumstance. And it, too, is a reaction to the Second World War, and is equally paradoxical. We've accepted, both at the national and international levels, a serious and irreversible obligation rooted in constitutions to protect the fundamental rights of individuals, even against the political tyranny of the majority. And we are the better for that. At a more general level, our political-juridical vocabulary has become a discussion of legal rights. The rights of a German citizen are protected by German courts, and, above all, by the Constitutional Court. But also by the Court of Justice of the EU in Luxembourg, and – again – by the European

Court of Human Rights in Strasbourg. It's enough to make your head spin. And this is true for the other EU Member States.

Just think about how common it has become, in the political discourse of today, to speak more and more about "rights." To try and turn any political action into a legal action about rights and entitlements. And using the courts, again and again, to achieve our political objectives. It's enormously important. One would never want to live in a country in which fundamental rights are not effectively defended. But here too – as with the banishment of patriotism – we pay a dear price, indeed we pay two prices.

First, and this is a common, by now even banal critique, the noble culture of rights does put the individual at the center, but little by little, almost without realizing it, it turns them into a self-centered individual. It atomizes the individual since most fundamental battles of rights pose an individual and their liberties against the collective good.

But the second effect of this "culture of rights" – which is a framework all Europeans have in common – has received far less attention. It produces a kind of flattening of political and cultural specificity, of one's own unique national identity.

Typically we refer to "identity politics" in pejorative terms, and there are aspects of such which do merit such hostility. But, like patriotism, identity has a more noble aspect tied to one of the values we cherish most – human dignity. The notion of human dignity, the primary value to be found in most European constitutions, can be explained in secular, Kantian terms as being rooted in the very ontology of human existence, or in religious terms as going back to the fact that we have been created in the image of God. From this perspective human dignity displays two facets: On the one hand, it means that we are all equal in our fundamental human dignity – rich and poor, Italians and Germans, men and women, Gentile and Jew. To suggest that the life of one is more worthy than the others is a grievous assault on human dignity. On the other hand, recognizing human dignity means accepting that each of us is an entire universe, distinct and different from any other person. To suggest that one person is fungible with another, to dismiss the uniqueness of our individual identity, is an equally grievous assault.

And the same is true for each of our societies. To deracinate the cultural specificity of each of our nations and societies is, in this sense, to compromise an essential element of our dignity. When this element of diversity is diminished or derided, we rebel.

And since with only small differences of nuance our supreme value as Europeans is our belief in the Holy Trinity of rights, democracy, and rule of law (and thankfully this is the case), the specificities of our identities are seen to be devalued.

The third process that explains what has happened to Europe is secularization. Let me be clear: This observation is not an evangelical rebuke. I do not judge a person based on their faith or lack thereof. And even though, for me, it's impossible to imagine the world without the Lord – The Holy Blessed Be He – I also know many religious people who are odious and many atheists of the highest moral character.

This process also began with the Second World War. Who among us, after having seen the mountains of shoes from millions of assassinated children at Auschwitz, didn't ask the question: God, where were you? What has this to do with democracy? The link is, as mentioned above, that it is just one, even if socially hugely significant, element in dismantling and eviscerating the element of duty and responsibility from our public life.

A voice which was at one time universal and ubiquitous, a voice in which the emphasis was on duty and responsibility and not only rights, on personal responsibility in the face of what happens to us, our neighbors, our society and not the instinctive appeal to public institutions, has all but disappeared from social praxis.

In Church you do not hear about your entitlements from the state and others but of your duty toward society and others. No politician today in Europe could or would repeat the famous Kennedy Inauguration speech of 1960 – Don't ask what your country can do for you but what you can do . . . etc. Anything that goes wrong in our society is always the responsibility of others, not of us.

The citizenship chapter of the European Treaties is a poignant example. It speaks of rights and duties which the citizen enjoys and owes – but then no duties are ever mentioned.

It is totally understandable why we had become suspicious of patriotism, of identity politics, seeing the abusive way they were instrumentalized in Europe's past. But we have thrown the baby out with the bathwater. And into this void has stepped the new populist with oftentimes the old abusive practices.

It is easy to understand the appeal of, say, nationalism: As a member of a national community, I have a past, a future beyond my individual self-interest. The national idiom emphasizes that which is special and unique and becomes as such part of the identitarian asset of the individual.

Calling on people's duty and responsibility empowers them, and gives their action a meaning which goes beyond their self-interest. Above all, it imbues persons with respect and self-respect.

Europe's historical mistake was to fail to understand the huge importance of collective values and to adapt them to a modern progressive narrative which combined the so-called Holy and Unholy Trinities of values. There is a way of celebrating and respecting love of society and country, the idiom of liberal patriotism, of coupling rights with duties, of having a healthy self-respect to one's collective identity and culture which is not atavistic and chauvinist. Of exercising the best in the Christian heritage even if one has lost religious faith.

But that way is not "out there" as part of the program of mainstream politics. All we hear is a narrative of employment and growth, of a more equitable distribution of economic deserts, of how better to manage our markets and our prosperity – all incredibly valuable, but failing to understand that not on bread alone does man liveth. Until we fill this void, the field will be left to the seductive and pernicious siren call of a politics of meaning which we had left behind.

Which brings us full circle back to Orbán. Whatever merit there is in the above analysis does not remove responsibility from the people who freely put him there and endorsed his programs through their votes. But it imposes on us, too, the same moral imperative of democratic responsibility – to reintroduce us to a more honest form of republican democracy, a form to which we have become less and less accustomed. What is happening in Europe is not a *coup d'état*. It is a long process of widespread degradation of democracy in many of our Member States and of collective democratic self-asphyxiation, of willed action, in a country such has Hungary which could have been stopped at the ballot box. Let us call it as it is.

11

Corona as Chance: Overcoming the Tyranny of Self-Interest

SUSAN NEIMAN

> What we learn in times of pestilence: that there are more things to admire in men than to despise.
>
> Albert Camus, *The Plague*

This is not prophecy.

That isn't a task for philosophers, though it's not clear who could do a better job today. Bill Gates and others gave us some warning of the pandemic, but the world was caught unawares. The political thinker Ivan Krastev says we're living with a radicalization of the imagination that embraces left and right. For years, climate change activists sought to curb air travel; what once seemed utopian happened overnight. Right-wing nationalists have long demanded closed borders; suddenly even the EU's most visible achievement, open borders between Member States, was cast aside. What else can we begin to imagine? We know the economy is collapsing, but that determines nothing. In Germany, the Great Depression sealed the triumph of fascism. In the United States it spawned the closest thing to social democracy the country ever knew.

Philosophy cannot make predictions, but it can expand your sense of possibility. We all tend to limit imagination by the frameworks we know. Life is easier when you never ask if other frameworks might be possible, for if they are possible, they could become actual, and that demands effort. If you believe, like most Americans, that health care, sick leave, parental leave, and paid vacation are a matter of generous benefits, you'll be grateful when they're offered, but you will not think to demand them. If you believe, like most Europeans, that they're a matter of basic rights, you cannot really imagine life without them.

In the wake of the coronavirus, many are insisting that the crisis is an opportunity. Going back to normal should not be our goal: What was normal was awful for the planet, and so many of its inhabitants. Most anyone who has time to read this chapter felt a stab of realization at the start of the lockdown: You are not essential. It's the supermarket cashiers and the trash collectors who keep the world going. Some have turned that realization into a call for working conditions which honor the fact that the rest of us would be helpless without the labor of those whose safety, status, and salaries are so different from our own. I support these calls wholeheartedly, but this is not another of them. My aim is to remind us that we are living in a conceptual framework that we barely perceive as such. By perceiving it, we can begin to imagine others that will help change the conditions themselves.

For over a century we've lived under the tyranny of self-interest, the idea that every human action can be reduced to a desire to maximize our own interests, themselves understood as nothing but expanding wealth and power. The ideology is hard to recognize as ideology because it seems unpolitical; both left and right have adopted it. – *Shouldn't that make it not ideology but unadorned necessary truth?* – In fact, the tyranny of self-interest has been criticized within moral and political theory as well as by empirical research in psychology, primatology, and economics. Many thinkers in these fields argue that the appeal to self-interest is not only a miserable basis for social norms, but an unconvincing way to account for much of human behavior. Yet the appeal to self-interest as the only honest explanation of human behavior has continued despite considerable evidence that it isn't an adequate lens for perceiving reality. This is good reason to view it as ideology, for neither the evidence nor the arguments penetrated much of the public world.

Coronavirus has changed that.

In the first weeks of the pandemic, pundits predicted descents into barbarism and battles over toilet paper. What were not predicted were new forms of solidarity that emerged. Outside my window, past linden trees waving their furious spring beauty, a group of musicians sings a reggae tune. I can make out the lyrics across the canal: "We can make a change / We must come together." To tell from the accents, they are African immigrants. Writing songs to fight corona has become a task for musicians across that vast, underresourced continent.

You can hear many of them on the website of UNESCO's #Don'tGoViral campaign. Despite the variety of musical form, all the songs express a message that would have been dismissed as kitsch just a few weeks earlier. For at least as important as the spread of information – wash your hands, practice social distancing – is the dissemination of hope. *We shall overcome, but only if we remember that we are all connected.* When did you last hear something like that? Earlier heroes were not only tainted by violence, but by constant unmasking: How could we admire a hero whose feet were made of clay? All of a sudden it doesn't matter what nurses' feet are made of; they are risking their lives to save yours.

Signs of solidarity haven't been confined to songs and words. Someone in Ireland remembered that the Choctaw Nation, newly off the Trail of Tears, sent $170 to save starving families in County Cork during the 1847 famine. They started a drive that raised hundreds of thousands of dollars to supply food, clean water, and health supplies to Native American tribes now hit hard by the virus. A doctor in San Diego, overworked and underprotected like most of his colleagues, found time to care about the fears of COVID-19 patients who now see only people whose spacesuit equipment suggests robots. He began a campaign that pinned the smiling photos of medical workers onto their protective clothing, a visual signal to patients that there were human beings inside. A biochemist in Berlin whose autoimmune disease prevents her from volunteering for lab work started a drive that led Airbnb to offer medical workers free housing where they could stay without fear of infecting their families. Notes nailed to trees in my neighborhood list numbers that strangers can call if they want someone young and healthy to pick up their groceries or their prescriptions. Many thousands have volunteered to be infected with the virus in the hope of contributing to a cure.

I began collecting bits of good news when the pandemic was declared, and I realized that my last purchase before lockdown was the most useless. The cover of my calendar – I still use paper – was worn to tatters, and I'd ordered a new one. Now every date in my calendar was cancelled, and the very sense of ordering my life according to calendars was thrown into question. "If you want to make God laugh," say the Irish, "Tell him your plans."

Keeping your life to a plan is one piece of human nature the virus upended. Here is another: It no longer made sense to consider whether you were doing something in your own interest or in the interest of the common good. Your interests collided so closely they could rarely be distinguished. You should wear a mask to protect others, and hope they will wear one to protect you. If you want to eat your steak, someone else will have to raise a cow, slaughter it, package it, and ship it. (If you've decided to go vegan you're likely to depend on undocumented workers from Romania or Mexico.) Once set down on paper, these truths are glaringly obvious, but we've spent no end of energy shielding ourselves from the glare. The simplest truths are those we try hardest to avoid, for

they create moral demands. Coronavirus makes it impossible to repress
how dependent we are on each other. At the most rock-bottom, life and
death level, your well-being and my well-being are one and the same.

***

The tyranny of self-interest has a history, and if it's a framework that was
created, we could create another. Self-interest was hardly self-evident to
the nineteenth century, when the practice of dueling was common. To be
a man meant being able to defend your honor, not harnessing all other
emotions to the pursuit of simple gain. The nineteenth-century gentleman who failed to respond to an insult with a demand for satisfaction
suffered public humiliation. It was not quite the same humiliation that's
felt by a man whose labor isn't paid enough to feed his family – or, if he's
a twenty-first-century gentleman, to buy them whatever objects are
considered necessities in the neighborhood (iPhones? Fast cars?). But
the difference reveals how shame was transformed. In the first case, it was
shameful to love your life more than your dignity. In the second, you're
meant to feel ashamed if you're enough of a sucker to let ideas such as
dignity or integrity hold more weight than self-aggrandizement. In one
short century our emotions evolved: From fearing the shame of being (or
seeming) insufficiently honorable to fearing the shame of seeming (or
being) insufficiently self-serving.

Yes, there are gang wars where insults lead to consequences even
deadlier than duels, but these now take place on society's margins. The
very codification of the rules of dueling, which put some limits on
fatalities, signals how central the practice was to the social order.
Dueling is the sort of practice that should immediately make you question contemporary assumptions about human nature. This is not, of
course, a plea for a return to dueling, but a demand to consider how
many views that now seem self-evident are products of history, and very
particular interests. In a remarkable essay written in 1906, just as the
tyranny of self-interest was taking hold, William James gave considerable
thought to the question of what should replace martial virtues in order to
avoid a "cattleyard of a planet," "a sheep's paradise," "a mass of human
blubber."[1] James was a socialist and a pacifist, and he wasn't naïve about
the cost of violence. Two of his brothers died of wounds they suffered
while fighting as abolitionists in the American Civil War. Yet in "The

---

[1] William James's address, "The Moral Equivalent of War," was originally delivered at
Stanford University in 1906. See William James, *The Moral Equivalent of War and Other
Essays* (New York: Harper and Row, 1971).

Moral Equivalent of War" he argues that a postwar society must find ways for a "life of strenuous honor" without which "history would be insipid indeed."

Though women have also been soldiers, martial virtues that pit love of honor against the impulse to self-preservation have usually been men's business. Normally, women were expected to uphold ideas of honor and sacrifice that took different forms. Of course we're right to condemn misogynist conceptions of honor, or expectations that women should sacrifice their own lives to play supporting roles to their men. Yet it's worthwhile to read letters of those women who were early feminists and abolitionists to see how they understood the risks they took. Though basic goals remain the same as those of contemporary struggles for racial and gender equality, the arguments for them have changed: What once was a matter of justice is now a matter of power. Should anyone wonder that right-wing white racists now respond with their own claims to power? The earlier arguments are now dismissed as rhetoric, quaint ideas we discarded as we became sadder and wiser about what makes people tick. But no reader of Leo Tolstoy or George Eliot could suppose the nineteenth century was naïve about what moves us, or the complex mixture of self-interest and other motives that most of our actions reveal. The difference is that until quite recently, we assumed that motives are mixed. It seemed clear that people are inspired by desires to behave according to certain standards, as well as swayed by passion or driven by greed. No single influence was seen to require deconstruction of another. Now pointing out selfish motives behind appearances is synonymous with transparency – or even courage, given the bleakness of the world it thinks to reveal.

The ideology of self-interest depends on a model called *homo economicus*: The human being considered "solely as a being who desires wealth, and who is capable of judging the comparative efficiency of means for obtaining that end." John Stuart Mill, whose work engendered the term, emphasized that it "is an arbitrary definition of man, as a being who inevitably does that by which he may obtain the greatest amount of necessaries, conveniences, and luxuries, with the smallest quantity of labor and physical self-denial with which they can be obtained."[2] He quickly added that no political economist "was ever so absurd as to suppose that mankind are really thus constituted." Mill's caveats were

---

[2] John Stuart Mill, *Essays on Some Unsettled Questions of Political Economy* (New York: Augustus M. Kelley, 1968).

ignored as many economists and policy makers found his arbitrary definition convenient, though many others criticized it for failing to describe us. Crucially, most of the criticism concerns the ways in which we *fall short of this model* of rationality, showing how passions and perceptual distortions routinely prevent us from maximizing utility in the ways the model demands. Too little of the criticism addresses the ways in which this model *falls short of us*. It's that which outrages those who refuse to view reason as reducible to a means of maximizing self-interest, or value as reducible to market value. People who have preserved that outrage can be found left and right.

To see that the model of self-interest is not a self-evident constant but a norm, consider the work of Ayn Rand. Even the most famous philosophical advocate of selfishness was unable to maintain it consistently. Rand did not, in fact, rest her case on *homo economicus*. Mill's hypothetical creatures whose lives are devoted to obtaining the largest amount of goods with the least amount of labor are the *villains* of Ayn Rand's novels. Her stories win followers not through their tedious speeches, or even their Dostoyevskian plot twists, but because their leading characters represent dignity, courage, and passion in a world rife with meanness and envy. For all their talk about selfishness, Rand's men and women are always depicted as great and noble souls engaged in battle against small-mindedness. Whether designing skyscrapers or inventing metals, her heroes are creators who embody human freedom. As surely as for any abstract laborer imagined by Marx or Hegel, it's the work itself – not the wealth it may bring – which is the truest expression of their humanity, and the act that gives them a claim to something meant to replace the divine. In the end, Rand combined a Cold War defense of free markets with a nineteenth-century conception of heroism.

If the *homo economicus* model of human motivation doesn't even work where we expect to find it, how did it become the dominant one? Albert O. Hirschman's classic *The Passions and the Interests* showed how the self-interest model was initially driven by progressive impulses. For many eighteenth-century thinkers, the appeal to self-interest promised an end to violence, offering a less destructive basis for action than appeals to honor and glory. It wasn't only dueling, which robbed us of extraordinary souls such as Alexander Pushkin and Alexander Hamilton, as well as many who never lived long enough to do something which stayed in memory. Whole wars were waged for reasons that now seem ridiculous. The appeal to self-interest was also democratic, providing a basis for social justice that considered the needs of every group and every class. No one who made those appeals could have imagined the commodification of everything. Advertising had yet to be invented, much less algorithmized.

Advertising was only one of the forces that made the self-interest model seem self-evident; the Cold War was another. It was comforting to think that the men who controlled nuclear arsenals large enough to extinguish life on earth shared a notion of rationality which insured they would not use them. Then the end of the Cold War seemed to make the appeal to anything *other* than self-interest look like folly. The Soviet Union's own flaws took calls for international solidarity out of circulation. They needn't have done so, but the inclination to view every such expression as propaganda designed to veil what was merely a will to power was supported by three ideologies that blossomed at the end of the twentieth century.

The philosophical assumptions that have shaped much of the world since 1989 depend on the idea that self-interest is the only force that moves us. That's a pre-Socratic ideology which goes back to ancient Athens, but it was given new life by neoliberal economics, postmodern theories of truth and power, and evolutionary psychology. All three combine to convince us that acting for any reason other than our own self-interest – or at most, that of our respective tribes – is not only foolish, but counter to the wisdom of science and history.

Though they may be opposed to each other politically, postmodern philosophy, evolutionary psychology, and neoliberal economics all presuppose a metaphysics of suspicion: Every ideal conceals an interest. Neoliberalism suggests, without actually asserting it, that there are no values but market values. Evolutionary biology reinforces this idea with unprovable scientific theories: Our ancient ancestors, and even our very genes, have been biologically programmed to reproduce as many of ourselves as possible. Both ideologies assume that claims to truth are claims to power. If there are any facts at all, they are facts about domination.

In every generation, this standpoint is presented as bold and new. In fact, it's at least as old as Plato, whose greatest work *The Republic* was written in large part as a rejoinder to the standpoint as expressed by the young Thrasymachus. On the left in recent decades, Michel Foucault has been its most important spokesman, curiously seconded by the Nazi legal theorist Carl Schmitt. An introductory logic course could have spared us some confusion: From the fact that some moral claims are hidden claims to power, you cannot conclude that every claim to act for the common good is a lie. But logic is seldom the strong point of such thinkers.

Though they tend to be fond of Friedrich Nietzsche, their writing is sufficiently obscure to merit one of his better put-downs: "They muddy the waters to make them seem deep."

Journalists are no less products of their time than anyone else. Even those who never opened a book of philosophy swim in the ideological currents that swirl around us. Or as *Breitbart News* put it, "politics is downstream from culture." You needn't have a complete theory of relations between thought and action to know that what you think is possible determines the framework in which you act. If you think it's impossible to distinguish truth from narrative, you won't bother to try. If you think it's impossible to act on anything other than self-interest, you will have no misgivings about doing so.

The ideology of self-interest became so dominant in the last decades that few people dared question it. What kept them from questioning wasn't fear of torture or exile, the sort of thing that regularly prevents people from questioning dominant ideologies. It was something both sillier and more sinister: Fear of embarrassment. As economist Robert Frank observed, "The flint-eyed researcher fears no greater humiliation than to have called some action altruistic, only to have a more sophisticated colleague later demonstrate it was self-serving. This fear surely helps account for the extraordinary amount of ink behavioral scientists have spent trying to unearth selfish motives for seemingly self-sacrificing acts."[3] *The Emperor's New Clothes* is a powerful fable, for it shows how shame – and its poor relation, embarrassment – is often more powerful than terror (a fact about which we should be profoundly ... embarrassed). Here there is no emperor, nor two swindlers pulling the strings. What forces combined to make us ashamed to name the better angels of our nature?

Conspiracies should rarely be ruled out entirely; sometimes people do conspire to put new ideas into practice. But the tyranny of self-interest is so ubiquitous, and supported by so many sources, that seeking any one cause is probably senseless. Even exploring all its sources in depth would require a long and looping journey. The trip would take you, at least, through William James's essay, "The Moral Equivalent of War," and most of his brother Henry's novels; Eva Illouz's study of how early industrial psychologists taught businessmen to redirect their behavior according to notions of self-interest; a similar body of work produced in

---

[3] Robert Frank, *Passion within Reason: The Strategic Role of Emotions* (New York: W.W. Norton, 1988).

1990s Russia to accompany the transition to capitalism; Adam Curtis's explorations of the invention of public relations; Lorraine Daston's examination of the Rand Corporation's construction of Cold War rationality. And that's without exploring the cultures of selfies and social media. In this short chapter my aim is not to add to the detailed historical work these and other authors have done so well. It is rather to underscore what Ludwig Wittgenstein called a fact we've failed to notice because it's always before our eyes: The tyranny of self-interest is an ideology that was created, and like any other ideology, it can be overthrown.

***

Toward the end of May 2020 I stopped adding to the file I'd named "Good corona news." For one thing, there was too much of it. For another, something was happening that dwarfed all the other good news I'd collected – so long as it didn't end in civil war. At the time of writing, the prospects for justice and peace look better than they have for a very long time, though I know as well as anyone that the future is wide open. That, after all, is the premise of this chapter.

One of the first sources of sadness the pandemic brought was the fear that struggles for racial and historical justice would take a backseat to COVID-19. The world would be too desperate to get back to normal: A careless walk, a run to the corner grocery when you need a quart of milk, the touch of a beloved hand. The desperation to get the simplest parts of our old lives back would be so strong, I feared, that the harder demands for justice would be set aside. As they were so often before.

Then all over the world, people stood up to demand an end to normality. Normal were structures, from policing to health care, that kill people of color. Normal were histories studded with lies. Normal had been wrong for a very long time, but the cup just ran over. George Floyd's death on May 25 was one black death too many. It wasn't the first we saw on video, but it was the most excruciating – not only because we heard a dying man cry out for his own dead mama, but also because we saw the face of another man, blank and banal in its brutality, who had nearly nine minutes to change his mind about murder. (Gunshots allow us to imagine that everything happened too quickly to be deliberate.) Now it looks as if this murder could break a herd of camels' backs.

The speed of events is so swift that what surprised us in one week is likely to be overtaken by the next. First is the fact that at least as many white people as black and brown ones have braved COVID-19 and teargas to demand an end to systemic racism. The polls are unequivocal:

A large majority of Americans see this as everyone's problem, not one that's mostly a concern for people of color. It's no wonder that the protests began in America. This is not just because, though racism is an international problem, more people die of it on the streets of America. (Or in their beds. See: Breonna Taylor.) Even more importantly, America is the first nation on earth that wasn't entirely a matter of accident. Other nations were formed as collections of tribes settled down in one place or another and created political structures. Unlike them, America claimed to be founded on a set of ideals. That Native Americans had a right to life, and African Americans to liberty, was a truth whose self-evidence eluded most of the Founding Fathers. Historians have long worked to show how far American realities diverged from American ideals. (Occasionally, even philosophers contributed: Think of Ralph Waldo Emerson's and Henry David Thoreau's support not only of the quieter sorts of abolitionist but their defense of John Brown, or William James's denunciation of burgeoning imperialism. None of this is taught in major philosophy departments.) But the way from archives to public consciousness is a long one, and public understanding of history is still based on an exceptionalism that may acknowledge divergences from American ideals, yet focuses attention on attempts to correct them. Significantly, African Americans have always played a major role in holding the nation's feet to the fire. Very few supported the Back-to-Africa movements. From Frederick Douglass to Paul Robeson to Toni Morrison, African Americans have been at the forefront of those who demand that America live up to the ideals it proclaims.

For several reasons, not least the fact that Great Britain managed to outsource most of its slavery to the colonies, the British have been even slower than Americans to face up to their national crimes. A recent poll showed that not one in five Britons feels any reason for shame about Empire. Hence the speed of change in Britain has been even more astonishing than in America. Statues whose significance had been debated for years, such as Cecil Rhodes, beneath the dreaming spires of Oxford University, will finally fall. Symbolic changes have been matched by demands for systemic ones: To make black and colonial history mandatory throughout the school system and to examine police practices which, though not as deadly in London as in New York City, are racist nonetheless. Lloyd's of London and other corporations announced reparations for slavery. In other countries, statues of King Leopold II – whose policies led to the murder of some 10 million Congolese – were splashed with blood-colored paint in Belgium, and are now coming down. Australians are insisting on offering more than apologies for injustices done to First Peoples. Listening to voices around the world, extraordinarily diverse in age, class, and ethnic backgrounds, two things become clear: Their well-informed solidarity with the Black Lives Matter movement in America, and their commitments to facing their own racist histories. Just one thing is certain: By the time this volume is published there will be more surprises. Not all of them will be happy ones. I am buoyed, however, that veterans of the original Civil Rights Movement, as well as some of our more pessimistic black critics – Ta-Nehisi Coates, Roxanne Gay – are expressing long-buried hopes in this outsized moment.

Here and there, cynics have suggested that the protests have been an excuse to release pent-up energy after months of lockdown, while lending it a moral edge. To be sure: Some people make a habit of seeking the worst possible interpretation of every bit of human behavior. Looking at the faces and listening to the words of those in the streets give rise to a simpler explanation. The coronavirus pandemic has given us a chance to see how deeply we are connected and vulnerable to the same diseases, as well as how inequalities persist even in cultures that purport to condemn them. Facing history is not a vaccine against racism, but it is a necessary beginning. With his usual eloquence and clarity, Bryan Stevenson drew connections:

> In medicine, you can't come up with a cure until you understand the nature of the disease. We're in the midst of this pandemic, and our scientists are desperately trying to figure out how this illness spreads and what are the features that allow it to sicken our population. It's our knowledge of the truth about the disease that allow us to create effective remedies, and we've hidden from the truth of our history of racial inequality.[4]

The pandemic has also shown us a wide array of possibilities that seemed unreachable just months ago. Housing the homeless? Feeding the hungry? *All very commendable aspirations, but in the absence of resources they will have to remain … aspirational.* The speed at which international funding was provided to prevent pandemic-related disaster has given us a taste of what other changes might have a chance.

I suspect there has been another factor in the swelling of protest besides the pain for murdered black people, and the hope that what was normal has now been thrown into question. US President Donald Trump provoked revulsion and rage long before the palette of obscene

---

[4] Bryan Stevenson in conversation with Ezra Klein, podcast, www.stitcher.com/podcast/vox/the-ezra-klein-show/e/76293210.

remarks about George Floyd that issued from the White House in the days that rocked first Minneapolis and then the world, or his use of violent troops to shut down a peaceful demonstration so that he could pose before a church holding an upside-down Bible, a stunt so insulting to people of faith that any child could see through it. He has a singular talent for performing humankind's most contemptible forms. If Barack Obama reminded us of Lincoln's invocation of the better angels of our nature, Donald Trump is not only determined to encourage our worst ones, but to commit sacrilege at the Lincoln Memorial. Many remember his "American Carnage" inauguration speech, but the carnage he enacted the night before has been forgotten. Surrounded by troops commanded to serve him, Trump could have ordered any song in the world as he strode with his wife through the monument. His choice was the Rolling Stones' anthem to heartlessness: "Heart of Stone," ringing out under the statue of Lincoln's resolute and melancholy face. Watching the footage, I shivered with fear.

I have argued that experts in many fields have worked for decades to undermine the tyranny of self-interest; the model just doesn't work for explaining much human behavior (or that of primates, elephants, or, according to some studies, even rats). But even without the help of science and scholarship, self-reflection could convince us that we do not *always* act as the reigning ideologies suggest. We care about asserting truth, not just power; we often act upon interests that are not material interests; and our behavior is rarely guided by the impulse to reproduce as many copies of ourselves, or our names, as possible. Donald Trump is an extraordinary exception: Unlike the rest of us, he doesn't seem to understand any other combination of motives – much less to exhibit them. As the world looks on with horror at the *reductio ad absurdum* of the self-interest paradigm, is it any wonder we are moved to reconsider?

***

There is not much time for detours. At the moment, we need only outline the fact that self-interest *has* a history to show that the model is not eternal. Climate scientists told us we might have another decade, but no one in power behaved as if they believed it. Now coronavirus made everything stop. We have a chance to begin something different – if we understand that all the voices who ever told us something different was impossible were caught in a framework of possibility that we could reject.

It might, of course, go just the other way, and powerful interests are actively trying to make sure that it does. All the worst predictions could come true. Authoritarian leaders may coopt the pandemic for their own vested interests; we've seen it with Viktor Orbán and Benjamin Netanyahu. Others may use the virus as another tool to whip up nationalism; we've seen it with Trump and Narendra Modi. Domestic violence has been rising, along with divorce – I read bad news too. And just for the record, I was never persuaded by Pangloss. I've written a lot about evil.

But I'm interested in possibilities, not predictions, and there I take lessons from Immanuel Kant. He thought that we cannot know what people are like apart from society, for we'll never have access to the earliest state of nature. Nor can we know whether humankind is progressing to a better state, for the future holds twists and turns we cannot foretell. If one is too distant in history to be an object of knowledge, the other lies too far ahead in the future. Yet whichever kind of sin you may find original, how you imagine human nature has moral repercussions.

When a question that has moral repercussions is truly unknowable, Kant offers you rational faith. It is not wishful thinking, just enough conviction to allow you to act toward achieving the best you can. If you believe that a post-COVID-19 world could escape the tyranny of self-interest, you can work to achieve it. If you believe such a world is impossible, you'll kick back and have another drink. Self-fulfilling prophecies are not in fact prophecies, but they have their own ways of coming true.

Economic laws are not laws of nature. When the Great Depression began in America, labor organizers feared a decline of union activity. With so many people out of work and in need of a paycheck, wouldn't solidarity seem a luxury? It did not. Labor organizing and union membership increased till they led to the New Deal. We know that depression stoked fascism elsewhere, and could do so again today. But with so much at stake in the outcome, don't you have a moral obligation to bet on the outcome that gives you a chance to make it right?

If this chapter isn't prophecy, it also isn't theodicy, that ancient attempt to find meaning in suffering that seemed to justify pain. People have sought meaning in suffering since Job cried to God. Despite all the efforts of the Enlightenment, it's a form of magical thinking to which most of us incline. Earlier ages divided horror into natural evils and moral evils, and made one the meaning of the other. *If you suffer, you must have sinned* is a thought just as old as Job's friends. It was the Enlightenment that distinguished between natural evils – such as earthquakes and plagues – and moral evils – such as torture and tyranny. This meant that natural evil could no longer be declared punishment for a sin you cannot fathom. If you get sick, it's not because you skipped a prayer. Perhaps you're undernourished? How's the water in your neighborhood? Are you living in social conditions that contributed to your illness? On the hope that these suppositions will prove true, we can begin to do something about the social conditions. The Enlightenment taught us not to execute people for allegedly poisoning wells – nor even make them feel guilty for disasters they didn't cause.

It was a bold, progressive move. To grasp how radical it was, consider this: When was the last time you flinched inwardly, thinking *this misery I'm feeling is because I've done wrong.* (Fill in the blank for your favorite regret. If you're one of the rare souls who never experienced bad luck or illness as punishment, you should simply be grateful.) But however useful and progressive it may have been in the eighteenth century, the distinction between natural and moral evils is hard to maintain.

For we now have the power to change nature itself in so many ways that natural evils are returning in force, despite all we did to mitigate them. We discovered dykes and earthquake-resistant construction and vaccines and public health policies. In enlightened countries, we created rights to basic health and welfare. Still we are now hit by a plague that threatens every facet of our former lives. Shouldn't we conclude that Mother Nature is paying us back for the wrongs we have done her – clogging the seas with plastic, filling the skies with poison?

It's a conclusion as natural as that of Job's friends, though their image of the sins for which Job deserved punishment never reached to the seas and the skies. They thought he must have prayed wrong. It's a stance we're likely to take when we meet pain or sorrow, for anything seems better than meaningless suffering. You needn't be a Freudian to see an easy explanation for that stance: Our parents, if they were decent, only punished us when we did wrong. Of course we are likely to blame someone, be it only ourselves, for the plague.

Mother Nature is a natural image, but it's not a helpful one. Love of the earth will not save us, at least not without the political will to heed warnings about consumption and climate, inequality and waste. This makes the distinction between natural and moral evils less absolute, but still useful for reminding us that natural evils are not just deserts. If people of color are dying in America in greater numbers than others, it's because they've been living in conditions that made decent health care and nourishment impossible. Those are neither determined by God nor nature; they are things we can change.

This is not theodicy, for nothing can absolve the pain of those struck by the plague. Nor of those who loved someone who died alone amid masks and machines. Even if the pandemic turns out to be a crisis that opens doors to a better future, it would be obscene to try to justify it.

Still, the Renaissance followed the Black Plague, and there's a reason people are recalling that now. Sometimes, just sometimes, men and women who preserved body and soul through catastrophes unfolding around them went on to remake the world.

12

Reimagined Democracy in Times
of Pandemic

KALYPSO NICOLAIDIS[*]

Never before has a majority of humanity focused collectively and simultaneously on the most elementary gift of life: Breath. We watched as the most vulnerable gave out their last breath in droves. We watched out for each other's breath. We watched for our kin and our neighbors and for the breath of strangers. We watched, as thousands of health workers around the world sacrificed their lives so that the rest of us could breath. And amid a universal lockdown, we watched a lone black man in Minneapolis breathe his last under the lockdown of a policeman oblivious to his haunting cry: I can't breathe. In the months preceding this moment, we had willingly held our democratic breath, only for the urge to speak out to erupt again, on the part of populations grasping for air around the world. "If White People Didn't Invent Air, What Would We Breathe?" echoes Dread Scott's old ironic cry, bringing together those intertwined threads.

So what has COVID-19 done to "democracy," we ask – whatever we each put under this broad umbrella. There is little doubt that democratic practices have been and continue to be among the deeper casualties of the pandemic, as vividly symbolized by the emptying of our public spaces around the world. As many authors in this volume illustrate, the months of lockdown brought into sharper relief existing trends of democratic erosion around the world from Hungary to the United States, from India to Indonesia, as governments used states of emergency to grant themselves new executive powers. As ordinary citizens we are falling prey to the curbing of our freedoms and mobility and to the intensification of surveillance in a game of one-upmanship as people die. But there is also another story to tell here of democratic freedoms helping to navigate the

---

* I would like to thank Miguel Maduro and Daphne Saunders for their insightful feedback.

pandemic as much as constraints do, as civil society groups and free media keep governments on their toes.

I will not try to adjudicate here between these two opposite democratic sides of the pandemic coin. All we can say is that this moment will eventually count as one episode in a long process of mutation of our societies over decades, which has been redefining the grounds for public authority, shining light on the pathologies of capitalism and the unsustainable social contract underpinning its twenty-first-century variant. We will find that the pandemic pushed the fast-forward button on what some have called "the grand acceleration" of our age. And that in the process it has exposed both the fragility and the resilience of our democracies. The ledger is open.

Instead of observing or predicting actual changes in our democratic makeup, I ask here a different question: *How is the pandemic affecting our democratic imagination?* I do so in the spirit of Yaron Ezrahi's proposition that democracy, like any other political regime, must be imagined and performed by multiple agency in order to exist.[1] Beyond the picture of a deliberative self-governing polity of informed free citizens envisioned by Enlightenment thinkers, he argues, the grounds for governmental authority lie in the political imagination of its citizens. To be sure, these rolling waves of global lockdown and let-up have induced a veritable tsunami of imaginings, musings about the world afterwards, where everything is up for grabs, from the ways we move, interact, play, and work to the reconfiguration of our global politics. Whatever happens, we may hope that somehow we have become more self-reflexive, not only as individuals but also as societies. And that in the process, space has opened up for our political imaginaries. To be sure and at this early stage, we can only collect impressions, possible keys. The impressions may fade away, the keys be misplaced. But at the very least we will have been empowered to acknowledge our choices in a new light.

This is a "pandemic moment" when we might realize and reimagine what we have lost and what we have gained, what we might want to reclaim or retain. What if, half a century after the Franco-Greek philosopher Cornelius Castoriadis deployed his idea of the *imaginary institution of society* in the wake of May 1968, we were one step closer to fulfilling the conditions of "self-institution" by which we truly come to own our own

---

[1] Y. Ezrahi, *Imagined Democracies: Necessary Political Fictions* (Cambridge University Press, 2012).

laws, whether as individuals or as societies?[2] For if democracy was born from the fall of authority figures, gods, kings, emperors, and nations, it not only needs to be permanently reinvented to stay alive, but societies need to be fully self-aware as the authoritative originators of this reinvention. While conventional accounts of democracy center around collective self-rule, having a say over the rules that govern us, it is imperative to resist the centralization of power and ultimately state capture of all levers of authority. Democracies may be about fusing demoi and cratos, horizontal togetherness, and vertical governing, but ultimately, the democratic promise lies in the collective imagination of the governing demoi, a reassertion of the horizontal bond between all of us. Hence the question: If radical democracy calls for the dispersion of social, political, and economic power and the assertion of our mutual responsibility, how does society imagine itself doing so?

In the following pages, I suggest where we may start or pause in exploring the eclectic patchwork of reimaginings offered by the pandemic, through the metaphors of theatre, bubbles, strings, circles, and mirrors. First, the exposed politics of life and death offer a starting point for reimagining and claiming our democratic agency. Second, the obligations imposed on us by the state open up a space for the social appropriation of R, whether as reproduction rate or as responsibility. Third, the Jewish institution of the 'eruv' can inspire us as we renegotiate democratically the boundaries of our social space. Fourth, we are coming to picture the management of interdependence as a horizontal maze of different, overlapping, or nested circles of autonomy. And finally, we may start to see ourselves as defined by new "glocalities" whereby multitudes involved in new modes of contagious contestations help redefine a new anthropo-scene, a scene where humanity invents novel democratic performances across time and space for the next generation.

Theatre, or the Democratization of Necropolitics

The ultimate expression of democratic health lies in our mortuaries, where the dead speak of how they got there. In his *Necropolitics*, Achille Mbembe, offered a critique of the use of social and political power to dictate how some people may live and how some must die,

---

[2] Translated from the French by the author. C. Castoriadis, *L'institution imaginaire de la Société* (Paris: Collection Esprit,1975); C. Castoriadis, *The Imaginary Institution of Society* (Cambridge, MA: MIT Press, 1997).

focusing on the various forms of political violence which have accompanied colonial subjugation and slavery.[3] But Michel Foucault who inspired him spoke of our own societies, where the (mis)management of death brings about more vividly than anything else the close imbrication between statecraft as stagecraft. As the relentless collective contemplation of variously shaped graphs and cross-country comparisons of death figures has provided the staging for this pandemic's necropolitics, we can ask what this theatre of death does for our democratic social contract.

For one, it seems to be the case that populations across the world have had an unprecedented say on what kind of theatre this is in the first place. Leaders who followed the old Schmittean securitization recipe that war-induced states of emergency justify power grabs and self-aggrandizement, and thus initially sought to frame the pandemic as a theatre of war, rapidly needed to change metaphorical gear. Those who didn't, populist leaders à la Donald Trump or Jair Bolsonaro, will be exposed. Instead, political leaders were rewarded who staged the moment as another kind of theatre: The theatre of care. Citizens across the world saw how these "care-theatre" leaders, including often female prime ministers, from Taiwan's Tsai Ing-wen to New Zealand's Jacinda Ardern to Finland's Sanna Marin, not only spoke the language of care, caution, compassion, humility, and empathy, and were more prone to listen to outside voices, but also organized their states' response with greater emphasis on citizen participation and empowerment.[4]

These two theatres redefine differently the dynamics between heightened expectations and popular control. Undoubtedly, the massive mobilization of state resources to nationalize infrastructure services, subsidize industries, and pay wages in the private sector responded to a public expectation about the state. But at the same time this mobilization is accompanied by a rising demand for greater citizen engagement in defining and running state functions that manage how we live on a day-to-day basis. Moreover, in a theatre of war, cross-comparisons are about enmity and therefore zero sum: My health-gun is bigger than yours. In a theatre of care, there may be emulation but ultimately societies can literally see that if your neighboring locality or country does well, you do well too.

---

[3] A. Mbembe, *Necropolitics* (Durham, NC: Duke University Press, 2019).
[4] For an insightful discussion of the care society, see for instance A. M. Slaughter, *Unfinished Business: Women Men Work Family* (New York: Simon and Schuster, 2015).

In other words, the theatre of care offers roles with agency. In a theatre of care, citizens mobilize instead of being mobilized. Irrespective of leaders' original leanings, we have witnessed how, for the first time in the history of capitalism, the right to life has been affirmed over the functionalist rational of the modern state. Human rights activists have long sought to enforce the value of life as the supreme right, and a right not merely to protect physical existence, but to protect "life with dignity."[5] We may be very far from the equal enjoyment of this right for the seven billion people on the planet, but in its absence we take greater notice. A disaster it may be, but one closer to Chernobyl than to Pompei. The graphs do not tell a story of fatality but agency, a story of avoidable deaths where we are the ones to fill the void. That each citizen be equally authoritative over matters of livelihood, that is the core definition of the democratic ethos. The democratic contract may involve a common agreement regarding the obligations citizens owe the state, but it ultimately rests on the moral power we each hold to engage into mutual obligations.[6] And it is precisely because our agency has been radically curtailed that we are more prone than ever to claim it anew.

In the theatre of care therefore, the collective is inclined to engage in a moral task, albeit through process rather than outcome-related obligations. Between lives protected and lives taken, the pandemic moment has shown the best and the worst of humanity – side by side, those who sacrifice *for* others against those who call for the sacrifice *of* others.[7] We may hence become more attuned to the election of sacrificial victims. While democrats rightly call for better understanding of the chains of cause and effects that may have led to where we are, others prefer to skip directly to the last stage, pointing the fingers at their favorite scapegoat, within and without. Donald Trump may crudely blame Chinese people wherever they might be, Europeans, or the WHO, but tomorrow, people everywhere will be tempted to blame refugees, migrants, foreigners, Romanies, and other would-be "carriers." Or it will be the fault of young people who took containment too lightly, or of old people whose lives have cost us too much, or of civil

---

[5] According to the UN Human Rights Committee. See C. Heyns, "The Value of Life," EJIL: Talk! (June 20, 2020), www.ejiltalk.org/the-value-of-life/.

[6] P. Pettit, *On the People's Terms: A Republican Theory and Model of Democracy* (Cambridge University Press, 2012).

[7] See K. Nicolaidis, "D'Œdipe au coronavirus, les pandémies et leur boucs emissaires," *Le Grand Continent* (May 19, 2020), https://legrandcontinent.eu/fr/2020/05/19/oedipe-et-le-coronavirus/, and "From Oedipus to Coronavirus: Homo Sapiens and the Making of Scapegoats," *Open Democracy* (September 2020), www.opendemocracy.net/en/can-europe-make-it/oedipus-coronavirus-homo-sapiens-and-making-scapegoats/.

servants who have not done their job properly. As anthropologist René Girard explained, societies that are in the grip of mimetic violence, whatever its source, need to shift the burden of that violence onto certain groups or individuals living among them, preferably people who are as much the same as they are different from the norm.[8] Despite ancient awareness, the scapegoat reflex seems to remain the civilizational trademark of *homo sapiens*. And yet mature democracies are reluctant to assign blame. The hope today is for what we can call "pandemic pedagogy" bringing to light complex causalities as we debate what failed us, from bureaucracies to executives to industrialized food systems, and as citizens' heightened self-reflexiveness turns them squarely against the scapegoating urge.

In sum, if our politics is reset from theatre of war to theatre of care, our sense of what responsibility our togetherness entails "in sickness and in health" may be recast too.

Bubbles, or the Appropriation of "R"

Picture a family watching their country's prime minister's address on their television screen. The leader explains that what their life will look like in the next few months, and who knows, possibly years, will be determined by a sliding scale of alert levels. And where we fall in turn will depend on a mysterious number "R," the COVID-19 reproduction number, or the average number of individuals to whom a single person passes the virus. The contract the leader offers our family is simple: Bring and keep "R" down and the authorities will ease restrictions. How fast this lockdown is modified depends on you. It is in your collective hands and will be wholly determined by whether we continue to obey various rules starting with social distancing. In short, this crisis is fundamentally about what I call *the social appropriation of "R."* This social appropriation expresses itself on a spectrum of regard to disregard for emergent social norms, and is clearly beset by risks of free riding. But this is a story of highly visible free riding, exposed for everyone to see.

Castoriadis built his theoretical edifice of the social imaginary around the mutual constitution between the *logein* or social representation and the *teukhein* or social doing. Individuals in our societies constantly negotiate the relationship between their public and private persona in interaction with others, with whom they literally create and recreate this relationship

[8] R. Girard, *La violence et le sacré* (Paris: Grasset, 1972).

between *logein* and *teukhein*.[9] At the same time, our citizen is conscious that what escapes them, behind visible social reality, is the infinite wealth of alterity present in the world itself, meanings that can never be permanently fixed. Society evolves each time it is faced with the shifting boundary between what is or is not feasible, desirable, meaningful, inside and outside, in us and in nature. The pandemic moment gives us such transformative potential.

First, the value of "R" and the size and transparency of "bubbles" serve as metrics of sociability. In this story, "R" also stands for responsibility, or rather mutual responsibility. And the question that it raises is whether citizens' awareness that the future is literally in their (clean) hands creates the conditions of possibility for moving closer to self-institution of society. The meme "bubbles" serves as a metaphor for the transformative potential. Before the pandemic moment, bubbles had come to refer to the closed networks of like-mindedness in which people locked themselves thanks to social media. Now bubbles have become the metaphor of choice for conveying responsibility to others within, and the desire to expand this responsibility outwards: I invite you in my bubble.

Second, the pandemic helps us leave behind phantasm of collective mastery of our destiny bestowed from above. We still need the King but the King is naked, unprepared and uncertain, like the rest of us. Everything seems about wide-open probabilistic ranges, whether for "R," appropriate social distancing, appropriate quarantine time, and so on. We can see that the public supplies at least in part the public goods. The social contract concerning who is responsible for our well-being seems up for grabs. At this moment, will society resist the melancholia of powerlessness and the shirking sirens, and learn that it is not instituted by something outside itself (a god, nature, reason, necessity, a historical law) but by itself and as itself?

Third, this moment is about mutuality and the sharing of social imagery – as the many memes on social media attest to. We understand ourselves as part of democratic societies not only because this is how we each know that we want it but also because we know that this is how other women and men around us want it and live it. In this story, everything we do is relational. If one person is not safe, no one is. As with religious rituals, what we have to do is less about outcome and more about process, the thoughtfulness of it all. There may be no such thing as "society know

---

[9] Castoriadis, *L'institution imaginaire*, pp. 493–6.

thyself," but there may be moments like this one where societies come closer to watching themselves know themselves.

Castoriadis saw in the birth of philosophy, together with the birth of democracy, the first historical example of a society that is able to radically question its own imaginary institutions and therefore earn its autonomy. But in doing so, he seemed to be forgetting the fact that the autonomy of a minority of the population, that of the male active citizens, was constructed upon the heteronomy of its majority, women, slaves, people of foreign origins.[10] If we are to cash in on the promise of societal self-institution, we must hope that as our bubbles burst open in the "world afterwards," "R" remains the afterglow of a covenant of absolute inclusiveness in our mutual concern.

String, or Freedom in the Eruvian Age

This brings us to a third image relevant to how our democracies may come to reinvent themselves: Strings, or more accurately, almost invisible strings attached to poles high up in the air to envelope part of our cities.[11] I am referring here to the eruv, that is the imaginary enclosure which serves to delineate a religious space in which it is permissible to overcome the prohibition to carry objects outside one's private space during the Sabbath. The eruv was introduced in Roman Palestine around AD 50 for a Jewish community where many of the daily activities were performed in the shared courtyard – deemed a public space – in order to enclose these commons and join the inhabitants in an imaginary private space. As the rabbis teach us, each inhabitant had to donate a dish to these new commons, and we understand that the allowance for enlarged social interaction was dependent on the participation of the whole courtyard community. In time, the size of eruvs grew to entire towns around Europe and later the United States. "Imaginary" enclosures everywhere transformed public spaces into private ones, including large swaths of Manhattan, the busiest city on earth.

Could it be that the pandemic is teaching us to treat as private what was previously considered public space, much as the rabbinic eruv has done for the past two thousand years? Reminding us that social space is always imagined and negotiated, the model of the eruv and its magical power for

---

[10] C. Bottici, *A Philosophy of Political Myth* (Cambridge University Press, 2007).

[11] An earlier version of this section was published as A. Mintz and K. Nicolaidis, "Towards the Eruvian Age," *Open Democracy* (May 2020), www.opendemocracy.net/en/can-europe-make-it/coronavirus-towards-eruvian-age/.

observant Jews may yet help secular societies at large think through the complexities of transforming public spaces into safe "user-friendly" ones. The prospect could be ominous if the line between unsafe and safe socializing was not ultimately up to us. As we reinvent our common space, the boundaries which define it, and the ways we can and should interact within it, we may be entering an Eruvian age when the insights garnered over time by these Jewish communities will be precious, especially when it comes to enlarging our circles of conviviality.

While the eruv was imagined in order to wave prohibitions, our new COVID-19 social space is about introducing prohibitions to a public arena we once traveled with little care or concern. And unlike the eruv, the rules apply to all, and at least initially, only temporarily. But like the eruv, our new shared space is meant to allow for interaction against the background of prohibitions as we all consider each other as a potential "carrier." In other words, like the eruv, we are reimagining our social space in order to avoid being quarantined, even if with COVID-19 each household may have its own allowed perimeter, its own radius defined by imaginary strings.

Perhaps most importantly and like in an eruv, this new theatre of interaction requires the participation of everyone in the community. These limits do not work if they are simply dictated by those in position of authority. Instead, they need to be internalized by each of us. If one person fails to abide by the rules, the space is no longer safe and therefore no longer shared. How ironic that a shared space redefined for greater distancing requires the same level of communal participation and cooperation as the eruv of old, defined in the first place to allow for greater interaction.

Yet, is it really ironic? The ability to share space is a right that we usually take for granted. Public space is by definition free and available to all of us. Of course, we have to be law-abiding citizens in that space, but not for the sake of maintaining the space itself. The pandemic reminds us that classical liberalism, the idea that people should be free to do what they want so long as they don't harm others, is not quite enough, albeit a solid start. Instead we must contend with the old message of the eruv, that public space carries with it responsibilities and a communal set of rules.

When we finally find ourselves on the "day after," it may be that religious and secular interrogations about our commons enter a new fruitful conversation. For one, workers cannot return safely to the factory, employees to the office, storekeepers to the shops if even a few of us ignore the responsibility of being part of the "community," a community that recognizes that empathy for self and for the other are intrinsically linked. Recalling the special value of the eruv for women in the Jewish community, who were thus enabled to carry out their business, we will ask about inequalities of access and recognize the invisible contributions to our common space by often unrecognized members of our communities. We will recognize the value of shared green spaces for those who have none of their own. And we will ask about the ways in which the modern technological equivalent of invisible strings tied to poles – such as Apps indicating that a space is "safe" (as well as our data) – can help empower individuals within our future commons rather than curtail their freedoms from above.

Further afield, we will need to reconsider the ways we have allowed for the creation of distance with refugees locked down at our borders without the corresponding care we are now associating with our reinvented public spaces.

The Eruvian age could offer an ethics of horizontal mutuality rather than vertical imposition, defined in part by the empathy and compassion that shared space creates for each of us.

Circles, or the Antinomies of Autonomy

In the end, however, each eruv defines a single circle for a single community. But of course, democracy is also a game of scales involving many types and sizes of circles. This is where we may ask how pandemic politics might help reimagine a more horizontal understanding of our polities and their interdependence. In other words, what if we could imagine away the vertical idea of "levels" of governance, with authority moving further away from citizens as issues fall under the edicts of "economies of scale" and "externalities"?

Instead, a democratic experience that is citizen-centric involves circles of autonomy of different sizes, each with its own logic even if they overlap.

Autonomy is first reinvented in the basic unit of confinement, households. It is then organized at the level of neighborhoods, metropoles, cross-border regions, states, and at the supranational level when necessary. Each circle organizes interdependence within while minimizing dependence without.[12]

---

[12] See K. Nicolaidis, "L'ambition première de l'UE devait être de devenir la gardienne du long terme," *Culture* (April 9, 2020), www.franceculture.fr/politique/kalypso-nicolaidis-lambition-premiere-de-lue-devait-etre-de-devenir-la-gardienne-du-long-terme.

In this picture of overlapping circles, our neighborhoods come to the fore as the critical locus where we experience the daily habits of coexistence, where the "collective effort to lead a private life" becomes a school of local democracy, *the democracy of everyday life*.[13] With the pandemic world, never before has it been so clear that neighbors are not just the closest strangers, they are the fabric of our lives, a universe of constant negotiation through micro-interactions. When minding one another's business was optional, it now becomes a matter of life and death. At the same time the routine self-distancing expected from the neighbor becomes ostentatious, a solicitous mutual distancing, a gesture becoming a paradoxical mark of closeness and care.

"Sovereignty" becomes experiential rather than ideological in this story. Individual functionality is the name of the game as circles of autonomy scale up or down and political units below the state take over. Even in Jacobin France, it is clear that regions offer different vulnerabilities and capacities, and thus have organized their response relatively autonomously with bridges between them. Citizens can experience optimal circles as more or less fluid, formed and reformed according to circumstances and contingent vulnerability, to past experience or other social criteria such as habitus of social interaction, intergenerational living, state–society relations, and so on. Patterns are explained by the heterogeneity of situations, both local and international, rather than intensity of affects.

To be sure, at least in the EU, the quintessential circles of autonomy remain the Member States, whose national fiscal power can almost instantly deploy funds to help businesses and individuals. It is not surprising therefore that the EU's first act was to strengthen the autonomy of the Member States by relaxing budgetary and state aid constraints – in effect reaffirming the primacy of national circles of autonomy. Beyond, the EU remains torn between championing global governance anew and establishing itself as an optimal circle of autonomy in a world where procurement, research, and investment seem to call for "European sovereignty." Here, as elsewhere, EU democracy is about organizing its diversity as the multiple actors that compose it come to grips with the new games of scale ushered in by this new era.

---

[13] N. Rosenblum, *Good Neighbors: The Democracy of Everyday Life in America* (Princeton University Press, 2018).

Mirrors, Space-Time in the Global Anthropo-Scene

Whatever we may think of the "wisdom of the multitude," it is hard to deny the irresistible sense that humanity seems to surf on the coronavirus wave to create a global scene where its own follies and potential redemption in the age of the Anthropocene are to be debated through a new kind of connectedness. We could be creating the first global "anthropo-scene," where slowing down helps us renegotiate not only the space but the time we inhabit together. As we learn to debate radical uncertainty and ask how to invest in collective resilience, we may be starting to lay the foundation of "democracy with foresight."[14] Fascinatingly, social movements have already cunningly subverted COVID-19-based "states of emergency" to amplify calls for a social and ecological state of emergency. When past pandemics yielded to collective amnesia, will this one entrench the urgency of the long term?

What is democracy if not a crowd, conscious of its collective power? If the pandemic has not spelled the end for contestation, it has changed the way we may imagine it and reinvent the act of being a crowd, starting with socially distanced mass protests. The disciplined and somber crowd of people voicing their anger at Prime Minister Netanyahu two meters apart in Rabin Square is hard to equate with the image of the "unruly mob" of anti-democrats.[15] By adapting the methods of civil disobedience to the COVID-19 era, the spatial posture subverts its interdictions for democratic aims. Social distancing may make visible the sociability that we have lost everywhere, but dissent, like water, continues to infiltrate our polities in new forms. A group of US and UK academics has identified more than a hundred new methods of nonviolent activism adopted during the pandemic, including car rallies, labor strikes, and consumer boycotts.[16] Whether connecting from cars or roof tops, or hanging the same sign on windows or doors, to mobilize while keeping apart calls for *imagining* ourselves as a crowd. As we watch each other, we are present to each other. When, in Brazil, millions bang their pots from their balconies to express their discontent with their President's handling of the

[14] K. Nicolaidis, "Sustainable Integration in a Democratic Polity: A New (or not so new) Ambition for the European Union after Brexit," in Benjamin Martill and Uta Staiger (eds.), *Brexit and Beyond* (UCLPress, London: 2017), pp. 212–21, https://ucldigitalpress.co.uk/Book/Article/56/81/4230/.

[15] Y. Serhan, "Israel Shows Us the Future of Protest," *The Atlantic* (April 23, 2020), www.theatlantic.com/international/archive/2020/04/protest-demonstration-pandemic-coronavirus-covid19/610381/.

[16] E. Chenoweth et al., "Methods of Dissent and Collective Action Under COVID – A Crowdsourced List," Crowd Counting Consortium (2020), Crowdcounting.org.

pandemic, political protest becomes symbolically and practically a global household action. Myriad acts around the world function as infinity-mirrors, creating virtual crowds looking together in the same direction, as if stretching all at once our projected togetherness in space and in time.

This digital world of mirrors has become more than ever the refuge of democracy. Global digital mobilization is exploding. And while online activism is not new, this time around it has allowed us to visualize our shared human experience and the power this may give us to make good on the ravages of the Anthropocene. To be sure, for speech acts and virtual worlds to foster social transformation, something else has to happen which has to do with democratic struggle.[17] Democracy depends in part on whether and how forms of power are appropriated by the multitude of ordinary citizens against elite entrenchment, as Machiavelli put it long ago: "in every republic are two diverse humors, that of the people and that of the great, and . . . all the laws that are made in favor of freedom arise from their disunion."[18] Political stability thrives on insur-rection, but contestation no longer need rest on violence.[19]

Our democratic aggiornamento can only be transnational, but it matters to see democracy reinvented in different ways. Glocality is a potent democratic idea grounded in the resistance to a homogenized world. No system can survive without interaction with others, but too great a degree of systemic coherence can be as lethal as too little: The universal is about the mutual recognition of the different ways in which we negotiate our differences. Anthony Barnett is surely right to argue that the potential for far-reaching change has been created all along by progressive movements and ideas in the last half-century, under governments of all political stripes, even if the emergent new reality has taken us by surprise.[20] When President Emmanuel Macron tells the *Financial Times* in May 2020 that COVID-19 "makes us refocus on the human aspect" and that "there is something more important than the economic order," many are tempted to exclaim: Welcome to the club!

---

[17] R. Celikates, "Forms of Life, Progress, and Social Struggle: On Rahel Jaeggi's Critical Theory," in A. Allen and E. Mendieta (eds.), *From Alienation to Forms of Life* (University Park, PA: The Pennsylvania State University Press, 2018).

[18] Niccolò Machiavelli, *Discourses on Livy* (University of Chicago Press, 1996), p. 16.

[19] I. Cockerell, "Under Lockdown, LGBT Russians Were More Isolated than Ever. Then, the Zoom Parties Started," Coda (June 4, 2020), www.codastory.com/disinformation/russia-lgbtq-zoom/.

[20] A. Barnett, "Out of the Belly of Hell – COVID-19 and the Humanisation of Globalisation," Open Democracy (May 21, 2020), www.opendemocracy.net/en/opende mocracyuk/out-belly-hell-shutdown-and-humanisation-globalisation/.

Conclusion

COVID-19 certainly constitutes a stress test for democracy, with hugely unequal impact. But I have argued that the test will be deployed in part in our political imagination. If this pandemic has demonstrated anything, it is that we can collectively push farther and faster the limits of what is possible. We have long sought ways of democratizing democracy itself via the invention of new modes of action and transnational citizenship. What if this was the advent of a new world of democratic effervescence, ushering in a third democratic transformation à la Robert Dahl, transnational and transgenerational democracy?

I have only offered here an impressionist landscape of potentials, detours, horizons. It will be up to citizens to cash in on this pandemic pedagogy, as they realize like never before the value of diverse viewpoints and distributed intelligence where each of us feels free to speak up, the imperative need to monitor the surveillance thrust upon us, and the inseparability between protection of the individual and commitment to the collective.

To be sure, the liberal democracy narrative went too far in its universalist pretentions. But even as we adopt a self-critical gaze, let us not indulge in the story told by strongmen that democracy is a Western invention, that others do things differently.[21] Whatever local idiosyncrasies, our modernity has produced the same condition across the globe: People demand to be in control of their destiny and deny the state a monopoly on the rules of togetherness. The unprecedented intimate globality brought about by this pandemic is only beginning to expose the power of a deeper universal: Our democratic imagination.

---

[21] L. El Amine, "Beyond East and West: Reorienting Political Theory through the Prism of Modernity," *Perspectives on Politics*, 14(1) (2016), 102–120.

13

Redefining Vulnerability and State–Society Relationships during the COVID-19 Crisis: The Politics of Social Welfare Funds in India and Italy

DEVAL DESAI, SHALINI RANDERIA, AND
CHRISTINE LUTRINGER*

Introduction

There is a general consensus that COVID-19 is rapidly and radically transforming the democratic relationship between state and society. Focusing on political and legal arrangements, some argue that the virus gives a fillip to authoritarian tendencies by eroding constitutional checks and balances, while others suggest that it will reshape the state and its constitution owing to new understandings of mutual interdependence and solidarity.

We make a different argument here: Democracy is also being transformed by significant changes in the state's fiscal arrangements and its political economy. We do so based on scrutiny of a specific type of fiscal vehicle that crystallizes and regulates state–society relationships: Special-purpose social welfare funds. These are collected pursuant to state law to tackle the vulnerability of specific social categories, such as unorganized migrant labor in the construction sector in India or the underdevelopment of certain regions in Italy. We argue that these funds are a site through which social actors, and especially the state, define social vulnerability, and more generally welfare. Since the COVID-19 crisis directly raises questions of health and welfare, these funds constitute an important vehicle through which state–society relationships are currently being renegotiated.

* The arguments of this chapter build on Desai and Randeria, "Unfreezing Unspent Social Special Purpose Funds for the Covid-19 Crisis: Critical Reflections from India," *World Development*, 136 (2020), www.sciencedirect.com/science/article/pii/S0305750X20302655. This work was supported by a Swiss National Science Foundation Spark grant, "The Puzzle of Unspent Funds: The Institutional Architecture of Unaccountable Governance," no. 190372.

Correspondingly, we aim to recast debates over the political consequences of COVID-19 away from constitutionalist analyses focused on
the USA and Europe at large, which are limited in their view of state–
society relations, and toward lessons from the fiscal sociology of the state,
drawing on examples from India and Italy. In particular, we contend that
the coronavirus crisis both reveals and accelerates a certain form of
governance in which the state's purported care for specific vulnerable
groups is used to generate fiscal liquidity, whose subsequent financial or
political profits the state can appropriate to further a variety of political
goals. We trace how a large pool of unspent funds, originally held for the
social welfare of certain vulnerable groups in Italy and India, are reappropriated and placed in the service of combating a new vulnerability –
COVID-19. We argue that in doing so, the state captures funds raised on
behalf of vulnerable social groups by reframing social welfare – as well as
the social contract more generally – in ways that no longer address their
specific vulnerabilities. The state has the latitude to do so because of the
weak political leverage of the marginalized beneficiary communities and
regions, as well as the deficient political and legal accountability for the
use of these funds. The capture of these funds is likely to further entrench
and institutionalize these two political trends.

Our argument is fourfold, corresponding to the sections of the chapter.
First, we contend that the COVID-19 crisis can productively be understood in political terms as the renegotiation of the place and meaning of
"vulnerability" as a basis of state–society relations. Second, drawing on our
examples from India and Italy, we demonstrate that certain social welfare
funds have remained significantly underspent in "ordinary" times – to the
tune of several billion dollars in each country. These states are now
reappropriating these funds to combat COVID-19. Third, we argue that,
in reappropriating these funds to mitigate the consequences of COVID-19,
the state executes two political maneuvers: (1) It redefines "vulnerability"
from a context-specific category pertaining to certain marginalized groups
and regions, to a general and inchoate political term; and (2) it does not
tackle the underlying institutional causes of decades of underspending, but
simply bypasses them by using executive fiat and emergency powers.
Combined, these maneuvers reveal state practices that turn social vulnerabilities into a pool of financial liquidity under the guise of combating
them. Accordingly, the piled-up funds are reappropriated and released
under emergency provisions, when political stakes are high and the state's
immediate political goals may be under threat. Instead of cynically using
the idea of an (external) enemy to justify its expansion of force, the state

184 DEVAL DESAI, SHALINI RANDERIA, CHRISTINE LUTRINGER

here revisits the idea of a vulnerability to expand its fiscal clout. Fourth, this concern does not seem limited to the Indian and Italian cases under consideration. On the contrary, among the sprawl of new social welfare funds that are being created in the wake of COVID-19, many are likely to be vulnerable to the same political maneuvers as outlined above.

Vulnerability and "Critical Events"

The COVID-19 pandemic is a "critical event" that invites us to rethink notions of the state, of society, and of the relationships between the two.[1] Accordingly, many North Atlantic political theorists have attempted to apply their longstanding theoretical tools to the crisis. Giorgio Agamben has resuscitated the exception-as-the-rule to warn of the state's use of the pandemic to justify an authoritarian lurch.[2] Jean-Luc Nancy and Slavoj Žižek, on the contrary, have seen in the pandemic the humbling of the state (which has been reduced to a "grim executioner"). They further see in the pandemic the potential to trigger a reconfiguration of social relations centered on a politics of mutual vulnerability.[3] Boaventura de Sousa Santos, in turn, reminds us that solidarities have limits – racism is on the rise again, and the burden of the virus falls heavily on the silenced and marginalized, such as refugees and migrants confined to camps.[4]

Such efforts are useful, as they direct our attention not only to the consequences of specific declarations of emergency or the quashing of protest, but also to the specific ways in which the pandemic reconfigures state–society relationships. The authors identify *vulnerability* as an axis on which the critical event and its political transformations unfold. The ontology, directionality, and sociality of vulnerability are some of the political stakes of the crisis. While Agamben's concern remains the vulnerability of the body to state violence and its effects on society, Nancy and

---

[1] V. Das, *Critical Events: An Anthropological Perspective on Contemporary India* (Oxford University Press, 1995).

[2] G. Agamben, "Chiarimenti," Quodlibet (March 2020), www.quodlibet.it/giorgio-agamben-chiarimenti/.

[3] J.-L. Nancy, "Eccezione virale," Antinomie (February 27, 2020), https://antinomie.it/index.php/2020/02/27/eccezione-virale. S. Žižek, "Monitor and Punish? Yes, Please!" The Philosophical Salon (March 16, 2020), http://thephilosophicalsalon.com/monitor-and-punish-yes-please/.

[4] B. de Sousa Santos, "Virus: All That Is Solid Melts into Air," Critical Legal Thinking (March 19, 2020), https://criticallegalthinking.com/2020/03/19/virus-all-that-is-solid-melts-into-air/.

Žižek are concerned with social transformations premised on the vulnerability of bodily life to a nonhuman virus.

We extend these insights in two ways. First, we refer to the obvious: Transformations of state–society relationships through such critical events are not easily reducible to oppression or solidarity. The play of vulnerability is varied, contested, and complex. The state is never simply a grim executioner or an oppressor, nor society simply its obverse. The state, too, partakes in the play of vulnerabilities. But its part cannot be understood solely in the idioms of constitutional theory or practice. It is situated in a *political economy of state and society*.[5] While crises such as COVID-19 may be political moments in which states appeal to political solidarity, the political economy of the crisis demonstrates whether and how economic and political elites may play the rules in such a way as to extract rents from solidaristic policies. Second, it follows that transformations of state and society cannot simply be mapped from and in western Europe and North America. They demand a sensibility that is both situated and transnational – attuned to capital flows and development practices across the North and South, as well as to the specific practices of states within them.[6]

We study *unspent social special-purpose funds*, and their mobilization by the state under emergency conditions to combat the pandemic, to examine the political economy of reconfigurations of state–society relations around a redefinition of vulnerabilities. "Social special-purpose funds" refer to, first, funds that have been collected directly pursuant to state law, for a specific social purpose that would otherwise be the domain of discretionary state policy. Such funds may be collected through hypothecated taxes, but also through alternative channels. Second, these funds are held in some vehicle that reflects their social purpose (such as a public or private trust, or a corporation) rather than simply being absorbed into ordinary administrative budget lines. By "unspent," we refer to instances where a significant proportion of these funds remains both uncaptured by other interests and undisbursed during the fiscal year to the beneficiaries for which they were earmarked.

We examine the pandemic's impact on the use of these funds in India and Italy, examples we deliberately choose from across the global South and North. Both societies reflect strong economic disparities – along class

---

[5] See e.g. Das, *Critical Events*, pp. 156–74.
[6] S. Randeria, "The State of Globalization: Legal Plurality, Overlapping Sovereignties and Ambiguous Alliances between Civil Society and the Cunning State in India" *Theory, Culture & Society*, 24 (2007), 1–33.

and geographic lines in particular – and have reacted to COVID-19 with a massive expansion of their fiscal deficits to prop up their social welfare systems. Both countries have also accumulated significant amounts of underutilized social welfare funds. In India, we look at funds collected through hypothecated taxation and other, indirect modes of fund collection, for the benefit of construction laborers and mining-affected communities; in Italy, we turn to large pools of EU cohesion funding (of which the country is one of the main recipients). In both contexts, these curiously underutilized funds are being repurposed to hastily disburse monies to cope with the unprecedented socioeconomic effects of the pandemic. At the same time, the two cases vary in productive ways. They are embedded in distinct political economies and institutional contexts, involve different types of actors (e.g. the EU in Italy, and large private construction and mining firms in India), and articulate varying conceptions of vulnerability.

Our argument combines two strands of theoretical literature on state–society relations. The first is the political sociology of emergency, mentioned above, in which those relations are transformed by the state's exercise of emergency powers. The second is fiscal sociology, in which the constitution and relationships between state and society are revealed through the *fisc*: "The budget is the skeleton of the state stripped of all misleading ideologies."[7] Studying the executive remobilization of certain funds affords insights into some of the institutional features of the state, through the perspective of "complex social interactions and institutional and historical context."[8]

Explaining Unspent Funds: Causes and Cases

Why do these funds remain unspent? Lack of spending might reflect a series of predicaments, including: Weakness of institutional design and implementation; unresolved issues of governance (such as delayed fund transfers within the exchequer); challenges in identifying beneficiaries in the absence of a robust mechanism to do so, or administrative difficulties with the mechanics and practices of disbursing funds. The latter issue includes, for example, difficulties in finding private or subnational actors willing to cofund a project as required by fund rules in Italy, or

---

[7] J. A. Schumpeter, *The Economics and Sociology of Capitalism*, Richard Swedberg (ed.) (Princeton University Press, 1991), p. 100.

[8] J. L. Campbell, "The State and Fiscal Sociology" *Annual Review of Sociology*, 19 (1993), 163–85, 164.

identifying migrant workers within India, who move from one construction site or brick kiln to the next. Such ad hoc explanations are undoubtedly relevant to each individual case. However, as Venelin Ganev points out, insights from fiscal sociology suggest that flows of money through the public *fisc* should be understood as political phenomena that constitute forms of statecraft.[9] Indeed, the scale and persistence of unspent funds suggest that case-by-case explanations are insufficient. Instead, we propose that unspent funds tell us something important about vulnerability, the state, and society.

We do so through a discussion of three cases – two in India and one in Italy – which each hold billions of US dollars' worth of unspent funds. In India, the "Building and Other Construction Workers' Cess" fund (BOCW) identifies construction workers as a vulnerable group, whose numbers have risen manifold due to the post-1970s boom in the Indian construction sector, but who remain outside the purview of weak *de jure* and even poorer de facto labor protection. Most of India's labor laws apply only to registered factories, plantations, and mines. Around 450 million workers, i.e. some 90 percent of the country's labor force, work in the informal sector without employment security and social protection. The BOCW is meant to provide a range of long-term benefits, including medical care, childcare, and pensions, to the largely unorganized labor in the building sector. It does so through a 1 percent tax on the cost of construction, to be paid by the employer at the site to the relevant regional government. The funds are administered and disbursed by a BOCW board appointed by the respective regional governments. It is a "body corporate" with equal representation between the state government, employers, and workers.

Across India, BOCW boards currently hold an unspent balance of INR 520 billion (US$6.88 billion), reflecting a range of challenges including lack of institutional and political pressure to expend, and low levels of registration of workers (which is ironic, given the effectiveness of the Indian state's biometric registration and citizen monitoring programs more generally, such as the Aadhar card). Following the COVID-19 pandemic, the central government has taken the political step of pressuring the fund's administrators to disburse some of its unspent balance as

---

[9] V. I. Ganev, "The Annulled Tax State: Schumpeterian Prolegomena to the Study of Postcommunist Fiscal Sociology," *Communist and Post-Communist Studies*, 44 (2011), 245–55.

direct cash transfers to the existing class of beneficiaries, who have survived on philanthropic aid in the absence of provision of food by the state or wages by employers during the lockdown. This repurposing of existing funds constituted approximately one-third of the Indian government's COVID-19 welfare package targeted at the poor and vulnerable, following the announcement of India's lockdown. Currently the bureaucracy is scrambling to identify and register those eligible. At the same time, the construction industry has asked for the BOCW tax to be waived as building activity has come to a standstill under the lockdown.

The "District Mineral Foundation" (DMF) identifies mining-affected communities as a special vulnerable group. It provides money for local development projects for these communities, as the massive expansion of mining activity, following liberalization of the sector in the 1990s, led to huge socioeconomic dislocations and environmental damage. The money is collected by way of 10 percent royalty on mining leases from the companies holding them. Here too the total unspent funds amount to INR 250–350 billion (US\$3.31–4.63 billion). Constituted as some form of a public trust, each DMF is supposed to have a governing body, although its legal form and composition varies across India. So far DMF trusts have been established in only about half of the districts with relevant extractive activity. Following the onset of the COVID-19 pandemic, the central government promulgated regulations pursuant to its emergency powers, allowing local administrators to redirect 30 percent of the unspent DMF balances toward pandemic relief, irrespective of whether or not the money is spent on mining-affected areas or communities.

In Italy, we focus on European Structural and Investment Funds (ESIF) – funds of EU origin that are governed in the main by EU rules. They are designed to promote cohesion and mitigate disparities in social welfare between different regions, especially those with a GDP-per-capita of less than 75 percent of the EU average. The state mobilizes these funds to address the vulnerabilities that result from the dislocations caused by single-market integration, on the basis that these dislocations are local or regional. ESIF fund expenditures such as labor market programs aimed to reduce unemployment and increase human capital and social integration. The funds are organized into either national or regional Operational Programmes (OPs), which delineate investment priorities, and specific objectives and activities. OPs are governed by a "Managing Authority" – which can take a range of legal forms, so long as they follow EU financial management principles. ESIF monies are allocated and spent on seven-year cycles; the current one runs from 2014–2020. If they are unspent, they are returned to the EU budget.

At an EU level, underspending is a persistent problem. A *Financial Times* investigation in 2010–2011 found that only around 10 percent of ESIF had been spent, more than halfway through the 2007–2013 cycle.[10] As regards the current spending cycle, €37 billion still has to be spent before it ends in 2020. Italy has one of the lowest levels of spending and the lowest level of allocation of ESIF monies available to it among the EU-27 (as of June 2019), having allocated only 73 percent of its available funds. In past cycles, Italy has expended much of its ESIF at the last minute; and delays in the use and allocation of funds constitute an important part of the politics of spending. The later in the spending cycle it gets, the higher the risk that funds have to be returned to the EU. Under this time pressure, the greater the chance that state authorities might gain political leverage and discretion in the use of ESIF monies.

In response to COVID-19, several key principles and mechanisms governing the allocation and use of funds have been reversed, which has shifted institutional balances toward national governments. EU Member States are now allowed to use ESIF monies for measures that are usually not supported by the European cohesion policy, such as strengthening health systems. They are also able to move existing and future resources between programs, between funds, between regions, and even between priorities. And even though ESIF are aimed at the least developed regions of the EU, Member States can now move resources for the fiscal year 2020–2021 to richer regions that have been hit hardest by the crisis. Italy has received 9.67 percent of these funds.

Redefining Vulnerability and Capturing Unspent Funds in Emergency Times

We suggest that states have participated in the politics of redefining vulnerability within society by changing types of remedial expenditure in response to the pandemic. In the BOCW case, vulnerability is temporally transformed from long term to short term as monies are deployed not for pensions for construction workers, for instance, but for immediate cash transfers to workers left in dire straits during the lockdown. The social identity of the vulnerable group thus also shifts, from people

[10] P. Spiegel, "EU Structural Funds Investigation: An Update" *Financial Times* (February 3, 2011), www.ft.com/content/a1eefebf-5fdb-3d6a-a948-575d15575a1f.

vulnerable to harms specific to working on building sites (e.g. requiring health care for accidents due to lack of safety measures and protective gear on construction sites; compensation for the family in case of death or permanent injury to a construction worker), to labor migrants in need of immediate cash under the lockdown (to which their profession is epiphenomenal). Similarly, in the DMF case, the identity of the vulnerable group is transformed from a specific social group (the mining-affected community) to a broad-based concern for the health of the general public. In the Italian ESIF case, vulnerability itself is transformed from a set of social characteristics to health and economic ones; the geography of vulnerability is in turn transformed from a differentiated map of poorer and richer areas, to a map that is at once pan-European (since ESIF can be transferred to richer regions also), and national (as Member States take on greater control over the allocation of unspent ESIF monies across a broad range of sectors). This flexibility is given by the EU to Member States, and in Italy the redistribution is likely to be pronounced. Northern Italy and parts of its central regions account for more than 75 percent of Italian GDP. Five "less-developed" southern regions (Campania, Puglia, Basilicata, Calabria, Sicily) received 71 percent of Italy's ESIF in 2014–2020. However, wealthier northern regions were worse affected by COVID-19 – and are thus likely to be the main beneficiaries of a redistribution of unspent ESIF to pandemic-impacted areas.

More broadly, states have redefined "vulnerability" from a contextual phenomenon specific to certain marginalized groups and regions, to a more general and inchoate phenomenon. Accordingly, administrators now have greater discretion to deploy these otherwise special-purpose funds as they see fit. The emergency reappropriation of these funds also demonstrates institutional conditions by which the state works to transform vulnerability from a status into a set of discretionary resources that it controls. In other words, through these institutional conditions, states generate *liquidity* from vulnerability, and capture political or fiscal rents from that liquidity.

In India, the special-purpose vehicles in which we find unspent social funds are generally public–private *institutional hybrids*, which exist to recognize and remedy a particular social vulnerability (e.g. mining-affectedness or the informality of labor relations in the construction industry). These hybrids blend very different areas of law and policy – trusts, public administration, corporations, social policy – which entail very different institutional forms and practices. These forms may fit together poorly, or produce a great deal of ambiguity in terms of the types of activities they can fund, as well as when, how, and for whom money is spent at all. For example, DMFs are *inter alia* both an administrative instrument (established by regulation in furtherance of social policy objectives) and a public trust.

Unspent funds heighten the institutional contradictions in these special-purpose vehicles. Unspent funds are, by definition, the *absence* of a decision made by those responsible for social funds. The special-purpose vehicles we discuss do not impose a positive duty on functionaries to spend, but leave it at the discretion of administrators or trustees whether or not to spend in order to meet the fund's overall policy objectives. This is coupled to a series of restrictive provisions on expenditure designed to make it difficult to disburse the money. For example, requiring workers to have registered with the BOCW board to gain benefits in practice places a significant burden on illiterate construction workers in the informal sector, who are not only far away from their home villages but also migrate from one building site to another across the country, and thus find it impossible to deal with the necessary paperwork to maintain eligibility.

In the absence of effective political pressure, accountability mechanisms, or any sanctions for keeping funds dormant, administrators have little incentive to get the money flowing. For the BOCW, until the COVID-19 crisis there had been limited efforts on the part of the boards to actively register eligible construction workers – despite some pressure from actors such as national trade unions, who petitioned the Supreme Court. The order by the apex court to spend the funds remained unimplemented. It is thus unclear from where the practical pressure to expend, as well as scrutinize the mode of decision-making and delivery of funds, may come. Instead, we see buck-passing for nondecision from bureaucrat to bureaucrat and stakeholder to stakeholder.

The emergency use of these funds further entrenches the ambiguities that give rise to the institutionalization of nonspending. In the case of emergency redirection of DMF funds, by allowing them to be used for the general purpose of combating COVID-19, the central government has subsumed the interests of mining-affected communities to the general good, the definition of which is left to the discretion of the District Collector, the most powerful bureaucrat at the local level. In doing so, however, the claims of the affected communities that were the designated beneficiaries of these funds – and the specific hardships that the DMF was meant to remedy – are politically eroded. And the redirection of funds may further preclude mining-affected community members from holding officials to account for failing to uphold their interests.

In the EU, the institutional structure of ESIF is also complex and hybrid as it cuts across scales. Everything from beneficiary identification to anti-corruption mechanisms, monitoring and evaluation, and the funds themselves runs through a complex assemblage of institutions. (The EU's regulation that sets out the different institutional competencies for the management of ESIF – 1303/2013 – runs to 150 pages.) OPs are broken down into regional operational programs (ROPs) and national operational programs (NOPs), with distinct Managing Authorities. The competencies of and communication between these institutions is rarely smooth. Accordingly, the emergency mobilization of ESIF monies – and concomitant provision of executive flexibility at the national level – can be understood as a way to suspend or bypass the existing mechanisms for the distribution of these funds.

Italy currently has the largest amount of unallocated ESIF monies in absolute terms among EU Member States. Its room for maneuver is therefore significant. The Italian government announced that it was planning to reallocate around 20 percent of available funds. Statements by both Italian and EU administrators further point to the current crisis as an opportunity to rethink EU funding instruments more generally, and to introduce greater flexibility in ESIF spending. This would entail greater discretion for Member States beyond the life of the current crisis – which might be in tension with the basic objective of ESIF as supranational instruments.

To summarize: Vulnerable population groups are promised welfare through the EU budget or the collection of hypothecated taxes in India. Thus, special-purpose funds can be seen as a state response to meet the expectations of dispossessed citizens. The massive accumulation of unspent funds reflects how the state's promise to meet these expectations is continually deferred. COVID-19 has finally forced states to cash out some of this deferred promissory note. Yet the emergency use of unspent funds works through existing institutional mechanisms, while only suspending the *de jure* or de facto conditions that blocked spending. Money continues to be collected on the back and in the name of particular vulnerable groups. However, DMF trusts remain unestablished for the most part, with the funds often sitting "temporarily" in central government coffers and administrators having no incentives to disburse it. The BOCW has yet to improve its worker registration process (although there is significant variance between states: Kerala's board, for instance, has comprehensively registered workers and expended all of its funds). And so on.

Suspending rather than eliminating these conditions keeps alive the special purpose of that vehicle to a limited degree – the District Collector spends money in mining-affected districts, the BOCW boards target construction workers, EU Member States respond to vulnerable regions. Thus, emergency use implies that the state continues to recognize a special political class of vulnerable beneficiaries with rights and entitlements, but bears little practical obligation to meet them.

State actors thereby *liquidate* those rights and entitlements. The accumulated unspent monies are available to spend at some point in the future – for example, as all-purpose rainy-day funds, or election season war chests. They may be appropriated under residual or emergency powers of the state, or through political pressure (for example, just to get money out of the door, as the end of the seven-year lifespan of an ESIF round approaches). Alternatively, we see in India that the monies might be appropriated *indirectly* through monetization practices. In the name of fighting COVID-19, the government of the mineral rich eastern Indian state of Odisha borrowed up to US$1.5 billion (INR 170 billion) at a low interest rate, from a balance of unspent funds to mitigate the environmental effects of mining on local communities. This specific vulnerability was thus turned into cheap liquid capital for the state's general coffers.

Moreover, in the context of COVID-19, this liquidation is tied to life. Having recognized the special vulnerabilities of groups long enough to turn them into resources – vulnerabilities which are exacerbated by the pandemic, as the plight of migrant construction laborers demonstrates – the state then redeploys these resources in the pursuit of a recast notion of vulnerability, thereby determining which lives are to be saved, and which are dispensable.

COVID-19 and Social Welfare Funds

Our cases demonstrate a set of political and institutional effects of the emergency mobilization of unspent social welfare funds under COVID-19. Politically, it changes what "vulnerability" – and more broadly what "welfare" and "social" – might mean. The emergency mobilization of these funds is thus a vehicle by which the state extracts political and economic gain from vulnerabilities while simultaneously redefining both the temporality and scope of welfare with all-too-limited public debate or scrutiny. Institutionally, it not only reshapes state–citizen relations but does so in ways that recast the democratic accountability of the state more broadly. Emergency appropriation of funds is, of course, limited by the general accountability deficit of exceptional executive action. But this deficit is amplified as the appropriation of these funds reconfigures the identity of legitimate or relevant stakeholders, their modes of participation (*de jure* and/or de facto) in the allocation of the funds, and their standing to hold decision-makers to account for that allocation. Participatory mechanisms of decision-making may become a casualty of such emergency redirection of unspent funds, as may monitoring by civil society.

This mode of negotiating the state–society relationship is ever more salient, as special-purpose funds proliferate globally in response to COVID-19, some of which are marked by the political maneuvers we identify. In India, the central government introduced a major new fund to combat the effects of COVID-19, "Prime Minister's Citizen Assistance and Relief in Emergency Situations" (or "PM-CARES"), which received approximately US$858 million (INR 65 billion) within its first week of operation. It is run out of the Prime Minister's office but structured as a public charitable trust that is able to receive direct philanthropic donations. On this basis, the office claims that the trust is not publicly auditable, nor do the donations have to be disclosed. Its funding sources, governance, and accountability for expenditure are thus already controversial, with public commentators discussing it in terms of Prime Minister Narendra Modi's mode of rule.[11]

We have argued that such critical scrutiny of social special-purpose funds is crucial. But it should not be limited to decrying these funds as cynical ways of peddling influence (in terms of their contributions) or as slush money (in terms of their expenditure). Even if overt misfeasance does not take place, our analysis of unspent funds suggests that we must pay attention to the relationship between the lack of scrutiny of such funds and the different beneficiary classes the fund declares over time.

The state–society relationship that emerges from this view is one in which vulnerable social groups engage with the "cunning state" – a state which strategically proclaims its weakness (here, in its capacity to spend

---

[11] V. Bhandari, "Indian Companies Are Contributing Lavishly to PM-CARES – Even amid Layoffs and Pay Cuts," Scroll (May 9, 2020), https://scroll.in/article/961383/indian-companies-are-contributing-lavishly-to-pm-cares-even-amid-layoffs-and-pay-cuts;
P. Jebaraj, "How Different Is the PM CARES Fund from the PM's National Relief Fund?" *The Hindu* (May 10, 2020), www.thehindu.com/news/national/coronavirus-how-different-is-the-pm-cares-fund-from-the-pms-national-relief-fund/article31546287.ece.

social welfare funds) while selectively mobilizing its strength (here, its capacity not only to collect but also to absorb and reallocate those funds when the conditions are ripe); a state which promises to meet the expectations of dispossessed citizens but defers this promise ad infinitum by collecting monies without disbursing the funds to the supposed beneficiaries.[12] In short, this is a state that captures resources raised in the name of its vulnerable citizens. At the same time, it renders itself unaccountable to these citizens (as well as to the capitalists and others that have contributed to the funds) for fund management and distribution – by redefining "vulnerability" and "welfare" in ways that sideline their voice.

[12] Randeria, "The State of Globalization."

14

Democracy and the Obligations of Care:
A Demos Worthy of Sacrifice

PAUL W. KAHN

A pandemic arises when biology meets politics. The biology may be universal, but politics are local. Some nations suffer many thousands of deaths; some hundreds. Same virus; different politics. Economic development accounts for some of the differences, but even nations at the same level of development can have radically different pandemics. If politics is destiny, then our fate is in our hands.

The threat of the coronavirus to a community raises a political question: What is the nation prepared to do? In the United States and the United Kingdom, the initial answer was "very little." Other places – for example, China, Israel, or South Korea – were prepared to do quite a lot. The statistics show the consequences.

Just as pandemics begin with political decisions, so do they end. The very idea of an end suggests more a political than a biological condition. The virus may become a background condition of life for the indefinite future – rather like a potentially deadly cold. Short of a vaccine, each nation must decide what that life will look like. How much economic pain, how much disruption of ordinary life, should a community be asked to accept? There is bound to be much trial and error – experiments with social-distancing practices in schools, shops, offices, public transport, and entertainment. At stake in these decisions are the lives of citizens. Something close to a rewriting of the social contract is at hand. How much protection? How much security? At what cost, and to whom?

Decisions must be made while individuals remain deeply uncertain and divided in their values. Citizens vary in their willingness to assume risks to their health; they vary in their economic circumstances and their eagerness to return to work. They do not have access to the same facts as government; they may not understand the risks their behavior imposes on others. Economists and epidemiologists can help clarify facts, but they cannot decide for us. They can describe costs and benefits, but they cannot tell us what sort of costs matter most. There is no scale independent of politics by which to assess these costs.

Behind the biology of pandemic, then, a political discussion must take place among citizens, civic groups, political parties, judges, and representatives. Political leaders must respond to the variety of claims put forward by citizen groups. Citizens, in turn, look to political leaders for protection, but also for direction. The pandemic is like a war in focusing the entire society on the obligations of citizenship and the responsibilities of political leadership. In multiple ways, people are talking, listening, and trying to decide. We are all asked to consider what we owe to each other, individually and collectively. The pandemic is simultaneously a public health disaster and a political opportunity. Some nations will emerge stronger; others will add political failure to the costs of the pandemic.

The phenomenon of the decision is concrete rather than abstract. There are no universal rules to follow, only practices to interpret. In this chapter, I look at the variety of claims and justifications put forward in the United States. That nation's actions are not a standard by which to measure other nations' deliberations or decisions – for good or bad. At best, they are a source for comparative work. American politics is one iteration of the experience of the political in modern democracies. Other nations face similar claims, which range from law, to policy, to the sacrificial.

* * *

In the late spring of 2020, the United States found itself in a situation of considerable uncertainty. Two things, however, were certain: COVID-19 was both a public health catastrophe and ruinous to the economy. President Donald Trump and many of the nation's governors focused on the latter. They urged a quick reopening of the economy. Public health experts countered that the range of symptoms produced by the virus was much worse than had been thought and that the disease had not been contained in many parts of the country. They urged caution.

The President responded, "The remedy must not be worse than the disease." No one can disagree with that in the abstract. It suggests some sort of balancing of public health costs against economic benefits. There was, however, no agreement on how safe was actually safe or even how safe any particular course of action would be. Rather than cite calculations of costs and benefits, officials pushing for rapid reopening claimed political support: The people, they said, were demanding an end to the lockdown. These demands were often framed as claims of legal right – a right to decide for oneself how to balance competing interests. Those urging a more cautious approach cited more than public health: They raised issues of justice and care with respect to bearing the burden of the pandemic. We cannot balance these competing arguments; there is still a need to decide. At best, we can clarify the nature of the arguments and the grounds upon which they purport to stand.

Legal Rights as a Limit on Political Decision-Making

Those pushing for rapid reopening had the support of noisy demonstrators, claiming a right to be free to carry out their ordinary activities. As one judge on the Supreme Court of Wisconsin framed it, to be prohibited from leaving your home is the very definition of tyranny.[1] That court struck down the governor's lockdown order. In the eyes of these libertarians, the public health orders amount to home arrest without trials or convictions. Individuals, they claimed, should be free to decide for themselves whether to accept the risks associated with any particular activity, such as wearing a face mask or attending entertainment venues. These libertarian arguments gather particular support when they touch on religious freedom – particularly church services.[2] Some of the libertarians are also evangelicals who believe that God will provide.[3]

These populist libertarians pointed to no alternative public health plan. They framed their claim as a constitutional right to be left alone. This, they asserted, is a preemptory right, not to be balanced against other interests, including public health. They stood on principle, but also on the constitution.

This claim of right has little support in the history of political theory. The libertarian strand in Western political thought originated in writers such as John Locke, who developed a strong view of natural rights, including a right to property. John Stuart Mill set forth the boundaries

---

[1] *Wisconsin Legislature v. Palm*, __ N.W.2d __, 2020 WL 2465677, at *15 (Wisconsin 2020).

[2] See generally *Abiding Place Ministries v. Wooten, et al.*, No. 3:20-cv-006830BAS-AHG (S. D. Cal. April 9, 2020); *Our Lady of Sorrows Church Inc. et al. v. Dr. Amir Mohammad*, No. 3:20-cv-00674 (D. Conn. May 14, 2020); *Word of Faith Christian Center Church, et al. v. Whitmer*, No. 1:20-cv-00392 (W.D. Mich. May 6, 2020); *County of Riverside v. Church Unlimited, et al.*, No. PSC2002064 (Cal. Super. Ct. April 11, 2020); *Elkhorn Baptist Church v. Brown*, No. S067736, 2020 BL 193393 (Or. May 23, 2020).

[3] See, for example, K. Stewart, "Opinion: The Religious Right's Hostility to Science Is Crippling Our Coronavirus Response," *New York Times* (March 27, 2020), www .nytimes.com/2020/03/27/opinion/coronavirus-trump-evangelicals.html.

of such claims in the "harm principle." One has a natural right to invest oneself as one chooses only up to the point at which one's choices inflict injury upon another. The exercise of rights is not a warrant to act in such a way as to harm another. Government arises precisely at that intersection of rights and harms. There, it must set the rules. Arguably, when each of us is a potential biohazard to others, we are never free of the harm principle.

Of course, John Stuart Mill is not a source of legal argument: Failure to satisfy the harm principle does not defeat a claim of legal right in and of itself. A constitution may be more protective of certain kinds of claims than political theory can support. Every legal system makes choices about what sorts of harms to recognize. The judge's role is to decide cases, not to practice political theory in the abstract.

The constitutional libertarians showed up with guns at the Michigan State Capitol. That is not surprising, since they think of their right to ignore the state lockdown as analogous to the Second Amendment right to bear arms. There has long been a public health argument against guns. Purchase a handgun to protect your home, and the risk of gun violence to your family members goes up dramatically.[4] The exercise of your right causes injury to the innocent. This is apart from the dramatic increase in the likelihood of suicide to the rights holder. These substantial and undeniable costs are excluded from consideration by American Second Amendment jurisprudence, which relies upon a formalist reading of text and original understanding of the right.[5]

There are constitutional rights that we enforce independently of a balancing of interests. There are categorical exceptions to the First Amendment's protection of free speech – for example, obscenity – but judges do not pursue proportionality review to adjudicate an assertion of the constitutional right. My right to speak is not limited by the offense you feel from my speech. Is the right not to be treated "tyrannically" like this? Is communicating the virus to another a legally cognizable harm, or merely a cost of living in a free society?

We can give a legal argument that distinguishes the libertarian, anti-tyranny claim from the constitutional right to bear arms: There is no specific text upon which to rely; there is a long history of draconian, public health authority. For many citizens, however, the better

---

[4] A. Anglemyer et al., "The Accessibility of Firearms and Risk for Suicide and Homicide Victimization Among Household Members," *Annals of Internal Medicine*, 160 (2014), 101–10.
[5] See generally *District of Columbia* v. *Heller*, 554 U.S. 570 (2008).

argument runs the other way: The breathtaking disregard for the harm principle in the modern libertarian's argument suggests the anomalous character of our Second Amendment jurisprudence. The right to bear arms has become a warrant for death and mayhem in the home and on the streets. Why repeat this mistake with respect to a new assertion of right?

Framing the issue as one of constitutional rights does not remove it from politics, when the law itself has become a site of political contestation. Such a framing only shifts the point of responsible decision from elected officials to judges. Our situation is parallel to that of the Supreme Court in 1857, when it tried to settle as a matter of constitutional law the national, political debate over slavery.[6] It could not do so, and the decision became only another political step in the march toward the Civil War. The judgment in Wisconsin was on a 4–3 vote, and everyone knows the political affiliations of those judges. Everyone also knows that other judges would have decided the case in the opposite way. Under these conditions, no court can relieve us of the burden of political decision. Politicians neither can nor should expect help from the courts.

Justice as a Limit on Political Decision-Making

Absent an actionable claim of legal right, we must turn to political first principles. Among those first principles is majority rule. Political commentators regularly criticize the cautious advice of leading public health officials on the grounds that "no one elected them." Is the decision one that is appropriately left to elected officials to decide as they see fit? A majority does not have a license to do whatever it wants. Majority politics is not mob rule.

Those who rely on the electoral defense may still be criticized, for example, if their decisions advance the economic interests of the well-off, at a substantial cost to less well-off groups. We think that the rich are using the poor, and that the poor should not be put to life-threatening choices that the rich can ignore. This inequality of choice and risk becomes a legal problem when the cost-bearers are constitutionally protected groups and the discrimination is deliberate.

Even when there is no legal violation, however, such decisions can violate our justified political expectations. Consider the issues around the

---

[6] See *Dred Scott* v. *Sandford*, 60 U.S. 393 (1857).

outbreaks among low-wage workers in meatpacking plants, public transportation, and food service operations. Similarly, the incidence of infection raises compelling questions about lower-income and minority communities' access to quality health care. The pandemic is laying bare many of the structural injustices that remain in and between our communities. In ordinary circumstances, these injustices remain largely invisible. When the corpses are overwhelming the capacities of the mortuaries, they are impossible to ignore. This new visibility contributed to the explosion of public protests under the banner of "Black Lives Matter."

That the virus is disproportionately affecting communities of color is a fact that cannot be ignored. Less clear are the reasons for this pattern and the path toward amelioration. Is it a matter of housing, public transportation, participation in the workforce, preexisting conditions such as diabetes or obesity, or something else? Perhaps all of the above. Nor do we know how the affected communities themselves work the balance between reopening and public health. No doubt, they, too, are divided. Again, it is not enough to say that the majority should settle the issue.

We cannot ask that political leaders act on *our* idea of justice, but we can rightly expect them to act on *an* idea of justice – and to defend that idea against competing conceptions. Some argue, for example, that it is unjust to keep individuals from their jobs or to force businesses to close down, when they have done nothing wrong. Let them defend that conception against those who argue that it is unjust to put the burden of making unsafe choices upon minorities and the less well-off.

These arguments over the demands of justice neither begin nor end with polling data. There is no electoral defense to injustice. No politician will explicitly campaign on the proposition that they will distribute the burdens of sickness and death disproportionately to less well-off communities. Even privileged voters, who might be attracted to such a policy, will not defend it in these terms. Yet, individuals differ in their ideas of justice. We are not going to resolve those differences under the circumstances of crisis. Neither, however, can we ignore them. The responsibility of political leaders in a democracy is to take seriously their obligation to persuade. That obligation comes with its own ethical standards: To persuade properly means offering good reasons, rather than fear, lies, and propaganda. Only then can we respect leadership's choices even when we disagree with them.

Legitimacy as a Limit on Democratic Decision-Making

Claims of legal right and claims of justice are two limits on democratic politics. Is that the end? Can a majority do as it pleases within these limits? In this section, I will argue that obligations of care exist alongside those of law and of justice.

The political obligation of care is not exhausted in a legal right to health care. While some courts have upheld such a right in some contexts, those decisions respond to claims of individuals for particular treatments.[7] In the pandemic, the political decision is not whether a democratic government can deny me treatment were I to become sick, but rather, what consideration elected officials must extend to the fact that I might become sick.

To consider obligations of care, begin where feminist theorists began – with the family. It has an obligation to recognize the rights of each of its members, but also an obligation to care for each. Justice does not exhaust care. A failure of care is a form of disrespect that can sever the ties of family, just as much as a failure to respect rights. A sick child deserves more than a sicker stranger, for the family has obligations of care toward the former but not the latter. Rights recognition and care constitute two sides of a broad obligation of respect. To be treated justly, but *as if* a stranger, expresses a familial failure. This would be a family in name only.

Communities begin in acts of care for particular individuals. Political communities are plural because care is not universal. I owe the stranger justice, but not care. Conversely, I owe the members of my community care beyond justice. Obligations of right and obligations of care align with the distinction between justice and legitimacy. Justice operates as a negative constraint on the state. Legitimacy speaks to the positive burden on government to sustain citizen identification with the state.[8] Questions of legitimacy ask how we stand with respect to a government choice, and through that choice, how we stand with respect to each other. A failure of care produces the distinct political pathology of alienation.

---

[7] See V. Abramovich and L. Pautassi, "Judicial Activism in the Argentine Health System: Recent Trends," *Health and Human Rights Journal*, 10 (2008), 53–65; G. Annas, "The Right to Health and the Nevirapine Case in South Africa," *The New England Journal of Medicine*, 348 (2003), 750–4; A. Arrieta-Gomez, "Realizing the Fundamental Right to Health through Litigation: The Colombian Case," *Health and Human Rights Journal*, 20 (2018), 133–45.

[8] Compare Virginia Held, "The Meshing of Care and Justice," *Hypathia*, 10 (1995), 128–32 (considering a number of permutations of the relationship of care to justice).

Politics fails if it pursues injustice, but also if it produces alienation. Talk of the "democracy deficit" today often points to the problem of alienation, not that of injustice.[9] We want laws to be just, but we also want them to be our own. They are our own when we can imagine them as the product of our collective authorship. We govern ourselves, then, through law. That authorship must extend even to laws enacted by earlier generations. These laws, too, must be imagined as the product of our collective authorship – We the People – or we will suffer the alienation that comes from thinking that we are ruled by the dead hand of the past.

In a democracy, we do not insist on winning every vote, but we do insist on care. Decisions to reopen society raise precisely this issue: Do they satisfy the obligations of care, even if they meet the obligations of justice?

Care Beyond Justice

Care for and among citizens is related to, but not quite the same as, care among members of a family. It is thinner and narrower. There may be few boundaries on care among family members, but there is much about ourselves that we do not think an appropriate object of political concern. I care about my children as complete and full individuals seeking to realize themselves in multiple dimensions. I do not care about other citizens in this way, even as I acknowledge that they make a special claim upon me. A politics of care cares for the special meanings that are a stake in a political life. Conversely, a failure of care disregards those meanings.

Political care is not a psychological state but a public practice. Imagine a crazy king. Most people would think irrational behavior on his part would be grounds for deposing him. We do not think that a crazy king is fine as long as he is not violating any individual's rights. We think he is not doing the thing that is constitutive of kingship – advancing an idea of the public good. Absent that, he cannot care for those for whom he is responsible. Would we think the situation different if there were recourse to elections? Imagine a king subject to recall. That process formalizes a method to get rid of the king. It relieves us of the burden of ad hoc action – revolution – but it does not make legitimate that which falls outside of the boundaries of governance.

---

[9] D. Johnson, "A Democracy Deficit Plagues the US and the European Union," Aeon (August 1, 2016), https://aeon.co/ideas/one-way-the-us-and-the-eu-are-less-democratic-than-china.

Is a crazy democracy any different? If government is an institutional arrangement for advancing the public good, it is hard to see how craziness advances the ends for which it is instituted. Like the crazy king, a crazy democracy fails as a practice of politics. When critics of President Trump invoked the 25th Amendment, which allows the cabinet to displace a president who cannot carry out his responsibilities, they were appealing to this argument. The argument would remain even if Trump had majority support among the voters.

When Trump suggested ingesting bleach as a treatment, he could not legitimate that recommendation by pointing to majority support in the polls. Even if he won an electoral campaign on the promise of a "bleach cure," the policy would still not be legitimate. Democratic majorities cannot declare the earth flat. When they try to do so, they become instruments of coercion – a mob.

Arguments from the bleach cure and the 25th Amendment suggest the irrational state of American politics, but they do not get to the most difficult issue of care under exceptional circumstances. To approach this, we have to consider the President's claim that he is a wartime president: The pandemic is similar to, if not the equivalent of, a war. There is a serious argument here, but not that suggested by the President, who inverted matters when he described those returning to work as warriors. The proper analogy runs to the health care workers who risked their lives and even died to combat the disease.

People die in wars; many people suffer terribly. We give our elected officials the power to declare war. They are expected to make decisions in which they assess the threat to the public and its values against the likely death and destruction of citizens. What makes a situation "war-like?" After all, many ordinary policy decisions can involve loss of life; for example, decisions about environmental regulation, transportation safety, or investment in public health infrastructure. Modern government could hardly begin to act were it the case that a condition of legitimacy is protection of every life put at risk by a political decision. We are not necessarily careless, when we accept those risks.

For the most part, we justify the choice to bear these risks by calculating that they reduce costs in the long run. Lives will be better, or more life-years will be saved, when we adopt the practice or technology. A technology or practice that imposes disproportionate costs is one that should be reformed. There is no justification for imposing costs disproportionate to benefits. It is, once again, simply crazy – that is, it is careless in the double senses of that word. That some individuals may nevertheless suffer from a reasonable choice is unfortunate, but not necessarily an indication of political carelessness.

Many think that the response to COVID-19 fell into this pattern: Government had to reopen the economy; some individuals would get sick and die. Our concern should be with justice – i.e., distribution of costs – and rationality – i.e., benefits should exceed costs. I do not reject these concerns, but something else was at stake when Governor Andrew Cuomo of New York set off on his relentless – and very public – search for ventilators. At no point did he say that the state simply could not afford more or that enough had been spent, given that those likely to die had few life-years left anyway.

The most admirable moments of response were those that explicitly resisted the turn to calculation of costs and benefits. Entire societies locked themselves down for the sake of those least able to protect themselves. Most of those who stayed home and agreed to social distancing were not at serious risk from the disease. We acted together for the sake of the most vulnerable among us: The old, the sick, and the health care workers who take care of us. Again, Cuomo captured that attitude when he simply refused to acknowledge that anyone would be left behind. He framed a government response of care, meaning every person is entitled to recognition, regardless of costs.

Still, one might think that between the absolutists and the crazies there is a wide range for reasonable policy choices grounded in calculations of costs and benefits. We do not save every life in a war; we do not save every life on the highways. Yet, death in a war is not the same as death in a traffic accident, even if the government is responsible in some way for both. We capture that difference in the idea of sacrifice. No reasonable person says that highway fatalities are sacrifices for the sake of a higher GDP. Those who do speak that way, including an otherwise obscure government official in Texas, are seriously confused about the nature of a meaningful life.[10]

That confusion, nevertheless, tells us something important: The distinction between sacrifice and an unfortunate fatality is not carried by facts and circumstances alone. No set of observations will tell us whether to register a death as a sacrifice, a tragedy, or a cost. Indeed, all too often we register the battlefield not as a site of sacrifice but as one of needless

---

[10] See M. Hennessy-Fiske, "Sacrifice the Old to Help the Economy? Texas Official's Remark Prompts Backlash," *Los Angeles Times* (March 24, 2020), www.latimes.com/world-nation /story/2020-03-24/coronavirus-texas-dan-patrick.

slaughter. At that point, governments fall and decisions to use force appear illegitimate. It does not matter that they were supported by a majority, once they are seen to lack care.

The distinction between sacrifice and meaningless death depends upon what we, collectively, make of the situation. We invest death with a meaning or we do not; a sacrifice is an ultimate expression of care. More precisely, it is a response to the recognition of an ultimate value. Because these matters change over time, the circumstances of sacrifice tell us a good deal about the nature of a political regime. We have seen something of a transformation occurring right before our eyes, as health care workers and essential workers became "front-line troops" in the war on COVID-19. Their deaths registered as sacrifices in a way that had not been true before the crisis. Those for whom they sacrificed take on the value created by those deaths: They did this for us. We, in turn, are in their debt. This is the economy of care at stake in sacrifice. Lincoln gave voice to this idea at Gettysburg:

> It is for us the living . . . to be dedicated here to the unfinished work which they who fought here have thus far so nobly advanced. It is rather for us to be here dedicated to the great task remaining before us – that from these honored dead we take increased devotion to that cause for which they gave the last full measure of devotion – that we here highly resolve that these dead shall not have died in vain.[11]

Sacrifice is always an act of creative destruction. It puts a redemptive demand upon the survivors. We take on an obligation to be the people for whom they sacrificed. Thus, the Christian martyrs created the possibility of a practice of ultimate meaning for generations of Christians. Similarly, it has become our political responsibility to recognize the dimensions of the sacred that are developing in and around today's public health crisis.

When we stayed home, we were not calculating costs and benefits; we were affirming our care for each other. We were a sort of stay-at-home army, conscripted into a national campaign of care. We were standing with the health care workers who sacrificed for us; we were doing our part. When nations stopped to clap and cheer for those workers, they were expressing that care upon which legitimate politics depends. This is the contemporary equivalent of Memorial Day – the day on which we remember those lost in past wars.

---

[11] A. Lincoln, "Address Delivered at the Dedication of the Cemetery at Gettysburg, November 19, 1863," in R. Basler (ed.), *Abraham Lincoln: His Speeches and Writings* (Cleveland, OH: World Publishing Co., 1946), p. 734.

These investments of public meaning function as limits on democratic majorities. They remind us that politics is about ends – deadly serious ends – as well as means. Beside the crazy king, we have to place the sacrilegious king. A king who is careless of the nation's gods fails just as much as one who fails to pursue a public purpose. This lesson extends from kingdoms to democracies.

Politics is about reason, but it is also about our mutual and reciprocal capacity to create and sustain a transcendent meaning – a meaning that links us to those who came before and those who will come later. A democratic government must pursue reasonable policies, but it must also support and sustain the faith that grounds the state as a source of ultimate meaning. This is care beyond justice. Absent that care, even a democratic majority can be illegitimate.

Concerns of justice and legitimacy alone will not tell us whether or when to reopen. Politics remains a domain of freedom precisely because decisions must be made. In making those decisions, political leaders can sustain or destroy our political faith. When they act carelessly, they tell us that politics is no longer worth the sacrifice. If we support them in that act of destruction, we diminish ourselves by rendering acts of sacrifice senseless deaths. In that case, the form of politics may continue, but its substance is gone.